LEADERSHIP AT THE FED

LEADERSHIP AT THE FED

DONALD F. KETTL

YALE UNIVERSITY PRESS
NEW HAVEN AND LONDON

Designed by Sally Harris
and set in Caledonia type by
Brevis Press, Bethany, Ct.
Printed in the United States of America by
The Alpine Press, Stoughton, Mass.

Library of Congress Cataloging-in-Publication Data

Kettl, Donald F.
  Leadership at the Fed.

  Includes index.
  1. Board of Governors of the Federal Reserve
System (U.S.)   I. Title.
HG2563.K45   1986   332.1'1'0973   86–1551
ISBN 0–300–03658–2 (alk. paper)

The paper in this book meets the guidelines for
permanence and durability of the Committee on
Production Guidelines for Book Longevity
of the Council on Library Resources.

10   9   8   7   6   5   4   3   2   1

For James W. Fesler and Frederick C. Mosher

CONTENTS

TABLES AND FIGURES

Tables

Figures

PREFACE

This book began over dinner during the fall of 1981. A colleague asked several of us, "Why aren't there any books by political scientists on the Federal Reserve?" It seemed strange to him—a Latin American scholar—that experts on American government had ignored what was obviously one of the most powerful American institutions.

His question intrigued me, and I began casting about for work on the Fed. Economists had developed a whole subfield devoted to the Fed and monetary policy, and their work dominated the shelves and journals. Some of the work was politically quite sophisticated, like G. L. Bach's books.[1] It also turned out that political scientists had not completely ignored the Fed; there were in fact a few good works on the agency.[2] In the years since the dinner, furthermore, more political scientists have turned to the Fed. Nathaniel Beck has created excellent statistical models of the Fed's behavior, while John Woolley has written a fascinating book which argues that the Fed's behavior is bounded by its ties with external groups, like Congress, the president, and interest groups.[3]

These works, however, left me still puzzling over several important ques-

1. G. L. Bach, *Federal Reserve Policy-Making: A Study in Government Economic Policy Formation* (New York: Knopf, 1950); and *Making Monetary and Fiscal Policy* (Washington, D.C.: Brookings Institution, 1970).

2. A. Jerome Clifford, *The Independence of the Federal Reserve System* (Philadelphia: University of Pennsylvania Press, 1965); Don K. Price, "Control of the Monetary System," *Harvard Business Review* 40 (July/August 1962): 149–64; and Michael D. Reagan, "The Political Structure of the Federal Reserve System," *American Political Science Review* 55 (March 1961): 64–76.

3. Nathaniel Beck, "Presidential Influence on the Federal Reserve in the 1970s," *American Journal of Political Science* 26 (August 1982): 415–45; "Domestic Political Sources of American Monetary Policy: 1955–82," *Journal of Politics* 46 (1984): 786–817; and John T. Woolley, *Monetary Politics: The Federal Reserve and the Politics of Monetary Policy* (Cambridge: Cambridge University Press, 1984).

tions. First, while everyone who looks at the Fed notes its unique "independence" from the rest of the government, it is clear from even a casual reading of the newspaper that the Fed does not behave with complete independence. Given both the Fed's obvious connections to the rest of the government and also the rhetoric of independence, I puzzled over what "independence" means—and how an independent agency might be made accountable within the broader fabric of American government.

Second, I wondered about the base of the Fed's power. A casual look at the system that Congress created in 1913 shows a weak institution of uncertain authority. Since then the agency has acquired unquestioned leverage over the nation's—indeed, the world's—economy. For a student of bureaucracy, that metamorphosis is intriguing. I set out, therefore, to explore the Fed's history since 1913 to try to answer these questions.

The questions convinced me that a book on the Federal Reserve was worth writing. What was far less obvious was that the book could be done. The Fed has a public image of secrecy and impermeability. I worried over access to good sources about the Fed's decisions, not only for recent years but also for the early years of the agency's history. Several colleagues, in fact, urged me to give up the project because they feared I would not be able to get enough information.

Fortunately my problem turned out to be not too little but, in fact, too much information. Despite the public image of inaccessibility, members of the Federal Reserve Board and members of its staff gave more generously and openly of their time than I had any right to expect. They simply could not have been more helpful in answering my questions or in digging out documents that helped fill in the gaps. The same is true of officials in Congress and the executive branch. Forty-four interviews with key officials provided an important research base for this book. In return for their openness, many of the respondents were promised anonymity. Policymaking officials I interviewed are identified in the footnotes.

An even more surprising find was the rich collection of documents in the nation's presidential libraries. The Fed has long been of crucial importance to presidents, and the president has become one of the Fed's most important constituents. Most presidents, however, have had little background in economics, so their advisers have over the years undertaken to conduct seminars-by-memo. The result is a mother lode of data on White House thinking about economic policy. In the course of research for this book I have visited each of the seven presidential libraries (Hoover, Roosevelt, Truman, Eisenhower, Kennedy, Johnson, and Ford) as well as several other collections of papers. (With characteristic bad timing, however, I usually managed to schedule my trips to the deep south during the heat of summer and to the midwest in the chill of winter.)

These visits yielded several thousand pages of memos ranging from a shouting match between President Herbert Hoover and Federal Reserve Board members on the night before Franklin D. Roosevelt's inauguration to an evolving pattern of cooperation between Fed Chairman Arthur Burns and President Gerald Ford. The presidential libraries' documents on economic policy are among their very richest collections. The educational effort by presidential economic advisers has produced memos unmatched in number or detail; they typically lay out what the president ought to do and why in simple, persuasive text. Furthermore, the documents on domestic economic policy usually are not entangled in national security or privacy restrictions that make other parts of the collections sometimes difficult to use. The oral histories that supplement the papers often contain real gems. The result is an archival treasure that traces presidential concern about economic policy issues.

Finally, I relied heavily on government documents, especially congressional hearings. At every crisis in the Fed's history, members of Congress have called Fed officials to testify. The result is a fascinating record of congressional concerns about the Fed and the responses made by Fed officials. The many other persons who have come before congressional committees to testify have provided equally interesting information about public attitudes.

Thanks to the richness of these sources, I found writing the book a great deal of fun. As I worked through the Fed's history, a pattern emerged that became the central argument of the book: the Fed's history—and the growth of its power—is largely the product of the leadership of its chairmen. Over the years, we have come to expect more of the government in managing the economy, and the growing role of the government in stabilizing the economy explains part of the growing role of the Fed. That job, however, has often brought great technical uncertainty and political risk. The Fed has grown into the powerful agency it is today because of the way its chairmen have navigated their way through these uncertainties and risks.

This book thus is a story of the Fed's power and independence told through the history of the Fed's chairmen. It begins with the struggle to create the agency and continues into the chairmanship of Paul Volcker in the 1980s. It is more than a history, though. The book fundamentally is an analysis of the way the Fed's leaders have dealt with their external environment. In that story lie the answers to two related questions: What is the meaning of "independence" for a governmental agency, and what is the role of an "independent" agency in the American democracy?

In writing this book I have incurred enormous debts to the many organizations and individuals who have supported me. Generous grants supported the project: from the Earhart Foundation; the Hoover Presidential Library Association; the Harry S. Truman Library Institute; the Gerald R. Ford Foundation; and the University of Virginia, through the University Research Policy Council and the Sesquicentennial Fellowship Program. Dr. Thomas Johnson at the American Enterprise Institute provided office space during the Washington-based phase of my research.

I am also grateful to the many staff members and archivists who patiently guided me through the fourteen collections of papers I examined. In addition to the presidential papers, I have probed the following collections: the Marriner S. Eccles Papers at the University of Utah's Marriott Library; John D. Ehrlichman's papers at the Fenn Galleries in Santa Fe, New Mexico; the Walter Heller Papers at the Kennedy Library; the Arthur Burns Papers and William Seidman Papers at the Ford Library; and the Gardner Ackley and Paul McCracken Papers at the University of Michigan's Bentley Historical Library. The staffs of these libraries have my gratitude: at the Hoover Library, John Fawcett, Shirley Sondergard, Mildred Mather, and Robert Wood; at the Roosevelt Library, Elizabeth Denier and Susan Bosanko; at the Truman Library, Warren Ohrvall; at the Eisenhower Library, Kathy Struss; at the Kennedy Library, William Johnson; at the Johnson Library, Gary Gallagher, Linda Hanson, and Claudia Anderson; at the Ford Library, Don Wilson, Sandra Mitchell, and William Stewart; at the Marriott Library, Nancy Young; and at the Fenn Galleries, Forrest Fenn and Ann Brown. In addition, I would like to thank Marcie Schneider, on the staff of the Federal Reserve's Board of Governors, for her help in assembling the book's photo section.

Several of my students provided invaluable research assistance, including Barbara Keller, Laurene Semenza, and Tina Benyunes. They have my thanks.

In addition, I've been extremely fortunate to have colleagues who have generously shared their time in suggesting revisions to earlier versions of this book. I've received comments in far more depth than any author has a right to expect, and I have a lasting debt to those who have helped rescue me from mistakes or who have helped me sharpen my analysis: Michael Reagan, Charles Jones, Martha Derthick, Philip Cagan, and an anonymous reader. I am especially grateful to the two teachers to whom this book is dedicated, teachers who over the years have opened my eyes to new sights and my mind to new ways of thinking about policy issues: James W. Fesler and Frederick C. Mosher. I am also grateful to Marian Ash, Charlotte Dihoff, and Elizabeth Casey at Yale University Press for their enthusiasm for the project and their help in bringing it to fruition.

Finally, I owe a deep debt to my wife, Sue, who patiently put up with the slow genesis of the book. Her humor and love buoyed me constantly.

I simply cannot imagine a project in which I could have had more fun exploring such interesting sources and ideas, or one in which I could have had more support and help from family, colleagues, and, especially, the people at the Fed I was studying. The sense of discovery drove my research and writing, and I hope it captures you also as you read this book.

CHAPTER ONE

POWER AND INDEPENDENCE

By the 1980s, polls of leading Americans regularly rated the chairman of the Federal Reserve Board as the second most influential person in the nation, second only to the president.[1] The foremost economics textbook, written by Nobel laureate Paul A. Samuelson and William D. Nordhaus, a former member of the president's Council of Economic Advisers, concluded that the Fed "is the most important factor in the making of macroeconomic policy."[2] Unquestionably the Fed has enormous power over the American economy. Like other central banks, it has the job of keeping the currency stable by managing the nation's supply of money and credit. To nearly everyone, that means controlling interest rates, and the Fed has used that function to gain great influence over the nation's—and increasingly the world's—economy.

Such assertions would have astounded the Fed's founders, who recognized in 1913 that they had created an important agency but who scarcely conceived of it as one of the most powerful institutions in American government. Instead, they viewed it as a regulatory agency, in the spirit of the Interstate Commerce Commission, that would raise or lower the banking system's reserves according to the economy's needs, just as a damkeeper raises or lowers the level of water behind his dam according to the weather. The Fed was to steady the frequent wild swings in money and credit that had for a generation crippled the nation's commerce.

Even with this limited view of the Fed's role, many members of Congress believed that the new institution had to be insulated from the constant tug of political pressures. Financiers and populists had argued with each other

1. See, for example, *U.S. News and World Report,* May 20, 1985, 54.
2. Paul A. Samuelson and William D. Nordhaus, *Economics,* 12th ed. (New York: McGraw-Hill, 1985), 294.

1

for decades whether managing the nation's money and credit ought to be a private or a governmental function. If the job was to be done by government, the two sides could not agree on whether it ought to be accomplished by a strong and centralized bank or by a decentralized system with power dispersed around the country. Congress, as usual, compromised, creating a "Federal Reserve System" with uncertain powers. No one was quite sure what the new central bank ought to do—except that it should not be empowered to do too much.

Over the years since then, the Fed has discovered how to use its tools to manage the economy. It can increase the supply of money and credit (that is, it can make money more available and "easier") and nudge interest rates lower (that is, it can make money cheaper). It can also decrease the money supply (make money less available and "tighter") and influence interest rates upward (and make money more expensive). Easier money promotes economic growth, but money that is too easy and growth that is too rapid risks igniting inflation, a rapid increase in prices. Tighter money can cool economic growth that is too rapid to be sustained for the long term. However, slowing economic growth often costs jobs and drives interest rates up. The job of the Fed has thus come to be the politically sensitive task of balancing three different goals: keeping long-term growth as high as possible, keeping unemployment as low as possible, and keeping prices as stable as possible.

Balancing these goals inevitably involves conflict. Any given level of money and credit benefits some individuals more than others. Low inflation makes long-range planning easier for financiers, from mortgage bankers to insurance executives. Tight money helps keep inflation low; however, it also makes it more expensive for industries to borrow and expand employment. Furthermore, elected officials facing reelection campaigns often find it difficult to resist the lure of easy money. History is cluttered with leaders who inflated their economies for short-run gains at the expense of long-term economic stability. While politicians may sometimes preach the virtues of tight money to curb inflation, they rarely have the stomach for lasting restraint. The promise of a growing economy, whether a chicken in every pot or "full employment," is the traditional song of most presidential campaigns.

Monetary policy is thus the stuff of high political conflict, and during the nineteenth century these conflicts scuttled two attempts at American central banking. Financiers twice argued (in 1811 and 1836) that a strong economy demanded some central supervision of banking and credit—and twice populists killed the bank by contending that such concentration of power was a threat to American democracy and the prospects of ordinary citizens. Populists feared that a reserve bank under bankers' control would neglect

the needs of farmers and ordinary citizens, while bankers feared that populists would gain control of a central bank subject to political influence,
make money too easy, and unloose inflation.

When it created the Fed, Congress therefore decided to shield the Fed's
operations from this kind of pulling and tugging by giving it political independence. Establishing the Fed independently from the rest of the federal
government—and from the banking system—thus had double virtue. Both
populists and financiers were satisfied that neither group could work its will
to the detriment of the other. And Congress avoided having to settle the
conflict that had scuttled the earlier proposals for a central bank. It is the
spirit of political compromise embodied in the concept of legal independence that has enabled the Fed to survive over the decades since.

The Fed's legal independence has two elements: its unique place within
the federal government and its unique public-private structure. The Constitution vested in Congress the nation's monetary power—"to coin Money"
and "regulate the Value thereof."[3] Congress delegated the job to the Fed
with a broad grant of discretion. The Fed's mandate is exceptionally vague,
even by the standard of acts of Congress. According to the Federal Reserve
Act, the Fed should conduct its operations "with a view of accommodating
commerce and business."[4] The act also made the Fed self-financing and
thus free from the appropriations process.[5] The Fed is thus an agent of
Congress, but Congress has never exercised sustained and close oversight
of its operations.

Congress insulated the Fed's operations from political interference even
further by making it a joint public-private venture. The seven-member Federal Reserve Board, located in Washington, sets the system's basic policies
and oversees its operations, but twelve Federal Reserve banks conduct the
Fed's operations. (The banks are located in Boston, New York, Philadelphia,
Cleveland, Richmond, Atlanta, Chicago, St. Louis, Minneapolis, Kansas
City, Dallas, and San Francisco.) The reserve banks are not like other banks;
they do not take deposits or make loans to the public. Instead, they are
bankers' banks, which provide important services to the financial industry.
They hold the banking system's reserves and make loans to banks. They
also clear checks and supply the banking system with currency and coins.
They supervise the soundness of member banks, they administer a sophisticated electronic fund transfer system, and they act as agents for the U.S.
Treasury. In short, the reserve banks do the Fed's routine work.

3. Art. I, Sec. 8.
4. Federal Reserve Act of 1913, P.L. 63–43, Sec. 14d.
5. The Federal Reserve Board raises money for its operating needs from assessments on
the Federal Reserve banks. We will examine this issue later in chapter 1.

Compared with other agencies in American government, the reserve banks have peculiar public-private control. While the Federal Reserve Board supervises their operations, the reserve banks are owned by their member banks. The Federal Reserve Act required all national banks to join the system, and it allowed state-chartered banks and savings banks to join if they met certain conditions. Members must purchase stock in the Fed and follow the Fed's regulations. In return, member banks have the right to elect the board of directors of each reserve bank, which in turn chooses each bank's operating officers.[6]

In practice, it is the making of monetary policy that dominates the Fed, the Federal Reserve Board that dominates the reserve banks, and the chairman of the Federal Reserve Board that dominates the system. Members of the board enjoy unusually long (fourteen-year) terms, second only to the fifteen-year term served by the head of Congress's General Accounting Office and the lifetime appointments of federal judges. Once appointed, furthermore, members of the board can be removed only for cause, a standard never tested. The president can fill vacancies that occur on the board and name one member to a four-year term as chairman; such appointments are subject to Senate confirmation. Once appointed, however, board members are not responsible to the president, who has no official channel of communication to the Fed and no legal power over the Fed's policies.

The Fed thus occupies a unique place in American government: a public board supervising quasi-private reserve banks, a board free from congressional appropriations and presidential oversight, a board composed of officials exercising Congress's monetary powers yet possessing great autonomy and broad flexibility.

To accomplish the Fed's central purpose of governing the supply of money and credit, the Federal Reserve Board relies on three tools. First, it sets reserve requirements—the amounts banks must hold against their deposits.

6. From 1913 to 1980, the Fed's regulations and services extended only to the member banks. However, the Monetary Control Act of 1980 expanded many of the Fed's regulatory powers and financial services to all depository institutions.

The board and the reserve banks are also separate from the federal government's civil service system. The Fed administers a unique personnel system for its staff. The boards of directors of the reserve banks select, with the approval of the Board of Governors, the operating officers of the reserve banks.

Each reserve bank has nine directors. Member banks elect three Class A directors (representing the member banks) and three Class B directors (representing the public). The Board of Governors chooses three Class C directors (also representing the public) for each reserve bank. The reserve banks finance their operations from income on government securities they own and from fees charged on the Fed's services. Member banks are entitled by law to dividends on their stock. After the Fed has paid the dividends and the expenses of the banks and the board, all profits are returned to the Treasury.

Raising the reserve requirements decreases the amount of money banks have to lend and thus tightens the money supply; lowering the reserve requirements has the opposite effect.

Second, the Fed and the reserve banks set the discount rate, the interest rate at which banks can borrow from the Fed. (The Fed deducts the interest at the time the loan is made; the interest is thus "discounted" from the amount of the loan. Bankers often talk euphemistically about borrowing from the "discount window." In the early days of the Fed, there was a teller window in the reserve banks where bankers actually came to apply for the loans.) Raising the discount rate makes borrowing more expensive and tends to make money tighter; higher discount rates are typically a sign that the Fed is trying to slow economic growth in order to lower inflation. Lowering the discount rate has the opposite effect. By decreasing the cost to banks of borrowing from the Fed, banks can more cheaply increase their reserves and thus expand their lending.

Both of these tools are important, but they are also relatively inflexible. It is hard to adjust them subtly or often. The Fed thus relies most on its third tool, open-market operations: the buying and selling of government securities to raise or lower the supply of money. Open-market policy is set by the Federal Open Market Committee. The FOMC, established by the Banking Act of 1933, is composed of twelve voting members: the seven members of the Federal Reserve Board; the president of the Federal Reserve Bank of New York, who has a permanent seat on the FOMC; and four other members drawn by rotation from the remaining eleven Federal Reserve bank presidents. (The remaining seven reserve bank presidents, however, attend FOMC meetings as nonvoting members and take full part in discussions.) The FOMC meets about every five to eight weeks to discuss the state of the economy, review the Fed's options, and vote to set the Fed's open-market policy course until the next FOMC meeting. The Federal Reserve Bank of New York carries out the FOMC's instructions. By *selling* government securities, the Fed takes money in from buyers in exchange for the securities. It thereby decreases the money supply, makes money tighter, and reduces the ability of consumers to spend. The effect, therefore, is to slow economic growth. By *buying* securities in the open market, the Fed increases the amount of money available to consumers to spend (that is, it makes money easier) and thus helps feed economic growth. The Fed's buying and selling is often in large amounts, so over a short period of time the Fed can substantially change the amount of money in circulation and therefore influence interest rates and the economy.

For the Fed, open-market operations have many advantages. By working with several dealers in a constantly moving market, the Fed can subtly produce the effects it desires without making public pronouncements. That gives it considerable maneuvering room. Furthermore, since it can buy and sell in any amount it wishes, it has a large range of policy options at each step. Over the years, therefore, open-market operations have become the Fed's most important policy tool.

Although the Fed can, through the tools available to it, either promote economic growth or seek to prevent inflation, in recent years one ideology has predominated within the Fed: that inflation is bad and that it is the Fed's responsibility to prevent it. Many of the Fed's critics have argued that the agency has often (especially during the 1970s) bungled and made inflation worse. Despite some errors, however, the use of discretionary powers to prevent inflation has become a veritable house religion for Fed officials. They believe themselves part of a special priesthood, one former Fed official explained, that is dedicated to protecting the currency.[7] Indeed, there is great pomp and a rich liturgy. The Fed resides in a forbidding marble temple on Constitution Avenue in Washington, and it conducts its deliberations in technical jargon that most Americans do not understand. Secret meetings are a rich part of the Fed tradition, both to prevent speculators from benefiting from advance notice of policy decisions and to allow Fed officials to deliberate in collegial freedom.

One former board member, Nancy Teeters, enjoys telling a story that illustrates just how strong that priesthood is. In a conversation with Fed Chairman Arthur Burns one evening before her appointment, Teeters, a Democrat, realized that Burns was sounding her out about her views. Burns had been appointed by Republican Richard Nixon, and she warned Burns, "Arthur, you don't want somebody with known Democratic connections." Burns smiled and replied, "It doesn't matter, Nancy. In six months, everybody is a central banker."[8] Central banking means first fighting inflation, and the Fed's inflation-fighting priesthood urges its faith on all who sit around the Federal Reserve Board's table.

THE PROBLEM OF UNCERTAINTY

The Fed thus has great leverage over the economy, but its control is incomplete. In making monetary policy, the Fed faces enormous technical un-

---

7. Interview with the author. See also *Business Week*, November 21, 1977, 112; and Raymond Lombra and Michael Moran, "Policy Advice and Policymaking at the Federal Reserve," in Karl Brunner and Alan H. Meltzer, eds., *Carnegie-Rochester Conference Series on Public Policy* 13 (Amsterdam: North-Holland Publishing Company, 1980): 9–10.

8. Interview with the author.

certainties that make it impossible for Fed officials to predict with precision what results their decisions will produce.

If the Fed's job is to control the money supply, it is becoming ever more difficult to determine just what "money" is. Fed officials, in fact, have many different arcane definitions of money—the obscure M1, M2, M3, and so on that are reported in the financial pages—that range across currency, traveler's checks, checking accounts, interest-bearing checking accounts, money market funds, savings accounts, certificates of deposit, repurchase agreements, and savings bonds.[9] Many of these instruments have developed since the mid-1970s and have created substantial new problems for governing the money supply. For example, interest-bearing accounts on which individuals may write checks often double as checking and savings accounts. Since checking accounts influence the economy differently from savings accounts, how should the Fed count such "money" in predicting citizens' purchases? To complicate matters still further, new kinds of credit and debit cards, wire transfers, and other innovations in the payments mechanism have created many new—and harder-to-measure—forms of "money."

Even when the Fed estimates—and it is only an estimate—what money and credit are, measuring them is a difficult job. The only way to get prompt measurement of the money supply is to sample financial institutions, which means that the data are always incomplete estimates subject to constant revision. The same is true of other important statistics, from the utilization of manufacturing plants to the consumer price index, which provide information at best weeks old when released. It takes many months to get good gross national product figures, and it often turns out that what were thought to be "good" months were actually "bad" months, and vice versa. Then there is the difficulty of determining just what a given set of numbers means. Does an increase in consumer demand mean the economy is generating healthy consumer spending or renewed inflation? Does a decline in economic growth signal a welcome end to an inflationary boom or an emerging recession? There are lots of numbers, but little good, firm, reliable information that adequately paints an up-to-date picture of the economy. Even worse, there are very few reliable models about what figures from the past signal for the economy's future.

9. M1 consists of currency, travelers checks, demand deposits (checking accounts), and negotiable order of withdrawal accounts. M2 is M1 plus repurchase agreements, money market deposit accounts, small-denomination time deposits, and money market mutual funds. M3 is M2 plus large-denomination time deposits, Eurodollars, and institution-only money market mutual funds. There are numerous subcategories of these money measures, and there are other measures used less often (like L, M3 plus nonbank public holdings of U.S. savings bonds, short-term Treasury securities, and commercial paper).

Even if the Fed could determine just what the future will bring, it is never easy to decide just what to do about it. There is, economists suggest, a point beyond which attempts to lower unemployment will only increase inflation—the point of what is considered "full employment"—but they are unsure about just where this point lies. In fact, economists believe that the point has been changing over time. Furthermore, how long consumers hold onto money before spending it also affects the economy. Most kinds of "money" are spent over and over each year, and Fed officials must estimate how many times a typical dollar of money will be spent to determine how much economic growth any given level of the money supply will produce. Economists call this the "velocity" of money.[10] Unfortunately for Fed officials, velocity is often unpredictable, especially in the short run, and sometimes it is highly variable. Furthermore, the effects of monetary policy also depend on fiscal policy, and since the mid-1960s the future course of the federal budget has been nothing if not unpredictable. This uncertainty makes it difficult for the Fed to determine just how much restraint (or ease) to apply to achieve a given result.

Once the Fed has determined what it wants to do, the next problem is to decide when to do it. Some time always elapses in diagnosing an emerging problem, and more time goes by between a policy decision and the time the action takes hold. This lag is highly variable and unpredictable. It is always difficult, therefore, to guess how far in advance of an expected problem to apply the monetary brakes or press down on the accelerator. Furthermore, since a large part of the Fed's power comes from affecting the psychology and expectations of the markets, it is always difficult to predict accurately just how a decision will affect that psychology. As Paul Volcker, Fed chairman during the Carter and Reagan administrations, explained, "What seems technically right isn't right if the psychology is running in the other direction and it makes no impact." The important thing, he concluded, is "just conveying a message to the public. You've got to keep things simple in order to affect behavior."[11] This further increases the Fed's risks. It is not only technically difficult to diagnose the economy's condition and to prescribe the proper medicine; it is even more difficult to predict how the patient will receive it. The Fed can ill afford to damage public confidence or to court the wrong expectations about its policies.

The Fed's critics have long complained that outguessing the economy is impossible and that, in trying to do so, the Fed often makes problems worse.

10. Strictly speaking, velocity is the ratio of the gross national product to the money supply.

11. Andrew Tobias, "A Talk with Paul Volcker," *New York Times Magazine*, September 19, 1982, 70.

Milton Friedman has contended that the Fed is always too easy, except when it is too tight, and that it tends to deliver the wrong medicine at the wrong times. Instead, he argues, the Fed should simply increase the money supply at a steady and predictable rate rather than try to outmaneuver the economy's trends.[12] Congress has been unwilling to put itself on the line by stipulating just what level of money supply growth the Fed ought to try to achieve. For their part, not surprisingly, Fed officials have resisted Friedman's efforts to restrain their flexibility. Over the years it has proved politically more palatable for the Fed to accept criticism for its mistakes than to make elaborate attempts to avoid them.

The Fed thus has long faced enormous political risks in an environment of great technical uncertainty. Inflation-fighting usually means higher interest rates, while lower interest rates usually stir fears of inflation. Rarely can the Fed make everyone happy. Usually its policies make some powerful political force unhappy, and sometimes Fed officials succeed in making *everyone* unhappy. To make matters worse, the Fed's political risks are greatest when economic problems make effective monetary policy most important.

In the face of these technical uncertainties and political risks, the Fed's evolution into an economic power of first-rate importance is the most remarkable bureaucratic metamorphosis in American history. This book is an exploration of that metamorphosis. It asks two questions. First, how has the Fed acquired this remarkable power? Second, what does its "independence" mean for the Fed and, more broadly, for American democracy?

There are two common answers to these questions. One, put forward by economists, argues that the Fed like all bureaucracies seeks autonomy to protect its existence. The Fed wraps itself in its legal independence in defense against the short-sighted demands of elected officials like the president and members of Congress. It guards its autonomy against any intrusion. This argument is especially popular among monetarist economists like Milton Friedman who attempt to explain why the Fed does not follow what is (at least to them) the superior strategy of setting monetary policy by rule—fixed, regular increases in the money supply—instead of by discretion. In fact, Friedman has complained that "the unbelievable strength of bureaucratic inertia" prevents the Fed from learning from past mistakes. The Fed, he has argued, insists on acting in ways that strengthen its own power, and the result is unstable monetary policy and a tendency to make large, infla-

12. See Milton Friedman, "The Role of Monetary Policy," *American Economic Review* 58 (March 1968): 1–17; and "Monetary Policy: Theory and Practice," *Journal of Money, Credit, and Banking* 14 (February 1982): 98–118.

tionary mistakes.[13] These economists, in fact, contend that the Fed is *too* powerful and independent.

Other observers have concluded that, far from being too politically independent, the Fed is in fact too politically responsive, especially to presidents' short-term political needs. By this argument, the Fed's power is derived from currying the support of the president. The most famous tale is told in a 1974 *Fortune* article by Sanford Rose, who contended that Fed Chairman Arthur Burns caved in to pressure by Richard Nixon to pump up the money supply in time for the 1972 election. Monetary growth, Rose argued, boosted the economy and helped Nixon beat George McGovern. It also unloosed a frightful inflation, and Rose condemned the Fed for allegedly sacrificing the economy's health to Nixon's reelection.[14] Some political scientists have supported Rose's general argument. Edward R. Tufte examined the Fed's behavior around election years and concluded that the agency was a coconspirator in the electoral-economic cycle: the Fed tended to increase the money supply before presidential elections and to decrease it afterward.[15] This argument suggests that short-term political motives, rather than long-term economic conditions, govern the Fed's behavior. The results, the argument goes, are equally disastrous and inflationary.

Neither of these explanations, however, accurately describes the subtle bases of the Fed's power to influence the economy. Neither does the Fed's legal independence, which is only a precondition for its power. As Norton E. Long argued, legal authority and budgetary flexibility "are necessary but politically insufficient bases of administration."[16] The Fed's legal autonomy explains its ability to act flexibly but not the fundamental basis of its power.

13. Friedman, "The Role of Economic Policy," 102, 114–18. See also John F. Chant and Keith Acheson, "The Choice of Monetary Instruments and the Theory of Bureaucracy," *Public Choice* 12 (Spring 1972): 13–33; and Keith Acheson and John F. Chant, "Mythology and Central Banking," *Kyklos* 26 (1973): 362–79. This approach builds on work by Anthony Downs, *Inside Bureaucracy* (Boston: Little, Brown, 1967), and William A. Niskanen, *Bureaucracy and Representative Government* (Chicago: Aldine, Atherton, 1971).

14. Sanford Rose, "The Agony of the Federal Reserve," *Fortune* 90 (July 1974): 90–93, 180–90.

15. Edward R. Tufte, *Political Control of the Economy* (Princeton: Princeton University Press, 1978), 51. Tufte builds on several analyses by economists on the relationship between the economy and national elections. See M. Kalecki, "Political Aspects of Full Employment," *Political Quarterly* 14 (October–December 1943): 322–31; William D. Nordhaus, "The Political Business Cycle," *Review of Economic Studies* 42 (April 1975): 169–90; and Assar Lindbeck, "Stabilization Policy in Open Economies with Endogenous Politicians," *American Economic Review* 66 (May 1976): 1–19.

16. Norton E. Long, "Power and Administration," *Public Administration Review* 9 (Autumn 1949): 257.

THE SOURCE OF THE FED'S POWER

Bureaucratic power, of course, is not an abstract principle. It exists only in the degree to which an agency affects the outside world. The path to analyzing the Fed's power thus lies in understanding its relationships with its environment.[17] The Fed differs from all other American government agencies in the flexibility it has in making decisions. It shares with all other agencies, however, the need to build political support and to avoid debilitating attack. The Fed's power depends on the political support of—or the absence of opposition from—its political constituencies: individuals and groups that possess important sanctions and rewards to which the Fed must pay attention.[18]

Every decision with political implications—every decision that benefits some people more than others—attracts political pressure, and the Fed's decisions are no exception. The power of its decisions, moreover, depends more on the balance of political forces that stand behind them than on the force of the decisions themselves. The keystone of the Fed's power thus is not so much its legal independence as its success in winning political support for its decisions.[19]

In understanding the Fed's power, therefore, it is important to understand the relationship between the agency and its constituencies. If the Fed has greater flexibility than other agencies, it also has more varied—and more conflicting—constituencies. One important group of constituencies is within the government. Fed officials have long had a sibling rivalry with the Secretary of the Treasury, who as the top fiscal spokesman for the administration and the government's chief bond salesman has enormous impact on the markets in which the Fed deals. Members of Congress can help build or destroy public support for the Fed and can alter or even remove the Fed's perquisites. Other constituencies are outside the government. Farmers, automobile manufacturers, and home builders rely on cheap credit for prosperity. Bankers and insurance brokers, on the other hand, demand low inflation to make investing for the future less risky.

Among all of the Fed's constituencies, however, the president is the most

17. See John M. Gaus's explanation of the importance of an organization's "ecology" in *Reflections on Public Administration* (University: University of Alabama Press, 1947), 5–7.

18. See Long, "Power and Administration"; Murray Edelman, "Governmental Organization and Public Policy," *Public Administration Review* 12 (Autumn 1952): 226; Matthew Holden, Jr., "'Imperialism' in Bureaucracy," *American Political Science Review* 60 (December 1966): 944; Peter Woll, *American Bureaucracy* (New York: Norton, 1977), 65; and Francis E. Rourke, *Bureaucracy, Politics, and Public Policy*, 3d ed. (Boston: Little, Brown, 1984), 97–103.

19. Long, "Power and Administration," 257.

important. Especially since Franklin D. Roosevelt and the New Deal, the public has expected the president to provide the good life, and presidential candidates have encouraged these expectations. Presidents, however, have little direct leverage over the economy. Managing the budget means dealing with—and often compromising with—Congress, and since the late 1960s the federal budget has been an inflexible policy tool. That has made the Fed and monetary policy even more important for the president, for it provides a different way to affect economic growth. The Fed has thus become keenly important to the president, and the president has become the Fed's most important constituent.

If the Fed's environment is complex, it is also fluid. The support or opposition of any constituency is neither fixed nor guaranteed. The Fed might find itself simultaneously attacked by the president and some members of Congress for encouraging high interest rates while it enjoys the support of bankers and financiers for cooling inflation. At another time, the president might applaud the Fed's war on inflation while home builders and automobile manufacturers complain bitterly that high interest rates are destroying their industries. The same part of the Fed's constituency can at different times be the source of the Fed's bitterest opposition and strongest support. Even bankers, traditionally among the Fed's staunchest backers, have sometimes angrily attacked its policies. The Fed's constituencies are numerous, powerful, and typically conflicting. Their conflicts give the Fed greater flexibility than agencies with strong, narrow, single-minded constituencies. The Fed never faces a single, overpowering political force, and its many constituencies often cancel out each other's demands.[20] These multiple constituencies, however, also expose the Fed to greater risk, because it is never possible to please everybody.

In dealing with its contituencies, the Fed faces two conflicting expectations. On one hand, the agency is expected to counteract inflationary pressures in the economy. Guarding the currency fundamentally means protecting it from rapid changes, and in practice that means fighting inflation. That mission, however, sometimes brings the Fed into conflict with constituents who want faster economic growth. On the other hand, elected officials fully expect that Fed officials will cooperate by steering monetary policy in concert with the fiscal course they select. Because elected officials are directly accountable to voters—and the Fed is not—they often argue that the Fed has an obligation to cooperate.

Over the years, navigating the Fed through these technical uncertainties

20. See Marver H. Bernstein, *Regulating Business by Independent Commission* (Princeton: Princeton University Press, 1955).

and political risks has been the job of its chairman. His goal traditionally has not been to minimize risk. Eliminating risk is impossible given the complex environment in which the Fed must work, and conflicts among the Fed's constituencies create opportunities as well as dangers.

Rather, the job of the chairman is *managing* the risks the agency faces. The Fed operates on a bounded plane of politically acceptable behavior. Political pressures define the terrain within which the agency can operate without courting strong attack: interest rates that are not so high as to enrage populists, inflation that is not so high as excessively to worry bankers. The many conflicts the Fed faces define the boundaries beyond which lie political attack. Since the constituencies are fluid, so too are the boundaries on the Fed's politically acceptable behavior. Sometimes, when the economy is relatively stable, the boundaries are broad and the Fed's risks are relatively low. At other times, especially during crises and at turning points in the economy, the boundaries become narrow and the risks, political and economic, very high.

It is the argument of this book that the Fed's power has depended on the chairman's leadership: on his ability to deal with the Fed's external environment, to help the Fed adapt to changing economic circumstances, technical uncertainties, and political demands. It has been the principal responsibility of the chairman to recognize the politically acceptable boundaries on its decisions; to keep those boundaries as broad as possible; and to attempt to keep the Fed's policies within those boundaries.[21]

The chairman's power is far greater than that of the chairmen of other independent boards and commissions in Washington. In fact, to most observers, both among experts and the general public, the chairman *is* the Fed. Former Federal Reserve Board member Sherman J. Maisel rated the influence of the chairman on the Fed's decisions as nearly twice as strong as that of any other part of the Fed. The chairman, he argued, has "the paramount role" in the monetary process.[22] Such a role is remarkable given the weak status the position had in the early years. At that time the secretary of the Treasury chaired the board and the board's own chief officer, then known as the "governor," was in charge only when the Treasury secretary chose not to attend. Not until the Banking Act of 1935 was the Fed under the direction of its chairman, and the act simply provided that the president

---

21. Robert C. Tucker similarly describes leadership as the tasks of diagnosing problems, formulating a plan of action, and mobilizing support. See *Politics as Leadership* (Columbia: University of Missouri Press, 1981), 18–19.

22. Sherman J. Maisel, *Managing the Dollar* (New York: W. W. Norton, 1973), 110, 123.

could designate one board member to serve as chairman and act as "its active executive officer."[23]

The chairman's power has evolved since then through the ability of individual chairmen to build the position to a post of prominence. His power rests on five extralegal sources: his role as public spokesman for the Fed; his position as representative of the Federal Reserve System, especially in meetings with the president; his management of the Fed's staff; his role in chairing meetings at the Fed; and his ability to build coalitions for key votes.[24]

The Chairman as Spokesman   Few pronouncements from Washington leaders have the same effect as words from the chairman. He regularly testifies before congressional committees, and committee members—as well as the closely observing financial community—look on him as the personal embodiment of the institution. His listeners assume that his words represent the Fed's official position, and any hints he gives on the future direction of monetary policy can move the money markets. Because he is the Fed's official spokesman, his words have tremendous influence among members of the official Washington community and in the wider network of Fed-watchers.

The Chairman as Point Man   Because of the chairman's position, he is the person outsiders seek when they wish to communicate with the Fed. He is in such heavy demand from congressional committees that Fed staff members carefully weigh competing claims to determine which committee appearances must be delegated to other board members. The chairman is the board member with whom the president meets. The same is true with foreign dignitaries; during the international debt crisis of the early 1980s this task occupied much of Paul Volcker's time.

The Chairman as Manager   Congress gave administrative responsibility for administering the Federal Reserve—from hiring its 1500-member staff to preparing its budget—to the Federal Reserve Board as a whole. The board then delegated the job to the chairman. To relieve the chairman of some day-to-day work, individual board members have responsibility for overseeing individual parts of the Fed's bureaucracy, but the chairman has principal responsibility for managing the agency. That also means that the chairman's needs receive top priority from the staff. The Fed's staff is among the best economic staffs in the world and a job there is coveted by economists holding new Ph.D.'s from the major universities. In as arcane and

23. Banking Act of 1935, P.L. 74–305, Sec. 203b.
24. This discussion relies heavily upon Maisel, *Managing the Dollar*, 123–29.

complex a domain as monetary policy, the chairman's ability to call on such talent greatly enhances his ability to lead.

The Chairman as Agenda-Setter   The chairman's position gives him powerful leverage over the timing and content of the Fed's policy. He determines the order in which participants speak at Fed meetings and, more importantly, he determines the content of the Fed's agenda: which issues are raised, when, and in what fashion. Every meeting of the Federal Open Market Committee is dominated by briefing books that describe the current state of the economy and the Fed's options. By tradition, the FOMC gets three options: to keep monetary policy about the same, to make it tighter, or to make it easier. The chairman plays the pivotal role in defining these options and in leading the Fed from the status quo to tighter—or easier—money.

The Chairman as Coalition-Builder   Making monetary policy requires a majority of the seven votes on the Federal Reserve Board and of the twelve votes on the Federal Open Market Committee. By framing the agenda, the chairman can decide which issue to raise—and how. By relying on the staff's expertise, the chairman can build an intellectual case for the policy he favors. And by relying on the force of the chairmanship, he can win support for his views. Maisel contended that the prestige of the chairmanship automatically meant that when the chairman cast his vote he typically carried at least one other vote in Federal Reserve Board meetings and two votes at FOMC meetings.[25]

THE STRATEGIES OF LEADERSHIP

Fed chairmen thus have many resources in moving the Fed to policy decisions, but, as we have seen, they also operate in a world of great political risk and technical uncertainty. The key both to insuring political survival and to building political support has been managing the Fed's relations with its constituencies, especially its central constituency, the president. Over the years, relations with the president have followed three patterns.

The first is *accommodation*. Over most of the Fed's history, its monetary policy has coincided with what presidents have wanted. Sometimes this was because the chairman and the president have a fundamental agreement on the medicine the economy needed. Sometimes it was because the economy was moving in uncharted directions and the Fed and the president groped their way together. Sometimes it was because the chairman could not win

25. Ibid., 128–29.

enough support to move the Fed in a different direction, though he wanted to do so. The single most important feature about Fed policy making over the years, though, has been the need to win political support and, since the president's support has been most important, the dominant pattern has been accommodation.

At times, however, the chairman-president relationship has been one of *confrontation*. Deep conflicts between the Fed and the president—typically when the Fed's fundamental worries about inflation have run into presidents' pressure for high economic growth—have sometimes produced sensational conflicts. Such confrontations have been rare, but when they have occurred resolution has required fundamental changes in the relationship between the Fed and the president.

Finally, the relationship between the chairman and the president has sometimes been one of *transformation*.[26] Especially during confrontations with the president, some Fed chairmen have sought to use the Fed and its power to change the environment rather than adapt to it. These have been special times for the Fed, times of fundamental redefinition of both the institution and its relations with the president: of redefining the Fed's mission and the president's expectations; of changing its organizational structure; and of setting its basic ideology—how the Fed views the world. These periods of transformation have been the product of unique moments of time and visions of the future, of crises in which problems threatened both the economic health of the nation and the bureaucratic health of the Fed, of special leadership from unusual Fed chairmen.

The Fed's power thus has depended on the chairman's leadership: on his ability to build the institution and to cement political support from the president as well as its many other constituencies. The biggest crises of the Fed's history, in fact, have come at the times of weakest leadership. The Fed's story thus is a twin tale: the interdependence between the Fed and its environment and the leadership of its chairmen in managing that environment.

Its leaders have built the Fed into a powerful bureaucracy unrivaled in the American republic and the chairmanship into one of Washington's most powerful positions. This dual power is all the more remarkable when compared with the Fed's weak and uncertain first steps, which began with the creation of the Federal Reserve System in 1913. In the first years of the twentieth century, the nation's financial and political officials recognized that the paralysis of the banking system was handicapping the country's

26. James MacGregor Burns calls this kind of leadership "transformational." See *Leadership* (New York: Harper and Row, 1978), 4.

advancement into the industrial age. They agreed that something had to be done to rescue the nation's financial system—but they struggled fiercely over just what to do.

CHAPTER TWO

IN SEARCH OF A MISSION

Southerners and westerners had always feared the domination of powerful eastern bankers. In fact, at the beginning of the twentieth century, thirteen eastern states held two-thirds of the nation's cash. Woodrow Wilson's Treasury secretary, William G. McAdoo, later complained that "the large cities were draining the country dry."[1] To make matters worse, wildly different kinds of money circulated: gold, gold certificates, silver, silver certificates, greenbacks, and notes issued by many different banks. There was little coordination among banks in good times, and in bad times regional jealousies and periodic bank panics crippled the economy.

The banking system had two fundamental problems. One was that the currency was inelastic—it could not expand or contract with the nation's needs. The federal government required national banks, the country's largest and strongest, to back their notes with government bonds. Since the supply of bonds was fixed—and the supply of other forms of money like gold and silver varied little—the supply of currency was fixed as well. Demands for currency, however, varied with the season of the year. Farmers needed to borrow extra money in the fall to harvest their crops and to bring them to market. When they later sold their crops and repaid their loans, the money supply bulged. From month to month, therefore, interest rates swung wildly. From 1890 to 1908, the average rate in the second week of June was 2.31 percent, while in the fourth week of December it was 7.38 percent.[2]

The other problem was that the decentralized banking system had no way

1. William G. McAdoo, *Crowded Years* (Boston: Houghton Mifflin, 1931), 211.
2. The rates are the stock market call loan rates. See B. H. Beckhart, "Outline of Banking History: From the First Bank of the United States through the Panic of 1907," *Annals* 99 (January 1922): 14.

of mobilizing money in crises. In normal times, a country bank deposited its idle cash with a larger city bank, and most city banks deposited their reserves with a larger New York bank. The New York banks, in turn, lent out their idle cash, most often to investors in the stock market. The banking system's available cash thus was minimal and most of the reserves ultimately ended up in stock speculation. If the economy turned sour and depositors in the nation's interior demanded their cash, the country banks had to go to the city banks and the city banks to the New York banks. To get their money, the New York banks in turn would call in the stock market loans, but stocks were difficult to liquidate in the midst of such a panic.

An especially severe panic in 1907 led to strong calls for government action. In mid-October New York's third-largest bank, the Knickerbocker Trust Company, failed and investors began a run on New York's other banks. The city's financiers broke the panic in New York within a week, but by that time country banks, worried by previous panics when they could not get their cash, demanded currency for their deposits. When the New York banks restricted payments on the accounts, citizens everywhere hoarded currency. The banking crisis produced substantial unemployment; whole-sale prices declined 5 percent and on an annual basis the national product shrank by 11 percent.[3]

To explore reforms, Congress established a National Monetary Commission, chaired by Senator Nelson W. Aldrich. The commission toured Europe to compare banking systems and produced an imposing array of reports, some of which became classics. It concluded that the United States suffered from inadequate cash reserves, an inflexible supply of currency, and the lack of any agency to facilitate the exchange of cash and checks between regions. This, the commission argued, produced an unstable economy "tending to promote dangerous speculation" and "injurious disturbances in reserves."[4] Some portions of the country had difficulty getting inexpensive credit, and bankers had no market in which they could sell their loans and thus get cash to further expand their lending.

The answer, Aldrich concluded, was the establishment of a "National Reserve Association," a European-style central bank. The association would be a banker's bank that would discount loans (that is, buy loans from banks, at a discount from their face value, to supply more money for further loans) and would create an elastic note issue (which would expand and contract with the economy). The organizational structure of the association would be

3. Milton Friedman and Ann Jacobson Schwartz, *A Monetary History of the United States, 1867–1960* (Princeton: Princeton University Press, 1963), 156–68.
4. National Monetary Commission, *Report*, Sen. Doc. 243, 62d Cong., 2d sess., 1912, 8.

a decentralized one modeled on the American political system: the national association would have fifteen district associations broken down into local associations. Aldrich's new organization, most importantly, would be a private body with minimal governmental control. Federal officials would have only four of the fifty seats on its governing board. The president could choose its chief executive officer, but only from a list of three candidates submitted by the board. It was to be a central bank under bankers' control.

Aldrich's proposal became the cornerstone of William H. Taft's banking proposals in the 1912 election campaign. The prospect of bankers with even stronger control over the nation's finances, however, terrified populists who were already concerned about the "money trust" of New York bankers. Woodrow Wilson and the Democrats picked up this theme and hit hard at the monopoly issue in the 1912 campaign. Wilson rejected the concept of bankers' control that lay at the heart of Aldrich's plan and argued instead for banking reform, under government control and free from the money trust. "So long as that exists," he told a campaign audience, "our old variety and freedom and individual energy of development are out of the question."[5]

Wilson came to office determined to reform the banking system and place it under public control. With Senator Carter Glass, a Virginia Democrat who headed a newly organized banking reform subcommittee, he framed a banking reform plan based on federal control through an independent regulatory body like the Interstate Commerce Commission. Like the Aldrich plan, the new reserve system would provide for the rediscounting of commercial paper and for a flexible currency. And like the Aldrich plan, the system would operate through regional reserve banks. However, while the bankers and Republicans favored a small number of banks, perhaps only three or four, the Democrats argued for many more—at least eight and perhaps as many as fifty—to prevent eastern bankers from dominating the system.

From the beginning Wilson insisted he would not accept any banking reform under bankers' control. "There are only two choices, of course," Wilson told a press conference at the end of June 1913. "Either to give the central control to the bankers or to give it to the government." From the bankers' point of view, however, Wilson's plan for governmental control was dangerous because, they feared, a government-managed central bank would find inflation too attractive. A Chicago banker warned that Wilson's approach would "put the whole fabric of credits into politics."[6] For his part, Aldrich suggested that a governmentally controlled central bank might be

5. Woodrow Wilson, *The New Freedom* (New York: Doubleday, Page and Co., 1913), 185.
6. Quoted by McAdoo, *Crowded Years*, 225.

tempted to use the power to "insure the success of a political party." He contended, "no government has yet been found strong enough to resist the pressure for enlarged issue [an inflationary increase of the money supply] in times of real or imagined stress." For Wilson, however, the choice was clear. "My own feeling is that governmental control is perfectly safe. I can't imagine anybody audacious enough in a political office to play politics to that extent."[7]

The controversy threatened to scuttle the banking bill. To salvage it, Senator Glass and Treasury Secretary McAdoo suggested that Wilson allow the bankers a seat on the new board or at least permit them to recommend its members. Trying to strike a compromise, Glass took a delegation of bankers to meet with Wilson. Wilson remained adamant. "Will one of you gentlemen tell me," he asked the bankers, "in what civilized country of the earth there are important government boards of control on which private interests are represented?" The bankers could make no reply, and Wilson made clear that he would have a government board under government control. To assuage the bankers, though, Wilson suggested the establishment of a federal advisory council, composed completely of bankers, that would meet periodically with the reserve board to advise on policy.[8]

The bankers saw the proposal as a weak sop and mounted a new campaign in the Senate against the bill. If they were not to keep the government out of banking, they at least wanted to keep the number of reserve banks small. The more banks there were, they feared, the stronger the board would have to be to bring order to the system; fewer banks would make the system more powerful and thus would be greater insurance against government interference. The populists, especially from the South and West, naturally argued for a larger number to dilute the influence of eastern financial centers. Senator John Shafroth finally suggested a compromise. No bank, he said, ought to be more than one night's train ride from a reserve bank. In case of a run on his bank, a banker could climb aboard a train, secure the needed currency, and return to avoid a panic the next day. This, Shafroth said, argued for at least eight reserve banks.[9] Congress settled on no less than eight nor more than twelve reserve banks, which naturally led to the establishment of twelve banks to minimize the number of disappointed cit-

7. Nelson W. Aldrich, "Banking Reform in the United States," *Proceedings of the Academy of Political Science* 4 (October 1913): 37; and Arthur Link, ed., *The Papers of Woodrow Wilson* (Princeton: Princeton University Press), 27:559.

8. Carter Glass, *An Adventure in Constructive Finance* (New York: Doubleday, Page, 1927), 116.

9. *Congressional Record*, 63d Cong., 1st sess., November 25, 1913, 6021.

ies. And finally, on a near-party-line vote, the Democratic Congress gave Wilson his bank reform plan.

Wilson hailed the new "Federal Reserve System" as a plan to produce "accommodations which are going to secure us in prosperity and in peace," and he later ranked it among the greatest achievements of his administration. [10] He proclaimed the system's virtues: "Let bankers explain the technical features of the new system. Suffice it here to say that it provides a currency which expands as it is needed and contracts when it is not needed: a currency which comes into existence in response to the call of every man who can show a going business and a concrete basis for extending credit to him, however obscure or prominent he may be, however big or little his business transactions. More than that, the power to direct this system of credits is put into the hands of a public board of disinterested officers of the Government itself who can make no money out of anything they do in connection with it. No group of bankers anywhere can get control; not one part of the country can concentrate the advantages and conveniences of the system upon itself for its own selfish advantage." [11]

While Wilson praised the new agency, its creators were less sure just what they had wrought. Congress was very vague on what the Fed was to do or how it was to do it. The Federal Reserve Act gave the Fed the power to "discount notes, drafts, and bills of exchange arising out of commercial transactions." This language established the Fed's power to set the discount rate: the Fed could make loans to member banks that offered commercial loans as collateral. By borrowing from the Fed, the banks could increase their reserves and thus increase their loans. As we saw in chapter 1, Congress directed the Fed to set the discount rate—the rate of interest on these loans from the Fed—"with a view of accommodating commerce and business," a phrase that was to prove hopelessly vague. [12]

For the system's early supporters, however, the vagueness was not worrisome because they did not view the Fed as a powerful central bank. Instead they saw it more as a public utility whose function was simple: the reserve banks would expand and contract the supply of money with the economy's seasonal demands, while the Federal Reserve Board would oversee the system's policies. The job was to be relatively "scientific" and automatic. The regulatory commission model, in the tradition of the Interstate Commerce Commission, had for the Fed the obvious virtues of convincing

10. Glass, *An Adventure in Constructive Finance*, 231.
11. Link, *The Papers of Woodrow Wilson*, 31:172.
12. P.L. 43, 63d Cong., 2d sess., 1913, Secs. 13, 14d.

populists they would get a fair shake and disarming, if only partially, bankers' complaints about political control.[13] As Secretary McAdoo explained, the Fed "is really a public utility in the service of the nation."[14]

Further easing debate over just how the Fed was to behave were established economic theories that to many observers provided nearly automatic guides to monetary policy: the gold standard and the "real bills" theory. By the rules of the gold standard, the Fed needed to produce enough money in the long run to balance international payments. And according to the real bills theory, the money supply in the short run would vary with the needs of commerce; lending would be secured by "real" goods in commercial transactions. This theory held that central banks should expand and contract the money supply to accommodate productive borrowing. A banker, for example, would issue a short-term commercial loan, perhaps to a farmer to harvest his crops or to a merchant to finance his inventory. The banker could then sell such a loan, at a discount from the face amount, and use the proceeds to make further loans. As commerce expanded, the number of loans would increase and the money supply would automatically grow. The loans were self-liquidating: as the farmer sold his crops or the merchant his goods, he would repay the loan from the proceeds, and the money supply would shrink again. This made the currency "elastic" and kept interest rates stable.

The real bills theory posited that managing the dollar was a fairly automatic function. The central bank could expand the money supply as much as necessary to accommodate "eligible" borrowing. It was difficult, however, to define just which loans were eligible. The real bills theory set two basic standards—the loans should be short-term and for nonspeculative purposes—but just what that meant was anything but clear. One member of Congress complained that he had tried without success to get more than a dozen bankers to define what eligible loans were, and Congress despaired of doing any better.[15] It was not obvious just how "short" a short-term loan should be, and it proved hard to restrict loans to nonspeculative purposes. A clever merchant could shift idle cash to speculation and obtain an "eligible" loan to finance his inventory. The Fed was to be a public utility operating according to an automatic theory. Determining just how to apply that theory, however, left the Fed with great uncertainty and little guidance.

13. Richard H. Timberlake, Jr., *The Origins of Central Banking in the United States* (Cambridge: Harvard University Press, 1978), 204, 198.

14. McAdoo, *Crowded Years*, 222.

15. Timberlake, *The Origins of Central Banking*, 197.

UNCERTAIN FIRST STEPS

The Federal Reserve Board, the system's governing body, opened for business on November 16, 1914. Congress had created a seven-member board, with the secretary of the Treasury and the comptroller of the currency as ex officio members. The president was to appoint the other five members subject to the Senate's advice and consent, and he was to designate two members of the board as the system's chief administrative officers, the governor and vice-governor. When he attended a board meeting, however, the Treasury secretary was chairman. Even though he rarely attended, many Fed officials resented the secretary's dominant position in the new agency.

Wilson took his time in making the appointments. He told a January 1914 press conference: "I feel that is almost like constituting a whole Supreme Court. It's almost equal in importance."[16] The Supreme Court metaphor had become a popular one for the new Fed: it was to make policy with an eye toward the principles of science and business, just as the Court made decisions based in law, and it was to be scrupulously nonpartisan. For that reason, Wilson's advisers argued that, just as the Supreme Court appointments, it was important to insure that the appointees shared the administration's views. McAdoo contended that "it is most important, in fact, to my mind, vitally important, that at least four members of the Federal Reserve Board should be men of known sympathy with the spirit and purposes of the Federal Reserve Act and of undoubted loyalty to the Administration." Without such a majority on the board, the Treasury secretary added, "it would be most unfortunate and harmful to the Administration" if the secretary were to find himself in the minority "and be forced to act independently."[17]

When Wilson finally made his decisions, he settled on candidates who represented the interests that had clashed over the board. One, Paul M. Warburg, was a Wall Street banker. W. P. G. Harding was a banker from Birmingham, Alabama, and a geographic counterbalance for those who feared eastern bankers would dominate the system. Frederick A. Delano was a railroad company president, and Adolph C. Miller was a prominent economist who had served as assistant interior secretary in the Wilson administration. Wilson named Assistant Treasury Secretary Charles S. Hamlin to be the new system's governor. Treasury Secretary McAdoo and Comptroller of the Currency John S. Williams took their seats as ex officio members, and in the Fed's first meetings, as McAdoo feared, the board split

16. Link, *The Papers of Woodrow Wilson*, 29:138.
17. Letter, McAdoo to Wilson, May 20, 1914, in Link, *The Papers of Woodrow Wilson*, 30:50–51, 54.

into two blocs: Delano, Miller, and Warburg in opposition to the Treasury's McAdoo, Williams, and Hamlin, and Harding in the middle with the balance of power in early decisions.[18]

The earliest disputes arose about the Fed's independence, especially from the Treasury Department. Some members bridled under what they perceived to be the Treasury's attempt to control the board. Delano complained that Hamlin's previous ties with the administration might lessen his independence; he hoped that Hamlin's appointment, as he wrote Wilson, was not part of a plan "to control the Board's action through the power to designate the Governor and Vice Governor."[19] The location of board meetings also worried some members. Early meetings were held in the Treasury Department, and this greatly annoyed the anti-Treasury bloc. As long as the Treasury housed them, they feared, it would be impossible to speak with a truly independent voice. They suggested that although the Federal Reserve Act stipulated that the board's first meeting had to be in Washington, there was no regulation about the location of future meetings.[20] By moving board meetings away from Washington, members of the anti-Treasury bloc hoped to make it harder for the Treasury secretary and comptroller to attend. The board never acted on the suggestion; its location within the Treasury's walls proved a symbolic restraint on the Fed's freedom until 1935 when it got its own building—and when Congress also removed the secretary and comptroller from the board.

Also nagging was the question of protocol. Some board members worried about their place in Washington's social universe. As McAdoo sarcastically put it, "They were not to be pale and distant stars, lost in a Milky Way of obscure officialdom; they must swim in the luminous ether close to the sun!"[21] There was something more than vanity to the question, however. Hamlin wrote in his diary that members "felt degraded and humiliated" by the Treasury Department's treatment. Hamlin reported to Colonel House that board members believed the Fed was being made an adjunct of the Treasury Department rather than an independent body. The result, Hamlin warned, was that the president might not be able to attract first-rate men to the Fed in the future.[22]

McAdoo sent the question to a State Department protocol official, who

18. McAdoo, *Crowded Years*, 285.

19. Letter, Delano to Wilson, July 21, 1916, in Link, *The Papers of Woodrow Wilson*, 37:463.

20. Sec. 10.

21. McAdoo, *Crowded Years*, 286.

22. See Elmus R. Wicker, *Federal Reserve Monetary Policy, 1917–1933* (New York: Random House, 1966), 6–7.

replied that the members of the Federal Reserve Board ought to rank below assistant secretaries, with the Fed itself ranked fifth among independent commissions since it was the fifth one created. This did not satisfy Warburg and other members of the anti-Treasury faction, who argued that the Fed ought to have higher status if it were not to become the Treasury's subordinate. McAdoo remembered later that President Wilson was irritated by the request. "I can do nothing about it," he told McAdoo. "I am not a social arbiter." McAdoo replied, "I know that, Mr. President, but they want you to decide." "Decide what?" "Decide their rank in the scale of social precedence," McAdoo said. "Well," Wilson suggested with a smile, "they might come right after the fire department." McAdoo decided not to report back to the Fed on that conversation.[23]

The head of the New York Federal Reserve Bank, Benjamin Strong, concluded in 1916 that the Fed "will not establish itself with its members and with the country generally until it has met the test of a real crisis."[24] World War I provided just such a crisis, as the Treasury struggled to raise enough cash for the nation's war needs and put heavy pressure on the Fed to keep interest rates low. "The great temptation of Secretaries of the Treasury in time of war is to borrow cheap money," Strong argued.[25] Although low rates would help keep the Treasury's cost of wartime borrowing low, they also risked fueling inflation. Keeping interest rates low encouraged consumers to borrow more. Furthermore, since banks could use Treasury bonds as reserves against deposits, every extra dollar put into Treasury bonds became the reserve for six to eight dollars of checking accounts. (Reserve requirements varied according to the size of the bank.) This in turn encouraged more borrowing and purchasing.

Treasury officials, however, put heavy pressure on the Fed to support wartime borrowing at bargain rates. W. P. G. Harding, the swing vote in the early pro- and anti-Treasury disputes, had succeeded Hamlin as governor, and he and other Fed officials recognized the danger in such a policy. To oppose the Treasury in wartime, however, would have been unrealistic and, as Strong put it, would "be an invitation to Congress to have our powers

23. McAdoo, *Crowded Years*, 287–88. In succeeding years the Fed's chairman has been ranked with cabinet secretaries, its vice-chairman with under-secretaries, and other board members with assistant secretaries.

24. Letter, Strong to Henry R. Towne, director of the New York Bank, November 8, 1916, quoted by Lester V. Chandler, *Benjamin Strong, Central Banker* (Washington, D.C.: Brookings Institution, 1958), 101. This account relies heavily on Chandler's definitive biography of Strong.

25. Chandler, *Benjamin Strong*, 99.

modified—a perfectly unthinkable and most dangerous possibility."[26] The Fed had little choice but to support the Treasury.

Treasury Secretary McAdoo established an interest rate of 3½ percent for war bonds. The Fed agreed grudgingly to support the rate by making enough money available to keep the rate to that level. Since that rate was substantially below the prevailing rate in the market, Fed officials worried that the low rate might induce inflation. McAdoo countered that higher rates might make Treasury bonds too attractive an investment and drain money from banks to the Treasury, thus weakening the economy. He hoped instead to convince individuals to invest in government bonds as a patriotic, not a commercial, venture. The secretary's strategy saved the government millions of dollars in borrowing costs and insured the success of the Treasury's campaign, but it also created huge profits for financiers who borrowed money cheaply from the Fed and invested the money in Treasury bonds.[27]

If the war immobilized the Fed, the armistice only worsened the Fed's problems. The Treasury had a massive debt to refinance and naturally wished to retain the low rates. Harding and Strong, among others, pressed the Treasury to increase rates to bring inflation under control, but Treasury officials countered that a Fed policy of "direct action"—persuasion in the marketplace—could work instead. The Fed in January 1920 finally started to increase all interest rates, but the move came too late. The postwar inflation broke in the spring of 1920 with a worldwide decline in agricultural prices. The United States suffered one of the sharpest, if shortest, economic declines in its history.[28]

The episode demonstrated, if nothing else, that neither the Fed nor anyone else understood the dynamics of inflation and recession. To this point, the Fed had concentrated on manipulating the discount rate according to seasonal demands. The real bills theory told officials how to accommodate these cycles: to make enough money available to finance "eligible" loans. It did not, however, tell them how to distinguish between credit for eligible loans and credit for speculating on Treasury bonds, among other things. The theory, furthermore, did not tell Fed officials how to make permanent additions to the money supply to ease the economy out of decline. The Fed, therefore, made two serious errors. In the face of postwar inflation, it did not tighten money and raise interest rates to slow the boom. Then, when

26. Letter, Strong to Kemmerer, December 18, 1922, quoted in Chandler, *Benjamin Strong*, 120.
27. See McAdoo, *Crowded Years*; Wicker, *Federal Reserve Monetary Policy*; and Chandler, *Benjamin Strong*, 111.
28. Friedman and Schwartz, *A Monetary History of the United States*, 231–39.

the economy slumped, the Fed went a full year without lowering interest rates in the face of recession, since the real bills theory had no provision for situations in which demand dropped. The Fed's mistakes unquestionably made the situation worse, especially for farmers. [29]

The blunders predictably raised again the worries of farmers and small businessmen that eastern bankers would gain control of the Fed and choke off credit. Comptroller of the Currency John Skelton Williams, a Virginian and long a foe of Wall Street, contended that the Fed had conspired to plunge the country into deflation to drive up the interest rates for bankers' advantage. [30] Congress in 1921 established a Joint Commission on Agricultural Inquiry to investigate Williams's sensational charges. The commission concluded that they had no substance, but it did argue that the Fed had erred in the postwar years by allowing "the expansion, inflation, speculation, and extravagance" that led first to a boom and then to collapse. The commission had the sharpest words, however, for Treasury Department officials, who, they said, had the primary responsibility for the crisis. Even after the war had ended and the Treasury's financing needs had declined, the report said, "the discount policy of the Federal reserve banks was again subordinated to the Treasury policy." [31] Fed officials saw the report as a vindication of their own campaign to break free of the Treasury. For its part, Congress through the report made plain that it and not the Treasury was the Fed's ultimate judge.

The dispute spilled over in 1922 into the issue of reappointing Harding as governor. Some western senators accused him of taking advantage of his position to speculate in cotton during the deflation. Administration officials assured them that President Warren Harding, a Republican, had no intention of reappointing the governor, a Democrat. However, the governor's supporters, including the New York *Times*, argued that "his forced retirement would give a shock to the financial community" because it would signal "the intrusion of politics" and "sectional influences" into the Fed. [32] That argument won out, and the president reappointed Harding.

The Fed thus ended its first decade with the principles of formal independence from the Treasury and freedom from political and sectional interference reconfirmed. In practice, however, the Fed was still subordinate to the Treasury. Furthermore, Fed officials were still trapped by the weak-

29. See Wicker, *Federal Reserve Monetary Policy*, 52; and Friedman and Schwartz, *A Monetary History of the United States*, 223.
30. Chandler, *Benjamin Strong*, 177.
31. U.S. Congress, House of Representatives, *Report of the Joint Commission of Agricultural Inquiry, Part 2: Credit*, 67th Cong., 1st sess., Rep. 408, 1922, 15, 12.
32. New York *Times*, May 12, 1922, 18.

nesses and uncertainties of economic theory. As the economy went through booms and busts, it had no good guide for dealing with economic cycles. Hamstrung by the real bills theory and trapped by the pressures of the gold standard, the Federal Reserve still viewed itself—and was viewed by the Congress and the Treasury as well—as a banking utility, not a board framing monetary policy to counteract economic cycles. The congressional commission sanctioned experiments by the Fed in dealing with these cycles, but Fed officials had not yet decided just how that ought to be done, or who ought to do it.

THE DISCOVERY OF ECONOMIC MANAGEMENT

In addition to setting reserve requirements and the discount rate, the Federal Reserve Act also gave the Fed the power to buy or sell securities in the open market. In the first years of the agency, the reserve banks used open-market operations principally to enhance their earnings. Several of the banks, especially the Dallas bank, chronically had difficulty turning a profit, and interest on the securities provided a steady flow of income. The Fed naturally wanted to increase the number of members as much as possible, and the state-chartered banks that had the choice of whether or not to join wanted assurance that they would receive dividends on the stock they bought. If the reserve banks could not make a profit, the member banks would lose money on their investment in the stock. To meet the pressure for earnings, therefore, the reserve banks began buying government securities to obtain the interest.

During World War I, however, some shrewd Fed officials realized that buying or selling government securities as part of the Treasury's support program could also help speed up or slow down the economy. Before the war, there was only a limited supply of Treasury securities, but because the war had increased the national debt from $1 to $25 billion, the opportunities for discretionary open-market operations increased dramatically in the postwar period.

With the Fed's *Tenth Annual Report,* issued in 1924, the agency stepped gingerly away from the public utility model toward discretionary control. Although some Fed officials maintained allegiance to the real bills theory, the report argued that the Fed "cannot adequately discharge their function" by "the simple expedient of any fixed rule or mechanical principle." No rule, the report maintained, could possibly take account of the many different economic situations the agency might face. "Credit is an intensely human institution," the report continued. "In its ultimate analysis credit administration is not a matter of mechanical rules, but is and must be a matter of judgment—of judgment concerning each specific credit situation at the particular moment of time when it has arisen or is developing."[33] The elevation of judgment to preeminence marked the beginning of policymaking by discretion. In the report the Fed implicitly announced that it would seek positive control of the economy. Less clear, however, was just who would exercise that control. Leadership in the Fed was disorganized, and the governor had little real authority. The Treasury dominated the board in Washington, while the reserve banks, largely independent of the board, set their own course.

W. P. G. Harding stepped down as governor in 1923, and President Harding named Daniel R. Crissinger, a boyhood chum with whom he had attended school and played marbles, to replace him. Crissinger had managed several farms in Ohio and had served as president of a bank there, so his appointment reassured farmers and small-town bankers who feared after the agricultural collapse that the Fed would draw closer to Wall Street. He had come with his old friend to Washington, even though he was a Democrat and the president was a Republican. President Harding had named him comptroller of the currency, where he served until moving to the Fed.

As governor, however, Crissinger found he had relatively little power. Instead, most of the Fed's power rested in Benjamin Strong, governor of the Federal Reserve Bank of New York. Strong had special power both because of the importance of New York in the nation's financial system and because of the force of his own ideas. Born of old New England stock, Strong had managed securities before moving to banking and ultimately becoming president of the Bankers Trust in New York. He had opposed the passage of the Federal Reserve Act because, like most bankers, he feared a public central bank would produce inflation. This initially led him to reject the offer of the governorship, and he accepted the position only after two friends—including Federal Reserve Board member Paul Warburg—spent a weekend in the country convincing him that the new system needed his talents. Once on the job, Strong was one of the system's first officials to see the enormous potential that open-market operations offered. In 1922, he anticipated the board's 1924 report by writing that "the Federal Reserve System, as the central factor in the control of credit, must rely upon the application of wisdom and intelligence of the first order."[34]

33. Federal Reserve Board, *Tenth Annual Report* (Washington, D.C.: Federal Reserve Board, 1924), 7–8, 32.
34. Letter to economist O. M. W. Sprague, November 3, 1922, quoted in Chandler, *Benjamin Strong*, 198–99.

By early 1922, Strong and his associates in the reserve banks had tripled their holdings of Treasury securities. Treasury Secretary Mellon, in fact, complained that such substantial activity, uncoordinated with his own dealings, made it difficult for the Treasury to gauge the market in placing new issues. Largely at the department's insistence, the system in the spring of 1922 set up a new Committee of Governors on Centralized Execution of Purchases and Sales of Government Securities by Federal Reserve Banks. Under this awkward title, the Boston, New York, Philadelphia (and later Cleveland) reserve banks recommended a policy for all of the banks to follow. That policy was not obligatory, but it did provide a structure within which the leading banks could try to coordinate their actions with the economy's problems. The New York bank became the committee's operating office and Strong the committee's chair. The increasing importance of open-market operations made Strong the most powerful figure in the young agency.

The Treasury continued to complain, however, that the uncoordinated purchases and sales by the reserve banks made effective management of the public debt impossible. Some banks held on to securities to protect their earnings when the committee recommended that the banks sell to tighten the money supply. Mellon, annoyed by the confusion, urged the board to rein in the banks and set uniform rules for the system's open-market operations.[35]

The Federal Reserve Board responded in early 1923 by disbanding the old committee and reconstituting it with the same membership under tighter rules and a considerably shorter name, the Open Market Investment Committee. A year later, Strong got an opportunity to test the new structure. A recession began in late 1923 and hit especially hard at textile mills in New England as well as rubber, steel, and farming. There were numerous bank failures and large gold inflows from Europe. The shift of gold from Europe to the United States threatened to erode the bank reserves the Europeans needed to attack their own recessions and, at the same time, to flood the American economy with gold that would ignite a serious inflation.

Under Strong's leadership, the reserve banks took aggressive action, perhaps the first time in history that a central bank moved against an economic cycle to promote economic stability.[36] In the open market, the banks bought $500 million in Treasury obligations, which simultaneously had several ef-

35. Memo to board, March 10, 1923, quoted in U.S. Congress, House of Representatives, Committee on Banking and Currency, *Federal Reserve Structure and the Development of Monetary Policy: 1915–1935*, staff report, 92d Cong., 1st sess., 1971, 82–83.
36. Friedman and Schwartz, *A Monetary History of the United States*, 240.

fects. This eased the money supply, helped lower domestic interest rates, and made American investments less attractive to European investors. The strategy soaked up extra gold, reduced the danger of American inflation, and helped stem the gold movement from Europe to the United States. It helped restore stability to the banking system, especially for farmers who relied heavily on credit. Most of all, it prevented the widespread panic that had accompanied previous recession. Strong proudly proclaimed on the day after Christmas 1924 that the result was "a greater feeling of tranquility and contentment throughout the country than we have experienced at any time since the war."[37]

The policy was a monumental success for the system, for the new Open Market Investment Committee, for discretionary action by the Federal Reserve banks, and for Strong's leadership. The system had engaged in historic, untried action and had noticeably eased a national downturn and an international financial crisis. The Fed had shown it could be far more than a public utility technically governing the flow of credit. It had become a monetary authority of first-rank political and economic importance, but that authority was centered in Strong and the New York Federal Reserve Bank, not the Federal Reserve Board. Presidents Harding and Coolidge, meanwhile, cared relatively little about the Fed. Management of the economy had not yet come onto the president's agenda, and both presidents struggled mainly to keep recurring tensions between financiers and populists from becoming a political liability for them in naming board members.

By the middle of 1927, a slowing economy led the Fed to seek easier money once again. A mild domestic recession had started, and a new inflow of gold from Europe threatened a new crisis. Fed officials responded by easing the money supply once again. This time the Federal Reserve Board instead of the reserve banks took the stronger hand, and instead of working through the reserve banks' open-market strategy, the board voted to approve discount rate cuts from 4 to 3½ percent. However, some midwestern reserve banks, led by the Chicago bank, opposed the move. They did not really believe it necessary and feared that the eastern-dominated Fed was trying to force the policies of eastern bankers down their throats. Crissinger led a slim majority on the board to force the Chicago bank to lower its rate. The vote maintained the solidarity of the Fed's policy, but it also rekindled old sectional fears about who would control the Fed. One of the Fed's strongest congressional backers, Senator Glass, was angry that the central board had overridden the principle of decentralized money management he had helped craft.

37. Memo to file, December 26, 1924, quoted by Chandler, *Benjamin Strong*, 242–46.

The issue came to a head when Crissinger resigned soon afterward. Bankers speculated over which faction President Coolidge would favor in naming a new governor. His choice reassured the partisans of a weak board, for he appointed Roy A. Young, who had been for ten years the governor of the Minneapolis Federal Reserve Bank. Since Young had sided with the Chicago bank in its dispute with the board and since the Minneapolis bank was the last to fall in line with the lower discount rate, his appointment signaled that the board would play only a limited supervisory role over the reserve banks. Analysts speculated that Young would command a majority of the Federal Reserve Board that would stand against overruling the policies of the reserve banks except in emergencies. His appointment will be a great thing, the St. Louis *Star* argued, "if the new Governor of the Board can keep his Western atmosphere enough to realize that all of the banks and all of the money are not in New York, nor all of the nation's industries in Wall Street."[38]

The board's step back into the shadows left leadership of the system completely to Strong. The governor had an international view of the monetary system, due in large part to his close and long-standing relationship with Montagu Norman, governor of the Bank of England. Strong believed that international cooperation of strong central bankers could break monetary panics and runs on currency, and when weighing American economic problems he always looked as well to their international consequences. For Strong, the crucial problem in 1927 was the huge inflow of gold into the United States that the board's action had done little to stem, and the instability of European currencies.

In 1927, a delegation of central bankers, including Norman, visited new York and Washington to argue for an easier Fed policy to slow Europe's gold drain. Easier money would lower American interest rates and make American investments less attractive to the Europeans. Strong agreed and within a few months, the system's holding of government bonds nearly doubled to $526 million, while holdings of bills increased from $64 million to $335 million. The policy, led by Strong, successfully ended the flood of gold from Europe. Its supporters hailed it for stemming the international crisis, but its opponents criticized it for destabilizing the domestic economy. Bank reserves increased substantially and banks used the extra reserves to expand their lending. The loans fueled a boom in stock speculation that did not end until the bubble burst in October 1929. Adolph Miller, one of the board's original members, later blamed Strong for making a monumental

---

38. Quoted in *The Literary Digest* 95 (October 15, 1927): 84.

error. Miller believed that Strong had sacrificed the stability of the domestic economy to his concerns for international finance and, especially, for his friend Norman. As Miller explained to Herbert Hoover in 1934, "Of one thing I am sure, that he [Norman] exerted great influence upon Mr. Strong" and that he had "indirectly, at least, a large measure of responsibility" for the flood of reserves.[39]

Normally silent Calvin Coolidge added his own fuel to the speculative fires by suggesting in January 1928 that he saw nothing alarming about stock speculation and that, in fact, stocks seemed to him a good buy. As secretary of commerce in the Coolidge administration, Hoover was aghast at the president's statement and he worked unsuccessfully within the administration to quiet the speculation fever. By the time he took office as president, however, the boom had gotten out of control and the stock market's forces were building to the crash. He held the Fed principally responsible for providing the bank reserves that made the stock boom—and subsequently collapse—possible, and he bore a grudge forever after that the Fed had cared more about the international than the domestic economy.

The Fed's officials were in fact not blind to the dangers of stock speculation. They could not, however, decide on a clear diagnosis of the problem or the best way to solve it. By early 1928, for example, the reserve banks decided that the economy had recovered enough, and they made money tighter by raising the discount rate back to 4 percent and by selling Treasury securities. They were confused, though, about whether to buy short-term Treasury bills or longer-term bonds. Some members of the Open Market Investment Committee believed that buying bills would produce less speculation than buying bonds; others saw little difference.[40] The reserve banks' confusion only further encouraged stock speculation, while the board watched quietly from the sidelines.

Much of the drift, however, resulted from Strong's weakening health. He had become the most powerful figure in the Federal Reserve System; indeed, he was as close to a central banker as the nation had ever had. Since 1916, though, Strong had suffered from tuberculosis, and the disease forced him to take frequent leaves from the New York bank. By the mid-1920s the leaves became more extended and he was away from New York one-third of the time. In 1926 an attack of pneumonia nearly killed him, and a combination of illnesses kept him away from work most of the time until the disease finally killed him in October 1928. Without his guidance, the reserve

39. Letter, Miller to Hoover, October 31, 1934, PPI, Adolph Miller Correspondence, Hoover Library.
40. Chandler, *Benjamin Strong,* 464.

banks were adrift. During his life, no figure emerged to challenge Strong, and after his death decisions reverted to a committee of the twelve reserve bank governors. Since no one was willing or able to step forward to assume leadership, the system drifted along by inaction.[41]

In the midst of this confusion, the Fed faced a complicated problem: how could it limit the flow of credit for stock speculation without drying it up for other purposes? Credit, Strong had believed, was credit; "We cannot control it once it leaves our doors."[42] Limiting one kind while loosening another seemed impossible to many Fed officials. To tighten money enough to slow the speculative boom would stir up attacks from farmers and small businessmen who would have great trouble in securing credit. Not to tighten credit would give license to speculators.

The Fed could not determine just what to do. To try to tighten money, the reserve banks continued to sell Treasury obligations. Meanwhile, however, the Federal Reserve Board maintained the discount rate under the prevailing market rate, which helped keep money easy. Speculators used that as an invitation to continue the buying fever. On eleven occasions from February to May 1929, the New York Federal Reserve Bank voted to raise its discount rate, and on every occasion the Federal Reserve Board denied its permission. The board argued instead for "direct action"—public pronouncements—to discourage the use of credit for speculation. The board asserted that it "neither assume[d] the right nor [had] it any disposition to set itself up as an arbiter of security speculation or values." It added in a letter to the reserve banks on February 2, 1929, that the Federal Reserve Act did not "contemplate the use of the resources of the Federal reserve banks for the creation or extension of speculative credit," but the caution lacked teeth.[43]

Arguing publicly against speculation, the board members nevertheless reasoned, was the most effective step the Fed could take. To increase the discount rate further would have taken the rate to the unprecedented level of 6 percent. Even that, board member Adolph Miller later argued before the Senate Banking Committee, would have had only momentary psychological value on speculators while inflicting great pain on the nation's commerce. He told the committee that an increase "would have been nothing but a futile gesture" or worse: "It would have been a practical declaration to the speculative markets of the country that the doors of the Federal

41. Ibid., 51–52; and Friedman and Schwartz, *A Monetary History of the United States,* 413–16.

42. Quoted by Chandler, *Benjamin Strong,* 430.

43. *Federal Reserve Bulletin* (February 1929): 93–94.

reserve system were open to all comers." Raising the rate to 6 percent while stock market loan rates soared as high as 20 percent, he argued, "would have been an admission of defeat."[44]

Not all members of the system approved the board's "direct action" policy. Governor George W. Norris of the Philadelphia Federal Reserve Bank, for example, wrote to board member Charles Hamlin in April 1929 that "as long as we maintain a discount rate which is absurdly low," the boom would continue. "Our 5 percent rate is equivalent to hanging a sign out over our door, 'Come In,' and then we have to stand in the doorway and shout 'Keep Out.' It puts us in an absurd and impossible position."[45] Advocates of stronger action, however, had no success in rousing their colleagues.

In August the board finally allowed the New York reserve bank to increase its discount rate to 6 percent, but by then it was too late. Although the board's indecisiveness did not directly cause the boom and subsequent collapse, the easy money policy did feed speculation. The board, furthermore, lost the opportunity to restrain speculation, and it also refused to allow the reserve banks to take strong action for fear of raising rates too high for everyday commerce. The entire system wallowed in a vacuum of leadership, as it had since Benjamin Strong's death.

ENSNARED BY THE DEPRESSION

Although vilified for doing nothing about the Depression, Herbert Hoover did in fact have a conscious plan to end the financial crisis: to keep steady the flow of the federal government's expenditures; to try to keep wage levels up; and to keep the federal budget balanced. He was convinced that there was little the federal government could otherwise do. Federal expenditures amounted to only 2.5 percent of the gross national product in 1929, and even a massive increase in federal spending would have produced only limited relief. In any case, pushing the federal budget into deficit for this or any other purpose was unthinkable to Hoover. The president therefore felt he could be most useful by insuring that federal finances were well managed and by spurring on the private sector and state and local governments to tackle the Depression's problems.[46] That, he hoped vainly, would put the economy back on track.

44. U.S. Congress, Senate, Committee on Banking and Currency, *Operation of the National and Federal Banking Systems*, hearings, 71st Cong., 3d sess., 1931, 143.

45. Quoted by Chandler, *Benjamin Strong*. 468.

46. Herbert Stein, *The Fiscal Revolution in America* (Chicago: University of Chicago Press, 1969), 3–16.

Hoover also relied heavily on the Fed, and he followed its actions far more closely than did his predecessors. When Young resigned the governorship of the board in 1930, the president named Eugene R. Meyer to replace him. A Republican who had served under every president since Wilson, Meyer was by his own admission an "original Hoover man." He was a New York banker whose nomination predictably unsettled western farmers, and some senators called him "a decoy duck and trader sent in by the Wall Street crowd."[47] Meyer, though, was far more than a front for financiers. He had skillfully managed the Farm Loan Board since 1927. His variety of experience had earned him a reputation as an adroit politician, and stories about his boyhood training as a boxer led many observers to speculate that he would transform the Federal Reserve Board into a powerful and aggressive force.[48] However, the Fed's inability to mount a strong and consistent campaign to deal with the collapse and the bank failures it produced soon frustrated Hoover. "I concluded," he wrote in his memoirs, "it was indeed a weak reed for a nation to lean on in time of trouble."[49]

In the absence of any other idea, Fed officials reverted to the real bills theory. They argued that the Fed's role was to provide enough credit to help businesses operate, and since economic demand was sluggish and interest rates were low, they concluded they could do no more. In fact, since there was little demand for loans, the Fed, entangled in the real bills theory, reduced the money supply further. That proved a major error and undoubtedly worsened the Depression.[50]

Fed officials saw the Depression as the inevitable result of the 1920s' boom. They believed that the stock market crash and the economic slowdown were the wages of sin for an economy that had indulged in excesses. As the head of the Philadelphia Federal Reserve Bank said in 1930: "The consequences of such an economic debauch are inevitable. We are now suffering them. Can they be corrected or removed by cheap money? We do not believe that they can." Instead, he argued, the nation must reduce production and consumer credit and encourage individuals to accumulate savings. "These are slow and simple remedies," he concluded, "but just as there is no 'royal road to knowledge,' we believe that there is no shortcut or panacea for the rectification of existing conditions." Along with many other analysts, he argued that unemployment and the decline of prices had just "about run their course and that the foundations for business revival

47. New York *Times*, September 14, 1930, IX:5.
48. See *Business Week*, July 1, 1931, 27–28; and *The Literary Digest*, October 4, 1930, 42.
49. Herbert Hoover, *Memoirs*, vol. 3: *The Great Depression, 1929–1941* (New York: Macmillan, 1952), 212.
50. Friedman and Schwartz, *A Monetary History of the United States*, 407.

[had] already been laid."[51] The Depression seemed the unfortunate but inevitable prescription for economic overindulgence.

Not all members of the system agreed with this policy of pain. Board member Adolph Miller, a friend and strong supporter of Hoover, argued that the low interest rates were giving the board a false sense of security. "Money is sleeping," he told the Open Market Investment Committee in 1930, "and it is conceivable that a part of a constructive program is to wake it up and make it do something."[52] Miller proved unsuccessful, however, in stirring his colleagues to act. The agency had poor indicators of the state of the economy and could not determine just what employment and business activity rates were. If by purchasing government securities the Fed could increase prices, some members suggested, perhaps it should be done. Fed officials wondered, though, if indeed there would be such an effect, how long it would take to be felt, and whether it might simply promote the forces of socialism.[53] The Fed did not know what to do, and no one stepped forward to lead strong action. The Depression crippled the Fed in uncertainty.

Hoover's advisers criticized the Fed for a "policy of confirmed pessimism."[54] In the White House, staff members were urging on Hoover a conscious stimulative policy that relied on easier money from the Fed. "There is a need for inflation," presidential confidante Mark Sullivan wrote Hoover in 1931. "Lacking inflation, we are in for continuation of this depression, with rather accelerated suffering." The Fed could do this, he told Hoover, and in fact had privately promised to start pumping money into the market, but its actions proved timid and far short of the promises. The "Hoover man," Governor Meyer, had been prevailingly wrong on the course the Depression would take, Sullivan argued. If he could not be convinced to take stronger action, Sullivan suggested, Congress, "through the improper and dangerous means of great bond issues and great government expenditures," might act instead.[55] Hoover certainly had no stomach for such stimulative congressional action, but he also had deep reservations about appearing to put political pressure on the "independent" Fed and declined therefore to mount a campaign for easier money.

The Fed's ineptitude nevertheless proved a constant thorn in Hoover's

51. Quoted in House Banking Committee, *Federal Reserve Structure*, 128.
52. Ibid., 129.
53. Ibid.
54. Letter, P. J. Croghan to Secretary of Commerce LaMont, April 26, 1930, Subject File, Federal Reserve Board Correspondence, Hoover Library.
55. Memo, Sullivan to Hoover, July 18, 1931, PPF, Mark Sullivan Correspondence, Hoover Library.

side. After one New Jersey banker telegraphed the president in October 1931 urging him to convince the Fed to take strong action, Hoover wrote an exasperated reply: "I am afraid I cannot run the Federal Reserve Banks, much as you and I might like to have it that way."[56] The large supply of sound assets immobilized in failed banks especially discouraged Hoover, and he constantly sought some way of releasing them to fuel the recovery. Meyer, meanwhile, angered Hoover because he seemed preoccupied with international problems—like Britain's 1931 decision to abandon the gold standard—instead of the Depression and the growing bank crisis. He wrote Meyer, "I feel it is necessary for me to say that it seems to me an equal effort to serve our own people in the matter of the closed banks to that which has been given to foreign banks is now required."[57] Meyer replied curtly that the Fed was working on the problem, but the system never did produce a plan to deal with the closed banks.

Hoover then determined to develop his own plan, a $500 million program to release frozen assets. The economy's basic problem, he believed, was liquidity, not solvency, a problem that could be attacked by unleashing the sound assets of those banks. "The only real way to break this cycle is to restore confidence in the people at large," he wrote in urging the Fed to back the plan. "To do this requires major unified action that will give confidence to the country."[58] Once again the Fed refused. Banks were failing, many Fed officials believed, because of insolvency—the value of bonds and real estate backing loans was falling, and unloosing more money on the economy would do nothing to help this problem. These conflicting views immobilized them both.

Bankers continued to complain to Hoover, who sent several of the letters to Governor George L. Harrison of the New York Federal Reserve Bank. Harrison wrote back a cheery reply, arguing that the Fed's open market purchases "will, no doubt, prove beneficial." He told the president, "Already there are signs that [Fed policy] is relaxing the attitude of a great many banks and bankers" and "ought to be quite an influence toward changing the conditions" to which the letters referred.[59] Harrison was reading the wrong tea leaves, however, and the banking crisis deepened in late 1932 and early 1933.

56. Letter, Hoover to E. C. Stokes, October 13, 1931, Presidential Subject File, Federal Reserve Board, Hoover Library.

57. Letter, Hoover to Meyer, September 8, 1931, Presidential Subject File, Federal Reserve Board, Hoover Library.

58. Letter, Hoover to George L. Harrison, governor of the Federal Reserve Bank of New York, October 5, 1931, PPF, Financial Matters, Hoover Library.

59. Letter, Harrison to Hoover, May 3, 1932, Presidential Subject File, Financial Matters: Banking and Bankruptcy, Hoover Library.

The 1932 election made Hoover the lamest of lame ducks, but he tried on several occasions to produce a joint policy with President-elect Roosevelt. Better than anyone else, Hoover realized that he could take no effective action without Roosevelt's support. For his part, Roosevelt was determined not to tip his hand until the inauguration. In the long four months until Roosevelt became president, which Hoover later christened the "winter of the Roosevelt hysteria," nothing happened.[60] Hoover continued to try, and in February 1933 Hoover and his staff developed a new plan for a clearing-house, backed by all banks, that would cover the assets of troubled banks. It was a form of deposit insurance, but Hoover could convince neither the Fed nor Roosevelt to back the plan.

In fact, Hoover believed, some members of the Federal Reserve Board, in concert with Roosevelt, were deliberately obstructing his efforts. He told his associates emphatically that one of three things was true. The Fed was dumb or blind to the problems, or it was being deliberately obstructive, or Roosevelt was deliberately orchestrating the Fed's actions to precipitate a crisis. He came to believe that Governor Meyer, in particular, was "obstructive and disloyal." He confided years later to his friend Miller, "I have always had the impression that Meyer was coaching Roosevelt not to agree to our proposals."[61]

As the crisis worsened, Hoover told the Federal Reserve Board on February 22, "I wish to leave no stone unturned for constructive action." He asked the board to advise him whether they considered the situation "a public danger" and whether the board could develop something to protect the public interest. All of the board's members joined in a reply: "At the moment the Board does not desire to make any specific proposals for additional measures or authority, but it will continue to give all aspects of the situation its most careful consideration."[62] While the board deliberated, the banking system further deteriorated, but even so the board members rejected another Hoover proposal to guarantee bank deposits.

Hoover continued working nearly to the hour of Roosevelt's inauguration. On March 2, two days before the transition, he proposed invoking the World War I–era Trading with the Enemy Act, which gave the president emergency powers, to limit the use of gold, to declare a banking holiday, and to guarantee bank deposits. Some members of the Federal Reserve Board tried

60. Letter, Hoover to John C. O'Laughlin, March 25, 1933, PPI, John C. O'Laughlin, Hoover Library.

61. Ogden Mills Notes, PPF, 1933; and letter, Hoover to Miller, May 14, 1952, PPI, Adolph Miller Correspondence, Hoover Library.

62. Letter, Hoover to Board of Governors, February 22, 1933; and letter, Meyer to Hoover, February 25, 1933, Federal Reserve Files, Hoover Correspondence, 1917–33, Hoover Library.

to bring Hoover and Roosevelt together, but the president-elect signaled through an intermediary that Hoover had enough authority to do what he proposed without Roosevelt's support and, furthermore, that he had no objection if Hoover went ahead. Roosevelt, however, refused to commit himself to the plan and the board followed suit.

As late as March 2, two days before the inauguration, Hoover continued to solicit the board's support for an executive order proclaiming a bank holiday. Fed officials, though, continued to drift along without recommending action. Finally, on the night before the inauguration, Meyer surprised Hoover by proposing that Hoover unilaterally proclaim a bank holiday. Roosevelt had already made clear that he wished no further action taken until he was sworn in the next morning, and Hoover saw the suggestion purely as an attempt to embarrass him in the last hours of his administration. He angrily rejected the proposal over the telephone and went to bed. Several hours later, his aides woke him with another urgent message from the Fed, this time in writing, pleading for the proclamation of a bank holiday as the only way to avert a collapse. Hoover curtly wrote back, "I am at a loss to understand why such a communication should have been sent to me in the last few hours of the Administration, which I believe the Board must now admit was neither justified nor necessary."[63] One of Hoover's supporters on the board, Adolph Miller, agreed and thought Meyer had "kicked a man in the stomach when he was down."[64]

Roosevelt was about to outflank the board with his own banking program. The Fed had been created to prevent banking crises and had been immobilized for four years. In fact, the Fed had missed many chances to ease the burden and, to make things worse, it had tightened the money supply when easier money was needed. Its ineptitude undoubtedly worsened the depth and length of the collapse.[65] After grappling with the Fed for four years, Hoover was in no mood for last-minute compromises to help the Fed save face.

To the end, Hoover and the Fed struggled over just what ought to be done about the Depression. The president believed that the Fed had helped trigger the collapse with easy money, that it had paid more attention to

63. Hamlin Diary, March 3, 1933, Correspondence, Federal Reserve Board, Hoover Library; letter, Meyer to Hoover, March 3, 1933, Presidential Subject File, Federal Reserve Board, Hoover Library; letter, Hoover to Meyer, March 4, 1933, ibid. For a view less flattering to Hoover, see Laurin L. Henry, *Presidential Transitions* (Washington, D.C.: Brookings Institution, 1960), 343–65.
64. Memo for file, October 1934, PPI, Adolph Miller Correspondence, Hoover Library.
65. Friedman and Schwartz, *A Monetary History of the United States*, 330.

European central bankers than closed American banks, that the Fed had overlooked opportunities to ease the Depression, and that in the administration's last days some Fed officials had colluded with Roosevelt to embarrass him. For their part, members of the Federal Reserve Board were reluctant to take any bold action on their own and they passively awaited Roosevelt's inauguration. The era marked the signal failure of the agency and the decline of monetary policy as an economic tool from the heights it had enjoyed during the 1920s, when it was the key element of American macroeconomic policy.[66]

THE MONETARY MISSION

The Fed was born in controversy. Farmers and small businessmen wanted a decentralized organization under strong governmental control to counterbalance the power of eastern bankers. The financial community, on the other hand, feared that political control of the system would bring inflation. They sought instead a centralized body under private control. The compromise that produced the Fed resulted in a system with power scattered among twelve reserve banks, with a weak central board of uncertain purpose. The Fed, furthermore, had only a weak theoretical guide for its policy decisions. The public utility model quickly broke down under the pressures of wartime finance. The real bills theory failed both times it was seriously tested, after World War I and again during the Depression.

At the end of its first two decades, therefore, the Fed was in genuine peril. It did not know what it ought to do, why it ought to do it, and just as important, who ought to direct policy. Furthermore, it had proved impotent in dealing with crises it had been designed to prevent. Benjamin Strong had demonstrated that the Fed could exercise a powerful role, especially in stabilizing economic cycles through discretionary control of the economy. He also demonstrated that monetary policy could become the equal of fiscal policy in managing the economy. Following Strong's death, however, the leaderless Fed drifted through crises. The Depression demonstrated the Fed's potentially fatal weaknesses: the vagueness of its purpose, the disorganization of its structure, and the uncertainty of its territory.

Purpose When events outstripped the comfortable certainty of the real bills theory, the Fed was frozen. The public utility notion told Fed officials how to accommodate annual cyclical changes in the economy. It did not, however, tell the Fed what to do about periodic crises, and when crises

66. G. L. Bach, *Making Monetary and Fiscal Policy* (Washington, D.C.: Brookings Institution, 1971), 64.

threatened the Fed was without a lens through which to focus its options. The lack of such a focus, which a sense of purpose would have provided, at times immobilized the Fed and at other times led the Fed to wrongheaded policies.

Congress created a reserve system with great expectations but little guidance. Members of Congress could agree on little more than the fact that the country needed banking reform, and even by the usually nebulous standards of acts of Congress the Fed's charter was mushy. Strong's personal views gave the Fed what little sense of purpose it had during its first twenty years, but that guidance was so personal that his jealous colleagues abandoned it after his death. Without a clear idea of what it was to do, Fed officials had a difficult time in understanding the economy and their role in it. As Chester Barnard explained in his classic treatment of management, "The environment must be looked at from *some* point of view to be intelligible."[67] The Fed had no institutional point of view for most of its first twenty years. It therefore could not tell which problems were its problems, or which solutions best solved which problems. As a result, the Fed moved from the 1920s—what Friedman and Schwartz called "the high tide of the reserve system"—to the banking crisis that threatened the Fed's very existence.[68] No new president, and especially no president like Franklin D. Roosevelt, was likely to accept a do-nothing Fed in the midst of economic disaster.

Structure To make things worse, the Fed was simply disorganized. The agency was little more than a collection of twelve banks, each pursuing its own course. Conflicts between the board and the banks were signs of the board's own weakness and of the Fed's lack of purpose. Barnard argued that "purpose is the unifying element of formal organization."[69] Without such unity, the Fed was doomed to destructive conflict and drift.

Territory Worsening the Fed's problems was the fuzziness of its domain. In day-to-day operations, the Fed was captive of the Treasury. With the secretary of the Treasury and the comptroller of the currency having seats on the board, with the Fed housed in the Treasury Department, and with the Treasury secretary the board's chairman when he chose to attend a meeting, the Federal Reserve Board had little room for independent action. World War I demonstrated just how risky this could be. The Treasury's interest in cheap money, especially during wartime, posed a recurring prob-

67. Chester I. Barnard, *The Functions of the Executive*, 30th anniversary ed. (Cambridge: Harvard University Press, 1968), 195.
68. Friedman and Schwartz, *A Monetary History of the United States*, 240.
69. Barnard, *The Functions of the Executive*, 137.

lem for the Fed. At times of greatest inflationary danger, the Fed could expect insurmountable pressure to serve the Treasury's purposes and sacrifice its own goals.

The Fed's uncertain purpose, disorganized structure, and vague territory thus seriously threatened the young agency's very existence. The Depression crystalized serious problems with which the Fed had struggled for its first twenty years. What should it do? How could it win support and deflect the inevitable criticisms of its decisions?

Strong's leadership in the mid-1920s had demonstrated the preconditions for effective action by the Fed: a clear sense of organizational purpose; a center of action in the system; and a unique domain—a domain, in particular, clearly delineated from the Treasury's. But he also demonstrated that effective action in the Fed, as it was then organized, was critically dependent on entrepreneurs. For the Fed to survive and thrive over the long haul, it needed to move past a reliance on intermittent entrepreneurs to an institutional base of power. And that in turn depended on the emergence of a leader who could diagnose the system's problems, develop a strategy for solving them, and build support for his plan.

President Hoover recognized the Fed's importance. He blamed the Fed's intransigence for many of his problems and struggled vainly for greater influence over its decisions. Hoover's legacy was thus important for Fed-president relations. Even if he did not know quite how to marshal its powers, he demonstrated that presidents could no longer ignore the Fed's monetary policy. It remained for Franklin D. Roosevelt and the chairman he appointed—Marriner S. Eccles—to bring the Fed to new maturity.

CHAPTER THREE

THE STRUGGLE FOR INDEPENDENCE FROM THE TREASURY

veryone agreed that the Fed had failed the test of the Depression. The Fed badly mismanaged the stock market boom and the bank collapse. The real bills theory, which suggested the agency could create enough "good credit" for business while preventing "bad credit" for speculation, proved disastrous. To make matters worse, the Fed was also organizationally hamstrung. The ghost of Benjamin Strong still hovered over the reserve banks, and the reserve bankers were unwilling to allow any colleague such power again. That, however, was largely moot, because no one—board member or bank official—showed any inclination to take control. The Fed's tools, therefore, remained in weak hands, and the economy suffered from the Fed's immobilization.

In March 1930, the board took a few tentative steps to strengthen its control over open-market operations. It disbanded the Open Market Investment Committee and reincarnated it once again, this time as the Open Market Policy Conference, composed of representatives of all twelve reserve banks. The board could now call meetings and discuss open-market policies, but each bank retained the right to decide whether to follow the policy conference's recommendations. For the first time, the system had an open-market policy—but there was no obligation for anyone to follow it.

Many members of Congress were unsettled by the Fed's open-market maneuvers, especially since Congress had never approved the Fed's various open-market committees or the use of open-market operations to manage the economy. In the Banking Act of 1933, better known for creating the Federal Deposit Insurance Corporation (FDIC) to insure bank accounts, Congress finally formalized what the Fed had been doing for a decade. It authorized a Fed committee, newly and finally named the Federal Open

Market Committee, to set open-market policies. The committee would be composed of one representative from each reserve bank as well as all board members, but, apparently through a legislative oversight, the Federal Reserve Board still had no power to initiate or approve open-market policies. Earlier versions of the bill had authorized such a role for the board, but the provision was dropped in the last-minute rush to assemble the bill for final action. As a result the board still lacked the most important and sought-after power. It did gain added leverage over the reserve banks with a provision forbidding reserve banks from engaging in negotiations with foreign banks except as authorized by the board, an undisguised slap at the extensive negotiations Strong had conducted with Norman.

In the energetic first days of the Roosevelt administration, however, the Fed faced an uncertain future. In the five years since Strong's death, the New York bank had been unseated from its unrivaled dominance of the system, but the relationship between the board and the reserve banks was still vague, as was the question of just who controlled open-market operations and what those operations were to accomplish. With the creation of an FDIC independent from the Fed—a new banking agency squarely in the Fed's turf—Roosevelt served notice that he would outflank the Fed if it proved uncooperative.

Soon after Roosevelt took office, Meyer resigned the governorship, and in May 1933 the president named Eugene R. Black to replace him. Black, a personal friend of Roosevelt, was then serving as governor of the Federal Reserve Bank of Atlanta; he agreed to come to Washington for three months. He was a conservative financier who opposed the "rubber dollar" inflation policy that some public figures were recommending. Instead, he argued for strengthening business and for relaxing credit so families and farmers could pay their debts. Black suggested that the high American standard of living would have to be scaled back to a level where individuals could meet their obligations. "We have been living in an automobile, a frigidaire, a radio era," he had said in a famous 1930 speech. "We cannot pay our debts and continue in that direction. Let us not fool ourselves."[1] Black's three months turned into fifteen as he stayed on to help the financial system through its most difficult times, but then, anxious to return to Atlanta, his family, and the reserve bank where he contended he had "the best job in the world," he resigned.[2] The Fed was once again without a leader or a sense of direction, and it was up to Black's successor, Utahan Marriner S. Eccles, to restore both.

SEIZING CONTROL

Eccles's unusual economic notions intrigued Stuart Chase, a Roosevelt administration brain truster, during a visit to Salt Lake City in February 1933.

1. New York *Times*, May 12, 1933, 16.
2. *Newsweek*, August 25, 1934, 36.

Eccles was a prominent local banker who argued that the Depression resulted from a failure of leadership, both political and financial. The depth of suffering, Eccles contended, was the consequence of the nation's failure to marshal its strength to revitalize the economy. Contrary to what many businessmen were arguing, the problem was not excessive federal spending and an unbalanced budget but too little extravagance in federal spending. The federal government, he said, had the resources to put people back to work, and it ought to do so.

Eccles was planning a trip east in a few weeks, and Chase recommended that Eccles stop in New York to talk with Rexford Tugwell, one of Roosevelt's economic advisers. The two met in a drugstore booth near Tugwell's Columbia University office, where Eccles urged on Tugwell a program of "logical radicalism": large federal spending—and a large federal deficit—to begin putting people back to work.[3] Tugwell liked what he heard and invited Eccles to discuss his views with other administration officials. His message, repeated to officials from Commerce Secretary Henry Wallace to Interior Secretary Harold A. Ickes, was simple: that the Depression was no ordinary downturn in the business cycle; that the president's "ringing manifestos" would not by themselves put people back to work; and that the government needed a conscious program of deficit financing. Eccles did not believe in a perpetually unbalanced budget; a budget in surplus, he believed, could help "offset the danger of a boom on the upswing, just as an unbalanced budget could help counteract a depression on a downswing." For the times, however, he concluded that "the only way we could get out of the depression was through government action in placing purchasing power in the hands of people who were in need of it."[4] He was a Keynesian who had never heard of Keynes and who, in fact, publicly argued the virtues of compensatory fiscal policy before Keynes published his famous *General Theory*. While other administration officials were already planning to stimulate the economy through federal spending, few more forcefully put the case than did Eccles.

Eccles made such a good impression on the administration's insiders that the new Treasury secretary, Henry Morgenthau, Jr., asked him to join his staff as a special assistant. Eccles had barely settled into the Treasury when Black resigned from the Federal Reserve Board. At a White House conference in August, Morgenthau leaned over to Eccles and whispered, "Marriner, I've been talking to the president about your filling Eugene Black's

3. Marriner S. Eccles, *Beckoning Frontiers: Public and Personal Recollections* (New York: Alfred A. Knopf, 1951), 115.
4. Ibid., 129–31; 79; 81.

place." A few weeks later Roosevelt asked him directly if he would accept the job. Eccles boldly replied that he would find the job appealing only if fundamental changes were made in the Federal Reserve System. "What do you think ought to be done?" Roosevelt asked. "If you will let me come back, I will give you an answer in two weeks," Eccles replied.[5]

Eccles returned with a three-page memo and had a two-hour discussion with Roosevelt. "If the monetary mechanism is to be used as an instrument for the promotion of business stability," he told the president, "conscious control and management are essential." Discretionary control was important, and to get that control, Eccles argued, power would have to be concentrated in the Federal Reserve Board. The board should be given full control over the timing, character, and volume of open-market operations. Furthermore, he contended, the appointment of the governors of the reserve banks should be subject to approval by the board. "The relatively minor role played by the Board can, in my opinion, be attributed to its lack of authority to initiate open-market policy, and to the complete independence of the Reserve Bank Governors," he told Roosevelt. Without accountability to the board, he concluded, "The Governors cannot help but be profoundly influenced by a narrow banking rather than a broad social point of view." "Marriner," Roosevelt replied, "that's quite an action program you want." The president nevertheless agreed to support Eccles's proposals, and a week later, on November 15, 1934, Eccles became governor.[6]

Working with one of Roosevelt's economic advisers, Lauchlin Currie, Eccles early in 1935 developed a bill proposing three fundamental changes in the Fed. First, he set a more ambitious and aggressive goal for the Fed's monetary policy. Currie found Congress's original "accommodating commerce and business" mandate "vague to the point of meaninglessness."[7] Eccles and Currie instead proposed that the Fed be given explicit power and responsibility "to promote conditions conducive to business and to mitigate by its influence unstabilizing fluctuations in the general level of production, trade, prices and employment."[8] The plan moved the Fed from a passive to an active role in economic management, from simply "accommodating" the demands of business to promoting overall economic growth. After 1932, it was never again assumed that the two were synonymous. The

5. Ibid., 165; and Extemporaneous Statement to Chairmen of the Federal Reserve Banks, May 29, 1948, box 46, folder 17, Marriner S. Eccles Papers, Marriott Library, University of Utah.

6. Memo, Eccles to Roosevelt, November 3, 1934, OF 90, box 2, Franklin D. Roosevelt Library; and Eccles, *Beckoning Frontiers*, 175.

7. Memo, Lauchlin Currie to Eccles, April 1, 1935, box 14, folder 3, Eccles Papers, p. 17.

8. Ibid., pp. 17–18.

Fed was moving to a stronger position from which to influence the economy as a whole.

Second, the bill proposed to transfer substantial power from the reserve banks to the Federal Reserve Board. "Decentralized control is almost a contradiction in terms," Currie wrote Eccles. "The more decentralization the less possibility there is of control." With the current Fed structure, he concluded, "it is almost impossible to place definite responsibility anywhere."[9] The result was that the agency's most valuable tool, open-market operations, was in uncertain hands. Eccles and Currie proposed to shift control over open-market operations from the reserve banks to the Federal Reserve Board, which would be advised by representatives from five reserve banks.

Finally, they argued that the Fed's monetary policies had to be integrated far more closely with the administration's fiscal policies. To Currie and other administration officials, it was clear that the New Deal was going to require a large supply of inexpensive government credit. The Fed would therefore have to play an important supporting role. Currie contended that the old arguments about the Fed's independence from the presidency were dangerous, and he argued, "There is no economic problem more important than achieving and maintaining prosperity, and since the actions of the monetary authority have a direct bearing upon the strength of business activity they must be subject to the control of the Administration."[10] That in turn depended upon open-market operations under the firm control of a strong board, a board sensitive to the state of the economy and to the administration's needs.

At the same time, however, Eccles recognized the danger that plans for a Fed tied more closely with the president might draw attack from financiers who had long feared political control of the money supply. To deal with these criticisms, Eccles developed a clever formulation. The Fed, he said, had to act not as the captive of any administration but in the public interest. It was to be "publicly controlled"—by Congress's oversight and its own sense of the general public's needs—"rather than governmentally controlled" by the president's presumably more narrow interests.[11]

Eccles's plan to strengthen the Fed stood in sharp contrast to emerging monetarist theories that argued for an automatic monetary policy. The monetarists held that discretionary control of the money supply was inherently

9. Ibid., p. 2.
10. Ibid.
11. U.S. Congress, House of Representatives, Committee on Banking and Currency, *Banking Act of 1935*, hearings, 74th Cong., 1st sess., 1935, 273.

dangerous because the chance for mistakes was too great. In testifying before a congressional hearing, one monetarist argued that Congress ought to force the Fed to set monetary policy by automatic pilot, with steady increases in the money supply: "We propose to set up a body which will operate strictly within the lines prescribed by this Congress, who will be nothing but office boys, nothing but clerks, with nothing to do except to carry out the specific provisions of the law."[12] Economists like Henry C. Simons, one of the leading monetarists, criticized the Fed for having tried during the Depression to differentiate between "good" and "bad" uses of credit. He argued instead for "a simple, mechanical rule of monetary policy"; "We must avoid a situation where every business venture becomes largely a speculation on the future of monetary policy."[13] The answer was to make the Fed into a utility that supplied money at a predictable rate of growth regardless of political pressures or short-term economic problems. The Fed's critics argued that only an automatic guide, prescribed by Congress, would safeguard the currency system.

Currie and Eccles disagreed. In a twenty-page memo prepared in April 1935 to help Eccles in testifying on Capitol Hill, Currie reasoned: "The fatal objection to automatic controls is that the combination of factors that bring about a business situation is never the same. Each new business situation with which we are confronted is in a large and significant measure a situation which we have never confronted and will never confront again." He concluded, "The objectives of control may, and we think should be, mandatory, but the management, or the handling of the instruments of control, must be discretionary."[14] Eccles and Currie believed too strongly in the potential of discretionary monetary management to abandon it to automatic rules. The Roosevelt administration, furthermore, relied too heavily on easy credit to allow the possibility that automatic rules would not make enough money available for the planned recovery.

The Roosevelt administration sent Eccles's plan to Congress, but it quickly ran afoul of Senator Carter Glass (D-Va.), who had helped write the Federal Reserve Act in 1913 and who felt a keen sense of proprietorship over the agency. Roosevelt had ruffled Glass by not consulting him on the Eccles nomination, and Glass had done everything in his power to delay the Senate's confirmation. When the Senate finally confirmed the new governor, Glass stood alone in voting no. Now Eccles repeated the mistake.

12. Testimony of Robert H. Hemphill, National Monetary Conference, ibid., 497.

13. Henry C. Simons, "Rules versus Authorities in Monetary Policy," *Journal of Political Economy* 44 (February 1936): 16, 3.

14. Memo, Currie to Eccles, April 1, 1935, box 14, folder 3, Eccles Papers, p. 2.

He had promised he would discuss the bill with Glass before taking it up with anyone else, but the bill arrived on Capitol Hill before Glass had seen it. The senator was sure that Eccles and the administration were again trying to maneuver quickly around him. Eccles vainly tried to explain that advance consultation had become impossible because the interdepartmental committee reviewing the bill had worked until the last minute in making changes to the legislation; Eccles himself had not received a copy until it had gone to Congress. Glass ignored Eccles's apologies and intimated that Eccles was lying.

Ruffling Carter Glass proved a major mistake, for he felt a keen sense of proprietorship for the Fed. The senator explained his close scrutiny by his fondness for the agency. "Next to my own family," he told Comptroller of the Currency J. F. T. O'Connor, "the Federal Reserve System is nearest to my heart." Others were more direct. An old Wilsonian, Josephus Daniels, wrote Roosevelt that Glass was "obsessed with the idea that the Federal Reserve Act, of which Carter thinks he is the sole author, makes no other legislation whatever necessary." Daniels concluded that "Carter's mind is both closed and sealed to new ideas."[15]

Glass packed committee hearings with bankers who feared that a stronger board more closely tied to the administration would dangerously promote inflation. Winthrop Aldrich, one of the nation's best-known financiers who earlier had supported the bill, now charged that the bill was "a concentration of authority as had not been known heretofore in the United States."[16] The U.S. Chamber of Commerce asserted that "the centralized control of credit resulting from such a fundamental change would amount to little short of political dictatorship over the individual deposits and credit of our people."[17] The real fear uniting Eccles's opponents was that a stronger Fed under tighter political control would lack the courage to oppose inflation in the future when the economy recovered. "Politics necessarily involves doing the popular thing," one banker told the Senate committee, while "sound banking on the other hand frequently requires unpleasant and unpopular refusals."[18]

The problem of political control arose most sharply in the question of whether to keep the Treasury secretary and the comptroller on the more

15. Arthur M. Schlesinger, Jr., *The Age of Roosevelt, vol. 3: The Politics of Upheaval* (Boston: Houghton Mifflin, 1960), 296.

16. Ibid., 298.

17. New York *Times*, May 3, 1935, 4.

18. Statement of Elwyn Davis, Clearing House Banks, Wilmington, Delaware, U.S. Congress, Senate, Committee on Banking, *Banking Act of 1935*, 74th Cong., 1st sess., 1935, 262–63.

powerful board. Financiers insisted that both officials be forced off the board to insulate it from political control. Some administration officials suggested that the comptroller stay while the Treasury secretary leave. Treasury Secretary Morgenthau, however, insisted that both he and the comptroller "either stay on or go off together." For him it was a matter of pride; he refused to sacrifice his seat while a subordinate, the comptroller, kept his. When congressional conferees decided to remove them both, Morgenthau said with a smile, "If that is what they want, it's all right with me."[19] He was less confident than Eccles in stimulative fiscal policy, and he feared that without a balanced budget, "we cannot help but be riding for a fall." If that happens, he wrote in his diary, "I do not want to be the sole goat." A more powerful Fed was a potential ally and a convenient scapegoat in case of trouble.[20]

When Congress finally passed the Banking Act of 1935, Eccles won most of what he wanted. The act consolidated control of the system in Eccles, whose position was renamed "chairman." The president would choose a board member to serve as chairman for a four-year term.[21] The act also consolidated control over open-market operations in a reconstituted Federal Open Market Committee where, for the first time, the seven board members had a vote in open-market policy. Eccles had hoped to keep the reserve banks out of open-market decisions, but in a compromise the act left five of the twelve open-market committee votes with the reserve bank presidents, with the votes rotating among the twelve reserve bank presidents.

The act thus had passed, but it proved Eccles was far better at framing bold action than in negotiating his way through Washington's political avenues. He so bungled his first efforts at congressional relations that he nearly lost his bill, and only Roosevelt's personal intervention saved it. "Marriner was naive politically, particularly when he first came and at the time of the Banking Act," recounted Sam Carpenter, a close friend and secretary to the board. "Without Roosevelt helping him and standing behind him," Carpenter said, "he'd never have gotten the Banking Act in a million years." He was a pragmatic manager and a grand strategist, but he had little patience for political maneuvering, building coalitions, or paying respects to elder

19. New York *Times*, July 2, 1935, 1.
20. Morgenthau Diaries, July 3, 1935, 15, Roosevelt Library.
21. Two things are worthy of note. One is that the president was limited in his choice of a chairman to sitting board members. He could not necessarily choose his own person because there might not be an open seat on the board. The other is that the chairman, if not reappointed, could serve the remainder of his fourteen-year term as board member. That might worsen the president's problems in naming a successor and might place a disgruntled former chairman in a position to obstruct the president's policies.

statesmen. "He thought if he came up with the right ideas," Carpenter explained, "everybody would say, 'come on, let's do it.' "[22] Eccles had little hesitation in telling anyone—his staff, senators, even presidents—what ought to be done, and even his friends called him abrasive with both superiors and subordinates.[23]

Even if Eccles lost the stronger mandate he wanted, the act did not prevent him from choosing his own course. The act's very vagueness gave the chairman flexibility for his fundamental mission: to gain control of the Federal Reserve System and to cooperate with the administration in launching the New Deal. Eccles's power was thus what he could make of it. The agency's power had moved to Washington from the district banks, and with the control of open-market authority in the FOMC, dominated if not controlled by the board, monetary management moved into more concentrated political control. The board's own role expanded to the initiation of policy actions. The natural outgrowth of this new role was a new relationship among the chairman, the president, and the Treasury secretary.

Without consolidation and centralization of the Fed's power, the agency had faced heavy and perhaps fatal attack. Decentralization of the system had the great advantage of flexibility, but without a clear central purpose there was nothing to guide that flexibility.[24] Such amorphous monetary policy was no policy at all. Eccles seized the moment by arguing a coherent theory of what the Fed ought to do—support expansionary fiscal policy through discretionary monetary policy—and how to do it—through a stronger board with himself as chairman. That created new possibilities for Eccles, and Eccles exploited them to strengthen his role as leader of the whole system, to enhance the power of the board, and to develop a close relationship with the president. The New Deal required an adequate supply of inexpensive credit, and in Eccles Roosevelt found an enthusiastic supporter. Eccles argued strongly for stimulative action by both the government and by the private sector, and he worked within the administration for a monetary policy supportive of the New Deal.

For the first time in the Fed's history, there was close coordination between fiscal and monetary policies. Ironically, this coordination occurred only after the Treasury secretary left the Federal Reserve Board. Not so ironically, it occurred when the Fed became of central importance to the president. In a lesson that was to last through subsequent history, the ep-

22. Carpenter Oral History, 8, 10, Eccles Papers.

23. See, for example, Merritt Sherman Oral History, 22, Eccles Papers.

24. See Philip Selznick, *Leadership in Administration* (Evanston, Ill.: Row, Peterson, 1957), 113; and James D. Thompson, *Organizations in Action* (New York: McGraw Hill, 1967), 129.

isode demonstrated that formal institutional structure was not the decisive element in coordination between the president and the Fed. Rather, coordination depended on the informal relationship between the president and the chairman.

Roosevelt recognized clearly just how important that coordination was. As he dedicated the Fed's new Constitution Avenue building in 1937, the president told his audience that if the Banking Act of 1935 had been passed earlier, the Fed "would have been in a far better position to moderate the forces that brought about the great depression." With the act, he said, the Fed's powers "have been concentrated to a greater degree than before in a single public body, so that they can be used properly and effectively in accordance with the changing needs of the country."[25] The administration, as Roosevelt well knew, would have been on dangerous ground with the old Fed, which in its disorganized and conservative state might, by design or accident, have weakened or derailed the New Deal.[26]

The Fed chairman and the New Deal president thus found themselves in mutually happy company. Eccles faced the task of rebuilding the Fed and restoring confidence in the banking system, Roosevelt of rejuvenating the economy. Eccles's ambition met a happy coincidence in Roosevelt's pragmatic strategies. Neither one was an economic theorist, and although later observers suggested that both men had embraced Keynesian economics, neither Roosevelt nor Eccles had followed the famous economist's prescriptions. Eccles had never attended college and until the late 1930s had never even read Keynes. "We came out at about the same place in economic thought by very different roads," he later wrote Senator Harry F. Byrd (D-Va.) about the economist, "and we have had the common experience of being highly unpopular in orthodox circles."[27]

Roosevelt was more a tactician than a theoretician. He developed the New Deal for short-term, pragmatic reasons and made little use of broader economic arguments available to him.[28] Eccles therefore figured importantly

25. *Federal Reserve Bulletin* 23 (November 1937): 1062.

26. The physical move for the Federal Reserve marked a further important change. With the board no longer housed in the Treasury building, its officials and staff were no longer beholden to the secretary for its facilities and comforts. The construction of a handsome building some distance from the Treasury Department gave the Federal Reserve a new sense of pride and independence, as well as enhanced prestige to accommodate its new functions. But with the greater distance communication between the Treasury and the Federal Reserve was not as good, and Eccles complained at a meeting with Morgenthau that the Federal Reserve Bank of New York, as the Treasury's fiscal agent, seemed always to have better information about the Treasury's plans than did the board. See Morgenthau Diaries, October 13, 1936, 117–26, Roosevelt Library.

27. Letter, Eccles to Byrd, June 11, 1942, box 44, folder 1, Eccles Papers.

28. See James MacGregor Burns, *Roosevelt: The Lion and the Fox* (New York: Harcourt, Brace, 1956), 334; and Schlesinger, *The Politics of Upheaval*, 407–08.

in Roosevelt's plans, especially in the president's first term. The chairman's voice was one of the few inside the administration urging the conscious use of stimulative fiscal policy to bring about economic recovery, and Eccles's public speeches helped create an intellectual case in public forums for Roosevelt's tactics. Eccles was one of the few leading figures in Washington with a clear plan and a strong philosophy to support his views.

STRUGGLES WITH THE TREASURY

Eccles's eager support for deficit spending often brought him into conflict with his mentor, the more conservative Treasury Secretary Henry Morgenthau. The secretary fretted that continued deficits would impair the federal government's credit and would increase inflation. He was upset about Eccles's enthusiasm for stimulative federal spending and was jealous as well about the direct access to the president his protégé seemed to enjoy.

By mid-1936, however, Eccles himself began to worry that the economy was starting to overheat. Gold was flowing from foreign to American banks, and the rising reserves encouraged the banks to expand their lending. The specter of a speculative boom emerged once again; Fed officials worried about repeating the boom-bust cycle of the 1920s. The reserve banks maintained that the Fed should sell government bonds, soak up extra reserves, and quell inflation. Morgenthau, however, feared that this strategy, by tightening money, would increase the interest on the Treasury's bonds and he strongly opposed it. Eccles and the board nevertheless decided to move, first by raising the reserve requirements in July 1936 by 50 percent and following it in a few months with another 50 percent increase. The change raised the amount of money banks had to hold in non-interest bearing accounts to support their deposits and thus decreased the amount of money available for borrowing.

Morgenthau was enraged. He complained that Eccles had not consulted with him in advance about the decisions and that, in fact, he had learned about it in the newspaper. He called Eccles, argued angrily, and later wrote in his diary: "I certainly put the fear of God into him and doubt if he will pull off another fast one. I can't make Eccles out unless he wants to be important."[29] He then counterattacked by establishing his own vehicle for open-market operations: the Treasury Stabilization Fund, which would sell ninety-day Treasury bills to raise money and then use the funds to buy and hold gold. The strategy was christened a "sterilization" plan: Morgenthau

29. Morgenthau Diaries, July 15, 1936, 98, Roosevelt Library.

calculated that by buying gold, he could stop foreign gold from flowing into American banks and "contaminating" the domestic money supply. He thus hoped to soak up the gold and keep interest rates from rising. Morgenthau's plan was a blatant trespass on the Fed's role, and Eccles bitterly fought against it within the administration. Only under heavy White House pressure did he finally give in.[30] For months afterward, Morgenthau and the Treasury successfully used the so-called sterilized gold to blackmail the Federal Reserve into keeping the Treasury's borrowing costs low.

Continued bickering over the sterilized gold eventually produced a showdown with Roosevelt. Eccles argued that the Treasury was trespassing on the Fed's terrain, while Morgenthau insisted that the Fed be forced to keep an orderly market, Treasury shorthand for stable (and, usually, low) bond prices. Roosevelt sided with Morgenthau. To make sure the Fed would not back out, Roosevelt sent Morgenthau to the next meeting of the Federal Open Market Committee. "Now, I never threaten," the Treasury secretary said, but added that he hoped the committee would "use the machinery which you have and give us an orderly market." If the FOMC refused, he promised, "the Government will, and that's the whole story."[31] Morgenthau had promised Roosevelt not to release his gold if the Fed kept its part of the bargain. Faced with the choice—giving Morgenthau the policy he wanted or allowing Morgenthau to use his gold to produce the same result, Eccles and the FOMC caved in. To fight Morgenthau further risked losing their leverage over the money supply to the Treasury. For the Fed to keep to its newly emerging mission, it could not allow that to happen.

The episode taught an important lesson. Under the Banking Act of 1935, the chairman had won substantial new powers. He was the unquestioned leader of the system, and he could work closely if informally with the administration in coordinating policies. However, when the Fed's policies conflicted with the Treasury's central mission—financing the federal government's debt—Morgenthau served notice that he would not tolerate an independent agency that drove his interest costs too high. In any serious dispute with the Treasury, Eccles knew he would have to fight the president as well, and that was one battle he could not win.

Within the Fed, Eccles found that the continued strong voice of the reserve banks in open-market decisions meant he could not move far beyond their support. "I've got a tough job here with a tough group of fellows," he told Morgenthau. "I can't go into a meeting of 12 people and simply use a

30. Morgenthau Diaries, March 29, 1937, 204–27, Roosevelt Library.
31. Minutes of meetings, Morgenthau Diaries, April 3, 1937, 272–73, Roosevelt Library.

club, you know. After all, you wouldn't get cooperation."[32] Eccles himself resented the need to work hard within the Fed to build support for policies he was convinced were right. So long as the reserve banks held five of the twelve FOMC votes, however, Eccles reluctantly accepted the need to build internal support for his plans.

Eccles preferred the role of framing grand strategies to building support for them, but as he spent more time in the job he gradually became more adept at cultivating the support of the president, the Treasury, the public, and the reserve banks. Eccles thus had substantially more power than anyone had ever previously enjoyed in the Fed, but the reserve requirement dispute demonstrated both how important and how difficult it was to build the needed support.

After the conflict with Morgenthau, the administration installed new procedures to keep better informed of the system's likely actions. Morgenthau began weekly lunches with Eccles in October 1936, a pattern which has since become a tradition between Treasury secretaries and Federal Reserve Board chairmen.[33] In 1938 Roosevelt created a presidential advisory board, composed of the Fed chairman, the secretary of the Treasury, the director of the budget, and the chairman of the Advisory Commission on Natural Resources. Although the advisory board ceased functioning with the outbreak of the war in Europe, it was the precursor of more regular meetings (including the same participants, with the chairman of the Council of Economic Advisers replacing the chairman of the Advisory Commission on Natural Resources) begun during the Eisenhower administration, meetings that eventually grew into the better-known Quadriad.

Eccles had the self-assurance that came from clear views about what ought to be done, and he pressed those views on the president and on his colleagues in the Federal Reserve System. Often what he told the president conflicted with what his internal constituency wanted; the reserve banks certainly had no enthusiasm for "compensatory fiscal policy." He nevertheless garnered enough support within the system to maintain his effectiveness with the president, and his Roosevelt connection added greatly to his leverage within the system. By the time Roosevelt began his third term, Eccles had restored the Fed to a position of unquestioned prominence, if not preeminence, and had established himself as an intellectual force within the administration.

The consolidation of the Fed's power, however, also increased its conflicts with Morgenthau and the Treasury. Since its founding the Fed had been a

32. Notes on phone call, Morgenthau Diaries, April 3, 1937, 246, Roosevelt Library.
33. Minutes, Morgenthau Diaries, October 13, 1936, 117–26, Roosevelt Library.

natural competitor with the Treasury, because its monetary policy influenced the price the Treasury had to pay to finance the government's debt. In 1938, Eccles again enraged Morgenthau by seeking to consolidate bank regulation in the Fed. Over the years, federal bank regulation had grown in haphazard fashion. The comptroller of the currency examined national banks, one-third of all banks which held nearly half of all deposits. The Fed examined the state banks that belonged to the system, while the Federal Deposit Insurance Corporation examined the insured banks that did not belong to the Federal Reserve System. Ten percent of all banks were under exclusive state supervision. The multiplicity of banking agencies led to "competition in laxity" among the regulators; making rules too strict might induce banks to switch to another kind of operation and another regulator. The Fed's rules, in fact, were the strictest, and Eccles worried that the system would lose members.[34] He called the regulatory structure "a crazy quilt that makes for inefficiency, waste and above all, bad banking."[35]

The regulatory agencies, furthermore, were sometimes working at cross-purposes. Following the 1937–38 recession, the Fed was trying to stimulate the economy with an expansive monetary policy. The FDIC and the comptroller, however, were tightening bank examination procedures to help keep the banks solvent. The policies were running in opposite directions, and Eccles complained to Roosevelt, "Authority over monetary policy is largely useless unless such authority is closely integrated with bank examinations and investment policy."[36]

Morgenthau saw Eccles's proposal to consolidate regulatory procedures as nothing more than a grab for power at the expense of the Treasury. Eccles, Glass told Morgenthau, "wants to absorb every federal agency he can lay his hands on." The senator concluded, "He wants to be everything except President and he'd like to be that if he can."[37] The Treasury Department naturally opposed Eccles, and an internal Treasury memo argued that consolidating banking regulation in the Fed would "be far more perilous" than "all the defects of the present system."[38] Traditionalists within the administration and Congress saw bank examination as different from monetary policy. Examination concerned the solvency of individual banks; monetary policy governed the amount of credit the government would make available. Eccles never succeeded in convincing Roosevelt that the issue

34. Board of Governors of the Federal Reserve System, *Twenty-fifth Annual Report* (Washington, D.C.: Board of Governors, 1938), 10–11.
35. Memo, Eccles to Roosevelt, November 12, 1936, box 5, folder 6, Eccles Papers.
36. Memo, Eccles to Roosevelt, November 23, 1938, 9, box 4, folder 3, Eccles Papers.
37. Phone transcript, December 17, 1936, 255–57, vol. 48, Morgenthau Diaries, 256.
38. Memo, Gaston to Morgenthau, December 8, 1938, 83, vol. 155, Morgenthau Diaries.

was important enough to warrant a major push. And soon afterward, the Japanese attack on Pearl Harbor created even bigger problems for the nation's financial system.

THE PRESSURES OF WARTIME FINANCE

When war broke out, Eccles and the Fed immediately pledged "to assure an ample supply of funds" to win the war. Behind the Fed's patriotic promise, however, was a deep worry: The Fed also wanted to avoid the mistakes of World War I, that is, setting the Treasury's interest rates too low, which encouraged the expansion of bank credit and unloosed inflation. In the first days after the outbreak of war the Treasury suggested a fixed pattern of rates: from ⅜ percent for ninety-day bills, the shortest term obligations, to 2½ percent for the longest term Treasury bonds, twenty to twenty-five years. Eccles was worried that the rate for the Treasury bills was too low, but Morgenthau insisted on the rate, and in February 1942 the Fed committed itself to maintain this pattern of rates for the duration of the war.[39] The agreement, known as the "peg," guaranteed that no Treasury offering would fail during the war and that the Treasury would be assured of stable, low prices for its obligations during the campaign. If for any reason the public did not buy all the securities the Treasury needed to sell, the Fed was prepared to buy them itself. As Morgenthau told his staff, the Fed's commitment was open-ended, "the sky being the limit."[40]

While the Fed's peg guaranteed the success and low cost of the Treasury's war financing, it left the system with little effective control of the money supply. More than any structural tie between the Fed and the Treasury, the peg undermined the Fed's independence. Once it agreed to support the Treasury's pattern of rates, the Fed could take no action to tighten the money supply (and force rates up), since it would have to absorb the Treasury's offerings at the lower rate in any event. The short-term rates, furthermore, were set so low that smart investors could play against the interest rate pattern. Many individuals who had bought short- and medium-term securities during war drives sold them at a premium to the Fed in later drives and then bought longer-term bonds at even better rates.[41] By the

39. Board of Governors of the Federal Reserve System, *Twenty-eighth Annual Report* (Washington, D.C.: Board of Governors, 1941), 1; Notes, meeting with Treasury staff, December 18, 1941, box 50, folder 1, Eccles Papers; Phone transcript, February 11, 1942, vol. 495, 314–19, Morgenthau Diaries.

40. Meeting notes, April 30, 1942, 226, vol. 522, Morgenthau Diaries.

41. Board of Governors of the Federal Reserve System, *Thirty-second Annual Report* (Washington, D.C.: Board of Governors, 1945), 12.

end of the war, the Fed came to hold nearly all short-term securities. The Fed purchases, moreover, added to the expansion of bank credit and further fueled inflation, which began to increase rapidly.

Also encouraging inflation was Congress's unwillingness to approve the Treasury's wartime tax proposals that would have funded half the cost of the war.[42] As a result, the United States relied more heavily on borrowing to finance the war than did its major allies. Great Britain and Canada, for example, financed half their war costs through taxation and half through borrowing. In the United States, taxes raised only 40 percent of wartime needs, and of the amount borrowed, 40 percent came from the banking system. Consequently, the money supply more than tripled, creating what the Board of Governors warned was "an inflationary potential."[43] *Fortune* echoed the agency's fears in a long article that blamed the Treasury for financing the war so heavily and willingly on borrowing: "The forces making for inflation are certainly boiling."[44]

Morgenthau had far different worries: being able to sell enough securities, at low prices, to finance the war. The Treasury originally operated the program in the states, but in May 1943, to improve sales, Morgenthau proposed having the reserve bank presidents take over as bond chairmen in their districts. The presidents agreed with most of Morgenthau's plan and suggested only what they thought were a few minor changes: they wanted all war bond activities to be coordinated through the banks, since they were to be the campaign chairmen; and they wanted sales managers to work under the guidance of the presidents, paid by the Fed under reimbursement by the Treasury, rather than by the Treasury directly as had been the case previously.

Morgenthau, however, believed the reserve bank presidents were trying to subvert his plan. He told them about an incident he remembered from years before, soon after he was named Treasury secretary, when he visited the home of George Harrison, then president of the Federal Reserve Bank of New York. Morgenthau said that Harrison and Owen D. Young, a director of the New York bank, stood over the secretary and warned, "You will do what we want you to do, or we will not support your Government bond market." Morgenthau told the presidents that he resented Fed officials' putting a gun to his head, and he added that he was not going to turn

42. John Morton Blum, *From the Morgenthau Diaries*, vol. 3: *Years of War, 1941–1945* (Boston: Houghton Mifflin, 1967), 78.

43. Board of Governors, *Thirty-second Annual Report*, 1–2.

44. *Fortune* 31 (May 1945): 118.

government financing over to the system. The presidents' suggestions, he said, were part of a strategy to take control of war finances from him. "You think I am incompetent to handle my job," he said, "and that I should turn it over to you." Before that happened, he said, he would resign. "I can do this job with you on my terms, or without you," he concluded. "You can take it or leave it." Eccles and the presidents were shocked, for they believed that there were only technical differences between the plans. The presidents, furthermore, believed that they had fully cooperated with the Treasury and they deeply resented Morgenthau's complaints.[45]

Eccles met with Morgenthau the next week to try to patch up the differences. Morgenthau said that he had only wanted to set the record straight. Eccles replied that if the remarks represented the secretary's opinion of the Fed there was no way that he could work further with him. The secretary's statements, he said, demonstrated no trust in the reserve bankers who were to serve as district chairmen. It finally took a meeting with Roosevelt to soothe the bruised egos, but not before the deep dispute between the Treasury and the Fed had spread from the top officials to the lowest-ranking workers. Despite the bad feelings, however, the reserve banks did take a large role in selling the Treasury's securities. In fact, selling and processing government securities during the war occupied half of the Fed's employees.[46]

Financing and refinancing the debt was a massive job, and Morgenthau was determined to keep the peg steady to minimize the government's interest costs. Despite continuing Fed requests during the war, Treasury officials refused even to consider increasing the ⅜ percent rate for short-term Treasury bills. When the Federal Reserve allowed the rates on short-term certificates to creep up in late 1944, Morgenthau immediately objected to Eccles. He rejected the Federal Open Market Committee's requests for higher rates and called on the committee to keep to the pattern agreed upon in the first months of the war. The Fed called for higher Treasury bill rates because the low rates had eliminated a public market, but the Treasury continued to resist. If reducing the costs of the Treasury's borrowing were the primary goal, some Fed officials sarcastically complained, the Treasury

45. Memo, Eccles to Roosevelt, May 24, 1943, box 47, folder 6, Eccles Papers. The Treasury's minutes of the meeting confirm Eccles's summary to the president. See David Bell to Eccles, May 26, 1943, box 12, folder 6, Eccles Papers.

46. Memo, Eccles to Sproul, May 21, 1943, box 12, folder 6, Eccles Papers; and A. Jerome Clifford, *The Independence of the Federal Reserve System* (Philadelphia: University of Pennsylvania Press, 1965), 188.

could accomplish this simply by printing money. The peg in practice led to the imposition of inflation as a wartime tax. [47]

As the war drew to a close, Eccles began to warn the nation publicly about the dangers of inflation. In a memo to a congressional committee, he urged the need for prompt action. "If left uncontrolled, the vast and rising tide of war-created liquid funds could overwhelm the markets for real estate, urban and rural, and for stocks and commodities." That, he said, "would be calamitous for Government financing. It would wreck the stabilization program. It would make a mirage of the G.I. Bill of Rights." [48] Eccles followed that with an anti-inflation plan presented to President Truman in July 1946. The principal cause of inflation, he said, was wartime borrowing from the banking system. In accord with his Keynesian-style principles, he called for a large budget surplus, derived from higher taxes and reduced expenditures, to cool the economy. [49]

When the war ended, Fed officials kept up the drumbeat. Fed Vice-Chairman Ronald Ransom visited Morgenthau's successor as Treasury secretary, Frederick Vinson, on his first day in office to try—unsuccessfully—to convince him to abandon the Treasury's preferential rate structure. [50] Eccles himself argued that "the continuance of the rate can no longer be of service to the Treasury's financing program nor to the maintenance of credit policy." Rather, he said, it was "an element of weakness in our battle against inflation," but the Treasury refused to budge. [51]

In the next few months the Fed slowly began backing away from the preferential rate for the shortest-term Treasury obligations, the ⅜ percent bills. The move, Eccles suggested, would not affect the Treasury's financing costs, since the Fed itself held almost all of the Treasury bills. Vinson again sought a delay, contending that "it does not seem wise to rock the boat" during the transition to the peacetime economy. He acknowledged that the significance of the rate was "almost entirely psychological," but it was important, he concluded, to maintain the psychology of continued low rates to spur the economy's transition to peacetime. [52] But in early 1947, the

47. See letter, Morgenthau to Eccles, December 22, 1944, box 11, folder 1, Eccles Papers; Memo, L. M. Piser to Eccles, February 23, 1945, box 11, folder 2, Eccles Papers; and Ralph Turvey, "Inflation as a Tax in World War II," *Journal of Political Economy* 69 (February 1969): 73.

48. Statement, Eccles to Vinson Committee, February 8, 1945, box 32, folder 1, Eccles Papers.

49. Letter, Eccles to Truman, July 19, 1946, OF 229A (1945–47), box 831, Harry S. Truman Library.

50. Reported in letter, Vinson to Eccles, March 28, 1946, box 12, folder 9, Eccles Papers.

51. Letter, Eccles to Vinson, December 13, 1945, box 11, folder 2, Eccles Papers.

52. Letter, Vinson to Eccles, March 28, 1946, box 12, folder 9, Eccles Papers.

Treasury finally agreed to release the Fed from its commitment to support Treasury bills. The Treasury had become far more worried about the price than the yield of government obligations, and the Fed agreed to support them at par.[53] With the door finally cracked open, Eccles argued even harder that other interest rates ought to be allowed to rise to alleviate the "continuing pressure toward higher prices."[54]

Eccles's inflation campaign so aggravated Truman that the president decided not to reappoint him as chairman when his third term expired on January 31, 1948. When Eccles pressed him for an explanation of his decision—and for withholding the decision until the last minute—Truman replied that the reasons were best known to himself alone, a response that scarcely satisfied Eccles or salved his wounded pride.[55] They finally arranged an exchange of letters, in which Truman said that his decision not to redesignate Eccles as chairman "reflects no lack of complete confidence in you." Truman asked him to stay on the board and to become vice-chairman, and Eccles agreed.[56] Three months passed, however, and Truman still had not named Eccles vice-chairman. Eccles became convinced that Truman had no intention of ever giving him the job, so he finally withdrew his name from consideration to prevent further speculation and sniping in the press.[57]

Eccles believed that the Fed's investigation into the California-based Transamerica Corporation, in which the system suggested that the Giannini family was trying to monopolize banking in the West, cost him his job. The investigation, Eccles thought, might have jeopardized support in California for Truman in the upcoming election.[58] The reality, however, was far more simple. Truman and his new Treasury secretary, John Snyder, no longer trusted Eccles to continue supporting the Treasury's bond market. Presidential assistant John Steelman said that "the administration not only was uneasy about the specter of tight money but also felt that Eccles was too close to the bankers and not cooperative enough with the White House."[59] Snyder later said that he suspected New York bankers were struggling to regain control of government finances, and Truman himself complained: "I didn't like the way Eccles first spoke in the Senate. He talked one way to

53. Sproul memo to files, May 8, 1947, box 11, folder 5, Eccles Papers.
54. Letter, Eccles to Snyder, October 14, 1947, box 11, folder 6, Eccles Papers.
55. Eccles, *Beckoning Frontiers*, 436–39.
56. Letter, Truman to Eccles, January 27, 1948; letter, Eccles to Truman, January 27, 1948, box 3, folder 7, Eccles Papers.
57. Letter, Eccles to Truman, April 16, 1948, box 3, folder 7, Eccles Papers.
58. Eccles, *Beckoning Frontiers*, 443–56.
59. Quoted by Robert E. Weintraub, "Congressional Supervision of Monetary Policy," *Journal of Monetary Economics* 4 (1978): 352–53.

them and another way to the President. I didn't want a chairman like that."[60] Faced with a chairman who opposed his policies, Truman simply removed Eccles from the chairmanship.

Truman appointed Thomas B. McCabe, chairman of the board of the Philadelphia Federal Reserve Bank, to replace Eccles, but pressures from the reserve banks continued to build for a break from the peg. Eccles, now freed from the chairmanship, led an even more outspoken campaign against the peg and what he called the "surrender to inflation."[61] The Treasury continued to insist on keeping the peg, however, and this rendered the Fed impotent. So long as it was bound to support an artificially low level of interest rates, the Fed had no way to govern the money supply effectively. The peg, in fact, made inflation worse by forcing the Fed to pump more money out to support the Treasury's market. The peg robbed the Fed of its operating flexibility and made a shambles of the sense of mission Eccles had developed.

Secretary Snyder now proved even more adamant about keeping the peg. He faced a massive refinancing problem: in 1949, $1 billion in Treasury bills alone were maturing each week, and Treasury officials expected to refinance $33 billion in medium-term notes and certificates and $11 billion in the coming year. For calendar year 1949, interest on the debt was $5.7 billion, and Snyder estimated that only a ½ percent increase in interest would add $1.25 billion to the Treasury's costs.[62] Eccles, however, had a more simple explanation. He was convinced that Treasury officials had a "chronic bias for cheap money in all seasons."[63] Every Fed request for an end to the pattern of rates, however, met the same response. Snyder's advisers worried about "soft spots" in the economy and suggested postponing any decision "until greater confidence has returned to the Government bond market." Furthermore, they argued it would be better to attack inflationary problems in each sector instead of raising interest rates for everyone.[64]

The continuing Fed-Treasury controversy spilled over into the 1948 in-

60. Truman's comment in John Snyder's memoirs, 33, Truman Library. Compare Snyder's Oral History, Truman Library; G. L. Bach, *Making Monetary and Fiscal Policy* (Washington, D.C.: Brookings Institution, 1971), 80; and Robert J. Donovan, "Truman's Perspective," in Francis H. Heller, ed., *Economics and the Truman Administration* (Lawrence: Regents Press of Kansas, 1981), 15.

61. Speech to the National Industrial Conference Board, September 23, 1948, box 81, folder 23, Eccles Papers.

62. U.S. Congress, Joint Committee on the Economic Report, Subcommittee on Monetary, Credit, and Fiscal Policies, *Monetary, Credit, and Fiscal Policies*, hearings, 81st Cong., 1st sess., 1949, 389.

63. Eccles, *Beckoning Frontiers*, 422.

64. Memo, Haas to Snyder, October 27, 1948, Federal Reserve Bank-Interest, 1948, box 14, Snyder Papers, Truman Library.

vestigation of the administration of government, a commission headed by an old Fed nemesis, Herbert Hoover. Ironically, the Hoover Commission's draft report on monetary policy was critical of the Treasury's domination of the Fed and recommended the system be given a stronger formal role in the formulation of credit policy and an equal voice in its dealings with the Treasury.[65]

Snyder found the commission's draft report offensive. He complained that its contention for a more powerful Fed was "erroneous," for the promotion of economic stability "cannot be carried out by an agency such as the Federal Reserve, which has no responsibility to the electorate—or only in a very limited sense." To Snyder, "correct fiscal and correct monetary policy . . . can never be different." The only proper policy, he concluded, was one "most in accord with the overall interest of the economy." That, he said, must "be left largely at the discretion of the responsible authorities," which, of course, meant the president and his Treasury secretary.[66]

Snyder failed to convince the commission. Its final report concluded that the Fed's responsibilities were "not being adequately carried out" because of "age-old Treasury bias in favor of too-easy money in inflationary periods." It was important, the commission stated, to give the Fed "a more central voice" in economic policy and to make the Fed's chairman "a more intimate member of the President's official family." The final report suggested an even stronger board of three members that would have total control over open-market operations. It also picked up Eccles's old campaign on bank regulation and recommended all bank supervision be taken over by the Fed.[67] Administration officials were naturally not very happy about the report, and nothing came of its recommendations. The Fed remained tied to the peg.

The Fed had in thirty-five years gone from an era when the president reverenced its independence as he did that of the Supreme Court's to a time when the agency had little if any independence. Eccles enjoyed telling a story to the chairmen of the reserve banks: A central banker from another country was once asked, "Do you feel your bank has the right to defy the Government?" "Oh yes," he replied, "we value that right very greatly and

65. Memo, Haas to Snyder, undated, Federal Reserve Bank-Interest, 1945–47, box 13, Snyder Papers, Truman Library. No evidence exists, however, that Hoover had anything to do with these recommendations.

66. Letter, Snyder to Robert A. Bowie, September 16, 1948, Federal Reserve, 1946–52, General #2, Snyder Papers, box 13, Truman Library.

67. Commission on the Organization of the Executive Branch of the Government, *Task Force Report on Regulatory Commissions, Appendix N* (Washington, D.C.: U.S. Government Printing Office, 1949), 109–11.

wouldn't think of exercising it."[68] Since the Banking Act of 1935, the Fed in fact enjoyed great legal independence, but it found itself bound practically by the Treasury's policies. It had the legal right to resist and, indeed, to set any policy it chose, but to oppose the Treasury and the president publicly was in 1948 unthinkable.

The Fed saw greater danger in inflation than in the increased borrowing costs higher interest rates would bring the Treasury, but the Treasury believed otherwise. Aside from the experience of World War I, there were few technical rules with which to predict who would be right. For the Fed, however, either side of the equation was extremely dangerous. If the Treasury were right, the Fed risked having its hands tied permanently, for the Treasury might well never find it convenient to pay more for the money it borrowed. If the Fed were right but immobilized because of the peg, it risked losing its central, sacred mission, safeguarding the currency. No matter how strong the arguments, the Fed could not buck the Treasury and the president on its own. Yet without the freedom to tackle inflation, the Fed might well lose the reason for its existence.

The postwar era thus proved just as great a threat to the Fed's existence as did the Depression. Legal independence meant nothing if it could not be exercised. Indeed, it might mean less than nothing if the Fed, hobbled by the Treasury's peg, allowed inflationary pressures to build up into another boom that broke in another depression. For its survival—and for the health of the economy—the Fed needed to recapture a unique turf. In the months that followed, therefore, Eccles's joke about independence was to become a bitter one for the system, as it underwent a test of just what its independence meant.

MOVING TOWARD ACCORD

Even though he no longer held the chairmanship, Eccles became the Fed's leading spokesman against the peg and its foremost champion against inflation. "So long as the Reserve System is expected to support the Government bond market," he told the Senate Subcommittee on Monetary, Credit, and Fiscal Policies, "the System is deprived of its only really effective instrument for curbing overexpansion of credit." Eccles pointedly added, however, that as much as he disagreed with the Treasury's policy, it was not the Fed's policy "to enforce its will."[69] The final responsibility, he said, lay with the Treasury and the Congress. His message was clear: on its own the board

68. Notes of remarks, May 29, 1948, box 46, folder 17, Eccles Papers.
69. Joint Committee, *Monetary, Credit, and Fiscal Policies*, 216.

could not buck the Treasury, but with congressional support the Fed could wage a more effective (and independent) attack on inflation.

In late 1949, the Fed won support for its position from Senator Paul Douglas, chairman of the subcommittee. Douglas was a respected economist in his own right, a former university professor and a monetarist. He saw the Fed-Treasury dispute as an example of the inevitable tensions that arise in inflationary periods, tensions between the Treasury's preference for low interest rates and the Fed's battle against inflation.[70] Douglas agreed with Eccles and argued that "the Treasury and the Federal Reserve have become Siamese twins."[71] The report he authored recommended a stronger Fed with "an appropriate, flexible, and vigorous monetary policy." It supported many of the Hoover Commission's recommendations and concluded: "The freedom of the Federal Reserve to restrict credit and raise interest rates for general stabilization purposes should be restored even if the cost should prove to be a significant increase in service charges on the Federal debt and a greater inconvenience to the Treasury."[72]

Truman's economic advisers, predictably, criticized the report and contested its "long-range theorizing without qualification," which, they argued, might lead to a perpetually unbalanced budget. The White House also rejected any thought of a congressional resolution that might impair the Treasury's operations.[73] Truman made clear that he ranked the Fed below the Treasury. At a dinner given by the chairman and directors of the reserve banks, Truman said, "Now gentlemen, you represent the greatest financial institution in the history of the world, except the Treasury of the United States."[74]

To hold the Fed's support, Treasury began announcing future offerings weeks instead of days in advance. That continuously committed the Fed to support the Treasury's market; to do otherwise would likely have caused an offering to fail, an unthinkable option for everyone. The Council of Economic Advisers (CEA), meanwhile, pursued a different tack. Council members suggested a paragraph in its forthcoming *Economic Report* that stated, "Monetary and fiscal policy should be oriented to the needs of the Treasury," which "should have access to a market where interest rates are low

70. George S. Tavlas, "The Chicago Tradition Revisited: Some Neglected Monetary Contributions," *Journal of Money, Credit, and Banking* 9 (November 1977): 529–35.

71. Testimony of W. Randolph Burgess, chairman of the Executive Committee, National City Bank of New York, ibid., 178.

72. U.S. Congress, Joint Committee on the Economic Report, Subcommittee on Monetary, Credit, and Fiscal Policies, *Monetary, Credit, and Fiscal Policies*, report, 81st Cong., 2d sess., 1950, Sen. Doc. #129, 2–3.

73. Memo, Feeney to Truman, January 26, 1950, OF 396, PSF, box 1076, Truman Library.

74. Stein, *The Fiscal Revolution in America*, 260.

and credit is easy." Fed Chairman McCabe was furious and wrote Leon Keyserling, chairman of the CEA, to register "vigorous protest."[75] The Fed succeeded in keeping the argument out of the report but had little success in moving the Treasury.

From the president's personal staff to the CEA and the Treasury Department, the Truman administration shared a remarkably uniform view of the problem. Ending the Fed's commitment to the bond market would increase the cost of interest on the national debt, which they all wanted to avoid. Even ending the support of shorter-term securities might make investors suppose that support would soon be ending for longer-term bonds as well, and this might produce a decline in bond prices as investors waited for higher-yielding bonds.[76] At the same time, however, the Douglas hearings warned administration officials about rising congressional and public concern about inflation. In particular, Douglas's report forewarned Treasury officials that continued attempts to bring the Fed to heel would invite congressional intervention. The conflict was thus inevitably building to a showdown.

The struggle grew closer to open warfare with a June 28, 1949, announcement by the Fed that it would conduct its operations "with primary regard to the general business and credit situation."[77] By emphasizing that "general" conditions, instead of the Treasury's needs, would be paramount, the Fed signaled that it was ready to end the peg, which McCabe called "the strait jacket in which monetary policy had been operating for nearly a decade."[78] At the time, however, the pronouncement was less than revolutionary. The economy was in the midst of a recession and the new policy merely allowed interest rates to fall. Just what it would mean when growth resumed and inflation worsened again was far less certain.

The test came with the outbreak of war in Korea in June 1950. The war created for Treasury officials a double worry: they needed to refinance the old debt from World War II and the New Deal, and they now needed to finance new wartime needs. Treasury Secretary Snyder was thus more concerned than ever about keeping interest rates low and maintaining the Fed's support of the bond market. The Fed, as usual, had different worries. The economy had recovered vigorously from the 1949 recession, and spending for the Korean War added even more fuel to the economy. The two com-

75. Letter, McCabe to Keyserling, July 19, 1950, Federal Reserve System, box 22, Murphy Files, Truman Library.

76. Letter, John D. Clark and Keyserling to Joseph C. Mahoney, November 20, 1950, CEA, box 21, Murphy Files, Truman Library.

77. *Federal Reserve Bulletin* 35 (July 1949): 776.

78. Joint Committee, *Monetary, Credit, and Fiscal Policies*, hearings, 471.

bined to provoke an unprecedented expansion of consumer installment and real estate credit. Wholesale prices rocketed up 16 percent from June 1950 to February 1951, and the nervous money markets worried about the "threat of near-runaway inflation."[79] From the financial community, especially bankers and insurance executives, came strong pressures on the Fed to get inflation under control. A few months of double-digit inflation would quickly destroy the value of long-term bonds invested at 2½ percent.

Fed and Treasury officials resumed sparring in August 1950, when the Fed announced an increase in the discount rate from 1½ to 1¾ percent. Reserve requirements were already close to the legal maximum, and with the peg still in place the discount rate was the Fed's only available tool for tightening credit. Snyder, however, saw the change as "a body blow, a real shock." He thought he had an understanding with McCabe not to change policy, and he attributed the Fed's decision to pressure from Allan Sproul, president of the New York Federal Reserve Bank, and other New York bankers who wanted the Fed to show real independence.[80] Snyder tried to outflank the Fed by announcing the same day a $13.6 billion refinancing of thirteen-month Treasury certificates at the old rate of 1¼ percent. With the maneuver, Snyder dared the Fed to keep to its new, higher rates. To do so would surely cause the Treasury refinancing to fail, an unthinkable happening.

The Fed, though, proved more clever than Snyder had anticipated. It offered to buy maturing securities at par to prevent the offering from failing while it simultaneously refused to back down from the rate increase. The Fed lost billions of dollars in the gambit—within days it purchased $10.4 billion of Treasury securities—but since the Fed funded the operation with the Treasury's own securities, the Treasury paid the bill. Meanwhile, the Fed kept the higher discount rate and dislodged the peg from medium-term issues, leaving only long-term bonds pegged. Treasury officials condemned what they called the Fed's actions "to churn up the market and deteriorate its psychology," and they warned that the system "jeopardized the entire financial program" for the Korean War.[81] Unless the Treasury agreed to higher rates, the Fed's gambit threatened future Treasury offer-

---

79. Friedman and Schwartz, *A Monetary History of the United States*, 595, 611; and U.S. Congress, Joint Committee on the Economic Report, *Monetary Policy and the Management of the Public Debt: Their Role in Achieving Price Stability and High-Level Employment. Replies to Questions and Other Materials for the Use of the Subcommittee on General Credit Control and Debt Management*, 82d Cong., 2d sess., 1952, Sen. Doc. 123, p. 229.

80. Snyder Oral History, 1468–69, Truman Library.

81. Memo to Snyder, September 19, 1950, Federal Reserve Bank-Interest, 1950, box 14, Snyder Papers, Truman Library.

ings. The Fed, however, served notice that it would not allow the Treasury to dictate its policies.

The final battle, over the long-term 2½ percent bonds, began in January 1951. Snyder again thought that he had extracted from McCabe a commitment to continue the Fed's support. On January 18, 1951, he gave a speech to the New York Board of Trade in which he asserted, "I am firmly convinced that any increase in the 2½ percent rate would seriously upset the existing security markets." He, Truman, and McCabe had conferred, he told his audience, and all of them had agreed that new issues "will be financed within the pattern of that rate." Many financiers were arguing for at least a small change in the Treasury's bond rate—say, from 2½ to 3 percent—but Snyder held that such increases were too small to have any real effect on inflation: "The delusion that fractional changes in interest rates can be effective in fighting inflation must be dispelled from our minds."[82]

McCabe was stunned. He recalled making no such commitment to Truman and Snyder, and the FOMC had not authorized any such statement. A few days later Allan Sproul, president of the New York reserve bank, made a delicately worded speech rejecting Snyder's argument. The Fed followed that on January 29 by allowing the price of 2½ percent bonds to fall slightly from $100^{23}/_{32}$ to $100^{21}/_{32}$. When bond prices go down, their yield usually goes up (and vice versa), so the Fed's strategy was a clear signal that the Fed would soon back away from its support of the bond market. Snyder, of course, was upset yet again. The Fed's action came just after Snyder had gone into the hospital for an eye operation when, again, he thought he had extracted from the Fed a commitment for no changes until he recovered.[83] To make the move while he was hospitalized, Snyder thought, was a low blow.

Truman was just as adamant. Above all, he was committed to keeping the price of Treasury bonds at par, and to strengthen the Fed's resolve, he called the entire Federal Open Market Committee to the White House to meet with him at 4:00 P.M. on January 31, 1951, the only such meeting in the Fed's history.[84] Truman began the meeting by reviewing the world situation. "The present emergency," he told the committee members, "is the greatest this country has ever faced, including the two world wars and all the preceding wars." The United States needed to combat Communist influences on many fronts, he said, and one way to do this was "to maintain

82. *Wall Street Journal*, January 19, 1951, 3.

83. Snyder Oral History, 1471, Truman Library.

84. This account comes from the Federal Reserve's minutes of the meeting, recorded by Governor Evans; undated, box 62, folder 1, Eccles Papers.

confidence in the Government's credit and in Government securities." Loss of this confidence might risk losing all he hoped to gain from the military's mobilization. He then repeated a story he had told many times before: when he returned home from France after World War I, he found that he could sell his $100 government bonds for only $80; later the price ran up to $125. That, he said, he would not allow to happen again.

He was doing all he could to fight inflation, Truman told the FOMC, and he had just met with congressional leaders to ask for a $16.5 billion tax increase to stave off inflation. He thought the members of the committee had done a good job in handling the nation's finances, and he wanted the FOMC to continue to maintain the financial structure of the country. McCabe replied by thanking the president for receiving them, and he said that they shared his concern for maintenance of the government's debt policies. Although support of the government bond market was "something in the nature of an extracurricular activity" for the FOMC, the committee had performed the service for the past nine years and, he thought, had done a good job. The Fed, McCabe concluded, always carefully weighed its responsibilities to the government and the economy.

Truman said that he wanted the committee to continue its good work during the defense period—and he emphasized the defense period only. He added that he did not want to discuss details like small changes in the price of bonds, but he repeated that the FOMC "should do everything possible to maintain confidence in the Government securities market." McCabe replied that the president could depend on everyone to do what they could to protect government credit. There would be differences of opinion on how that might best be done, he warned, but the president said that he understood. McCabe suggested that the Fed consult frequently with the Treasury secretary and seek every means possible to reach an agreement on financing questions. It was a meeting, as Herbert Stein put it, that was "a masterpiece of deliberate misunderstanding."[85] Commitments were vague and each side could interpret the conversation as it pleased.

Truman publicly announced his version the next day. He sent a letter to McCabe and announced it to the press:

Dear Tom:

I want the members of the Federal Reserve Board and the members of the Federal Open Market Committee to know how deeply I appreciate their expression of full cooperation given to me yesterday in our meeting.

85. Stein, *The Fiscal Revolution in America*, 272.

As I expressed to you, I am deeply concerned over the international situation and its implications upon our economic stability.

Your assurance that you would fully support the Treasury Defense financing program, both as to refunding and new issues, is of vital importance to me. As I understand it, I have your assurance that the market on government securities will be stabilized and maintained at present levels in order to assure the successful financing requirements and to establish in the minds of the people confidence concerning government credit.

I wish you would convey to all the members of your group my warm appreciation of their cooperative attitude.

Sincerely,

Harry S. Truman[86]

The letter surprised the members of the committee, who remembered the meeting differently and especially did not remember a commitment to maintain Treasury bonds at current prices and rates. Eccles saw it as "a final move in a Treasury attempt to impose its will on the Federal Reserve."[88] (Indeed, the White House did secretly consider a plan to issue an executive order requiring all Federal Open Market Committee operations be approved by Truman.[88] Eccles leaked copies of the minutes to the Washington *Post* and the Washington *Star*, and the story appeared on the front pages of their Sunday editions. The minutes showed no commitment to maintain the peg and, indeed, only the vaguest of support for the president's overall policy. With the leak, as Eccles wrote in his memoirs in uncharacteristically understated fashion, "the fat was in the fire."[89] Senator Douglas seized on the account to attack the Treasury and to signal clearly that the administration would find little support in Congress.

When the FOMC met a few days later, Sproul silenced bickering over whether the minutes should have been leaked by arguing that the president had "wholly misrepresented" the meeting. His letter was "intolerable" and Eccles's maneuver, he said, had "temporarily retrieved our place in the financial community and with the public."[90] The committee quickly rejected the idea of a mass resignation and considered instead asking Congress to

<hr>

86. Letter, Truman to McCabe, February 1, 1951, Federal Reserve, 1951, box 13, Snyder Papers, Truman Library.

87. Eccles, *Beckoning Frontiers*, 494.

88. Executive order with attachment, undated, Federal Reserve, 1951, box 13, Snyder Papers, Truman Library.

89. Eccles, *Beckoning Frontiers*, 496.

90. Minutes, February 6–8, 1951, box 62, folder 2, Eccles Papers.

settle the dispute, but the FOMC finally agreed to confront Truman directly.

"You as President of the United States and we as members of the Federal Open Market Committee," they wrote Truman, "have unintentionally been drawn into a false position before the American public—as if you were committing us to a policy which we believe to be contrary to what we all truly desire and we as if we were questioning your word or defying your wishes as the chief executive of this country in this critical period." The committee tried to reassure Truman that it was "the policy of the Federal Reserve System and of its Federal Open Market Committee to adapt credit policy to the needs and requirements of the Government as well as of the country." The FOMC added, however, that "in inflationary times like these our buying of Government securities does not provide confidence. It undermines confidence." The letter concluded by stating that the committee would seek to work out a policy as quickly as possible "which is practicable, feasible and adequate in the light of our defense emergency, which will safeguard and maintain public confidence in the values of outstanding Government bonds, and which at the same time will protect the purchasing power of the dollar."[91]

At the same time, the committee also sent a letter marked "secret" to Snyder. The Fed "for the present" promised to purchase enough long-term bonds to prevent their prices from falling below par. However, the committee added, "We should like to discuss with you possible features for the new bond that would remove or reduce the need for Federal Reserve support of the market in the future."[92] The letter put the Treasury on notice that the Fed's support would be both short-term and limited, that it soon intended to end its automatic support of the market, and that it would not allow the Treasury again to commit the system to policies with which it did not agree.

Truman attempted to end the dispute by forming on February 26 an interagency committee. He asked the secretary of the Treasury, the chairman of the Board of Governors, the director of defense mobilization, and the chairman of the Council of Economic Advisers to study ways to restrain

91. Letter, McCabe to Truman, February 7, 1951, Federal Reserve System, box 22, Murphy Files, Truman Library. The committee also sought to educate Truman on the differences between the World War I Liberty Bonds and the World War II Savings Bonds. The Liberty Bonds were marketable securities and thus had fluctuating prices. Holders of World War II Savings Bonds, on the other hand, were always guaranteed the return of their investment with interest on demand.

92. Letter, McCabe to Snyder, February 7, 1951, Federal Reserve 1951, box 13, Snyder Papers, Truman Library.

credit expansion while maintaining stability in the government securities market. While the study was under way, he said pointedly in a memo released to the press, "I hope that no attempt will be made to change the interest rate pattern."[93]

At the staff level, however, intensive negotiations were already under way. Snyder, who was still in the hospital, gave Assistant Secretary of the Treasury William McChesney Martin permission to meet with Winfield Riefler, the Fed's top career economist and assistant to Chairman McCabe. They spent two hours over lunch working out basic arrangements for future Fed-Treasury relations, a truce which finally emerged on March 3 in a simple joint announcement: "The Treasury and the Federal Reserve System have reached full accord with respect to debt management and monetary policies to be pursued in furthering their common purpose to assure the successful financing of the Goverment's requirements and, at the same time, to minimize monetization of the public debt."[94]

No one but the participants knew just what this meant, and Fed and Treasury officials both refused for a year to comment further on the agreement. It turned out that the deal had four parts. The Treasury agreed to exchange the marketable 2½ percent bonds for nonmarketable 2¾ percent bonds with a 29-year maturity. That encouraged long-term investors to hold their bonds, took pressure off the market, and ended the Fed's support of the long-term bond market. Second, the Fed agreed to use its open-market operations to keep the market orderly while it adjusted to the new conditions. Third, the Fed agreed to keep its discount rate at 1¾ percent and not to change it without consulting the Treasury. At the same time the Fed would no longer support the Treasury's short-term market. Finally, the Fed and Treasury agreed to consult in setting the strategy for financing the debt. To ease the transition to an unpegged market, the Fed would agree to support the market for a short period with an indefinite amount of money.[95]

Shortly thereafter McCabe resigned as chairman, and Truman appointed William McChesney Martin, the Treasury's principal negotiator for the accord, to succeed McCabe as board member and chairman. Both the timing

93. Memo from Truman, February 26, 1951, Federal Reserve System, box 22, Murphy Files, Truman Library.

94. Board of Governors, *Thirty-eighth Annual Report* (Washington, D.C.: Board of Governors, 1951), 4. "Monetizing the debt" means purchase of Treasury securities by the Fed in quantities larger than would be needed to achieve the Fed's monetary policy objectives. The effect of such purchases is to translate the Treasury's debt into increases in the money supply— the Fed exchanges cash for Treasury securities—and this creates an inflationary danger.

95. See Edward S. Flash, Jr., *Economic Advice and Presidential Leadership: The Council of Economic Advisers* (New York: Columbia University Press, 1965), 80. Flash's account is based upon a participant's diary.

of McCabe's leave-taking and Martin's appointment led some observers to speculate that McCabe's resignation was part of the deal, and that the Treasury was indeed trying to take over the Fed. The White House and Treasury consistently denied that there was any connection between McCabe's departure and the accord, although that was not the case. Snyder had sent word from his hospital bed that "Mr. McCabe has lost his effectiveness in the Federal Reserve position, as he apparently was not able to make decisions." Truman, in discussing the incident later, was more blunt. "McCabe," he said, "was informed that his services were no longer satisfactory, and he quit." McCabe submitted his resignation on February 26, in the midst of the negotiations, but it was not formally announced until March 9, six days after the accord was announced.[96]

To replace McCabe, Snyder favored Martin, but Truman and his advisers preferred Harry McDonald, the chairman of the Securities and Exchange Commission. They discovered at the last minute, however, that he was ineligible for appointment because the board already contained a member from his Federal Reserve district. Martin thus became the new Fed chairman.[97] After having negotiated the new Fed-Treasury agreement, it fell to him to carry it out. If there was any doubt about whether the Fed break with the Treasury was real, Martin and his new colleagues ended it during the Treasury's April financing. The Fed withdrew completely from the market and bond prices slid slightly. Interest rates on the Treasury's bonds, meanwhile, increased to the 2¾ percent level specified in the accord. As John D. Clark of the Council of Economic Advisers noted, "The Federal Reserve has made good on its claim to complete independence."[98] The real question now was what that independence meant: especially, what the Fed's relationship with the Treasury would be after ten years of Treasury dominance.

THE MEANING OF INDEPENDENCE

Congressman Wright Patman (D-Tex.) led a Joint Economic Committee investigation in March 1952 to try to determine the meaning of independence for the Fed. Senator Douglas, a committee member, asked Snyder during the hearings just how free the Fed truly was. What should the Fed's policy be, he asked the secretary, in the event of a large sale of Treasury securities? Should the Fed support the market? Snyder replied guardedly,

96. Truman in Snyder's memoirs, 33, Truman Library, Snyder oral history, 1472–73.
97. Bach, *Making Monetary and Fiscal Policy*, 83n.
98. Memo, Clark to Murphy, April 12, 1951, CEA, box 21, Murphy Files, Truman Library.

"I think that the policy of the Reserve Board should be one of cooperation with the Treasury." When Douglas pressed him for more explanation, Snyder refused to elaborate. The senator told Snyder he was "very disappointed" in his evasive response, but the Treasury secretary refused to add any more. Snyder limited his comments to suggesting that the Fed should keep the Treasury informed of its intentions and should allow Treasury officials to offer their views before the Fed made decisions.[99]

Fed officials stressed instead the need for equality with the Treasury. "I do not think you should subordinate the Treasury to the Federal Reserve or the Federal to the Treasury," Martin told the committee. "I think that they have both got to be equals." What would the system do in case of conflict with the Treasury? Martin replied, "We would sit around the table and hammer it out."[100] The New York reserve bank president Sproul elaborated that the principle of consultation, toward a joint program, was the core of the accord, with neither the Fed nor the Treasury "being the superior authority telling the other what it is to do and why it should do it."[101] If the Treasury was concerned that the Fed would use its newly asserted independence to make decisions without consultation, the Fed's officials were eager to make clear that they desired equal (but not superior) status to their brethren in the Treasury.

There was more to the accord, furthermore, than simply the Fed's relationship to the Treasury. Many members of Congress, especially Douglas and Patman, were unhappy that the Treasury's dominance of the Fed had locked Congress out of monetary policy decisions. The Fed existed, after all, on the foundation of monetary powers given by the Constitution to Congress and then delegated to the Fed. The Treasury's wartime dominance of the Fed thus raised for many members of Congress worrisome questions about the executive versus congressional roles in monetary policy.

Sproul developed a clever solution to the problem that appealed to the subcommittee's members. The Fed's independence, he wrote in a letter to the subcommittee, "does not mean independence from the Government but independence within the Government." This cryptic argument had a clear meaning to the members of Congress. Sproul was contending that there ought to be a distinction between the Fed's responsiveness to its executive and legislative branch constituencies. "In performing its major task—the administration of monetary policy," he wrote, "the Federal Re-

99. Joint Committee, *Monetary Policy and the Management of the Public Debt*, 14, 31.
100. Ibid., 86. Fed officials were searching awkwardly for a short name for their agency. "The Federal" was popular in the early 1950s until "the Fed" gained currency.
101. Ibid., 534.

serve System is an agency of the Congress set up in a special form to bear the responsibility for that particular task which constitutionally belongs to the legislative branch of the government."[102] The Fed inevitably would have to coordinate its decisions closely with the Treasury, since it dealt largely in the Treasury's own obligations. It was to Congress, however, that the Fed ultimately was answerable. Sproul's formulation would work, though, only if members of Congress would step forward to counterbalance the pressures Treasury officials put on the Fed. Douglas wryly observed that it sometimes helps "to have a little legislative protection."[103] Sproul agreed by indirectly criticizing the Treasury. "The temptation to tamper with money for temporary gain or narrow purpose is always present," he said.[104]

However, if Congress insisted that the Fed in the end be responsive to Congress and not the Treasury, the members of the subcommittee could not agree on what goals the Fed was to pursue. The existing mandate, the subcommittee's report acknowledged, was "vague and diffuse," but when it came to drafting new recommendations, the subcommittee fragmented.[105] Only two of the subcommittee's five members endorsed the main body of its report, and dissent clouded its conclusions.

Even though the subcommittee's investigation ended in dissension, it did produce two principles that guided the Fed for a generation. First, the subcommittee made unmistakably clear that it would not allow the executive branch free sway over monetary policy. The power to coin money, after all, was a congressional function. When the Treasury dominated the Fed, it left the Congress with much less leverage over the economy (and, indeed, over its own creature, the Fed). The subcommittee served notice that this it would not accept. Even though Congress had for forty years been relatively quiet on the question of what monetary policy ought to be, the investigation established that Congress reserved the right to intervene, albeit selectively, in monetary policy and the Fed's affairs.

Second, the subcommittee members demonstrated that Congress found it no easier in 1952 to specify how the Fed ought to conduct monetary policy than it had in 1913. Members of Congress were far more likely to tell Fed officials what they disliked than what policy approach they approved. The delegation of power to the Fed was thus to remain vague. The Fed was not

102. Ibid., 983–84.
103. Ibid., 97.
104. Ibid., 983–84.
105. U.S. Congress, Joint Committee on the Economic Report, Subcommittee on General Credit Control and Debt Management, *Monetary Policy and the Management of the Public Debt*, report, 82d Cong., 2d sess., 1952, 39.

to be the Treasury's puppet, but Congress itself would not write the Fed's script.

With the hearings, therefore, Fed officials gained powerful allies in resisting executive branch pressure. At the same time, however, Fed officials were christened into a new political reality: they lived in a world with sharply conflicting expectations but without clear instructions to guide them. Renewed congressional interest in monetary policy thus increased the need for the Fed's leaders to be more politically sophisticated. It also increased the number of political constituencies to which the Fed had to pay attention.

After a decade of dominance by the Treasury—and a decade before that of careful attention to supporting the New Deal—these new constituencies greatly changed the Fed's environment. The most important constituency was obviously Congress, scarcely a new one but certainly a significantly more interested one. Also of keen importance was the banking industry, which had been seriously harmed by the Korean War inflation. Bankers continued to fear that a Fed tied too closely to the administration might encourage more inflation. In a resolution passed in 1952, the Investment Bankers Association voiced strong support for "the maintenance of a Federal Reserve System whose policies are independent of the executive branch of the Government."[106] The American Bankers Association said the Fed should not be "subservient to political influences." One of its spokesmen told the Patman subcommittee, "Even when inflation reaches more advanced stages and the danger of a crash is imminent, the cry in some quarters will always be for more money and lower rates of interest."[107] The Treasury did not fare well during the hearings and its officials discovered it could press the Fed no further.

Eccles's years at the Fed thus bridged two crises. He had proven himself a powerful chairman and, in fact, his leadership was the standard by which most observers judged his successors. Even though the Fed had existed for twenty years before Eccles became chairman, it was not until he developed—and won support for—his strategy for consolidating power in Washington that the Fed matured. Eccles had a clear sense of how the agency ought to work—with a powerful board setting policy for the reserve banks— and the purpose that policy ought to serve—support of Roosevelt's New Deal to bring the economy alive again. Eccles's leadership transformed the Fed from a weak agency with an uncertain mission into a powerful institution of unquestioned influence.

106. Inserted in record, Joint Committee, *Monetary Policy and the Management of the Public Debt*, hearings, 345.

107. Testimony of W. L. Hemingway, chairman of the Advisory Committee on Special Activities of the American Bankers Association, ibid., 330.

Marriner Eccles proved himself a powerful chairman, but much of his power rested on the personal relationship he developed with Roosevelt. If he institutionalized the Fed by concentrating its power in Washington, he did not institutionalize the power of the chairmanship. After Roosevelt's death, he lost the crucial support on which he depended. When he could not develop a way to work with Truman, he not only lost the chairmanship but he also left the Fed to muddle through a crisis that was to take five years to resolve.

As his successor, McCabe was determined to avoid Eccles's mistakes. The problem he faced, though, was a difficult one. It was never clear just how long the Treasury wanted the Fed's support or just how long the Fed could support the peg without courting serious inflation. The Treasury's requests were always for maintaining the peg just a little longer—and they were always accompanied by dire warnings about the fate of the Treasury's bond market if the Fed did not. The problem, the New York bank's President Sproul explained, was that "you cannot be dogmatic, you cannot be sure you are right." The Treasury had always expressed its requests in terms of keeping interest rates steady in the transition from war to peace and preventing the failure of the government bond market. "We had to exhaust all the possibilities," Sproul concluded, "before making a complete break."[108] It was a difficult problem: strong political pressures accompanied by substantial technical uncertainties.

McCabe's strategy was to be a mediator: to try to transform the Fed's decade-old ties with the Treasury by backing away from the peg as gradually as possible. This strategy, however, proved a complete failure. He found himself under siege from Eccles and his allies who wanted a quick break with the Treasury. Freed from the chairmanship, Eccles spoke his mind with even less reservation, and McCabe found his position eroded by the many Fed officials whose candidacies Eccles had supported.[109] McCabe tried to counter his opponents within the Fed by accommodating Snyder and Truman, but they never did trust the chairman. Truman contended McCabe was "just as bad" as Eccles, and Snyder complained that he didn't have an idea about how to handle the job.[110] In seeking a middle ground, McCabe found himself alone and without support. The failure of his strategy to transform the Fed, to release it from the peg, allowed the Fed to drift into the most serious crisis in its history.

108. Joint Committee, *Monetary Policy and the Management of the Public Debt,* hearings, 534.

109. Carpenter Oral History, 14, Eccles Papers; Sherman Oral History, 14, Eccles Papers.

110. Both comments in Snyder's memoirs, 33, Truman Library.

A MATURE FEDERAL RESERVE

After nearly forty years of struggle, the accord finally established the Fed as a mature agency. Eccles had consolidated the Fed's power in Washington, but how that power ought to be used had not been clear. Neither was it clear just *who* should manage the Fed's power. The accord, and the process that produced it, helped answer these questions. It defined quite clearly that the Fed was a political agency whose power depended on the balance of political support it could attract from its key constituencies: the president, the Treasury, interest groups like bankers, and Congress.

The preaccord days had illustrated just how dangerous to the Fed—and to the economy—was dominance of monetary policy by any one part of its constituency. A Treasury able to reign over monetary policy might wreck the long-range plans of financiers. It might push the economy in a direction opposite to that desired by members of Congress. The interests of these other constituencies depended on a politically "independent" Fed—that is, a Fed not under the control of any one constituency. The Fed's own interests depended on being able to balance the demands of its supporters. The Fed's emerging relationship with its constituencies was thus reciprocal. It gave them a voice in policies about which they were keenly concerned, and it provided the Fed with enough political backing to avoid surrendering to any one constituent. More, and more vocal, constituencies thus gave Fed officials more flexibility.

At the same time, however, this also greatly complicated the Fed's political world. For all the problems the World War II peg created, it had the signal virtue of at least making decision making easy. With the accord, the Fed had greater risk and a more complicated environment: more political pressures on its decisions and a less certain guide with which to make them.

This new environment put a higher premium than ever on leadership. Weak leadership had twice led the Fed to serious crises, in the Depression and again in the post–World War II era. Eccles helped rescue the Fed from the Depression, but his chairmanship demonstrates the great institutional danger of a personality-based leadership. To cement the Fed's maturity, the challenge was to move the chairman's leadership from a personal to an institutional base, to a style of leadership that could survive presidential transitions and flourish in a more complex and risky environment.

That task fell to William McChesney Martin, Jr., a relatively junior Treasury official who succeeded McCabe as chairman at the age of only 44. Martin's appointment depended in part on coincidence, in part on his unique ties with both the Fed and the Treasury. He was acceptable to the

Treasury because of his previous service there, acceptable to the Fed because he had helped negotiate the accord. If some Fed officials feared he would be the Treasury's stooge—and if Truman hoped he had placed a loyalist within the enemy's walls—they were quickly enlightened. Martin carved out his own path, a path to accommodate the administration's needs without yielding to its political pressure. He quieted the fears of financiers and members of Congress, and he created through his leadership an era of good feeling that lasted nearly twenty years. Most of all, he transformed the Fed into a powerful agency, an agency whose power endured long past his tenure.

CHAPTER FOUR
LEANING AGAINST THE WIND

The accord was far more than a declaration of the Fed's independence. It also marked the agency's passage to maturity: an equal footing with the Treasury matched by congressional support for its operating flexibility. As Senator Douglas wrote in 1952, "The Treasury and the System will be better neighbors in the long run, the less they invite themselves to play in each other's backyards." Borrowing from Robert Frost, he concluded, "The proper principle is, 'Good fences make good neighbors.' "[1] Behind Douglas's clever warning, however, was a formidable task. The Fed was to consult with but not bend to the Treasury, to cooperate with the administration without ignoring congressional concerns, to prevent inflation from reigniting without challenging fiscal policy, to determine which economic conditions warranted action when.

William McChesney Martin, Jr., was the very personification of the accord and its puzzles. He had a Treasury background yet was not captured by it. He was also part of an old and distinguished Fed family, for his father had served as chief executive of the Federal Reserve Bank of St. Louis. Martin in self-deprecating fashion came to call himself just "a bond man," but in his early years he was known as the "boy wonder of Wall Street." After earning a law degree at Columbia University, he joined a small stock brokerage, A. G. Edwards, in 1929 at the age of 23. He became a partner of the firm in 1931 and operated its membership on the floor of the New York Stock Exchange for seven years. He so impressed his colleagues that he became a governor of the exchange in 1935 and its first paid president in 1938. World War II interrupted his banking career but not his pattern

1. Douglas, "Statement of Views," in U.S. Congress, Joint Committee on the Economic Report, Subcommittee on General Credit Control and Debt Management, *Monetary Policy and the Management of the Public Debt*, report, 82d Cong., 2d sess., 1952, 76.

of quick advancement. He entered the army as a private but at the end of the war left as a colonel and then went on to become president of the U.S. Export-Import Bank. Here he attracted the Truman administration's attention and became assistant secretary of the Treasury for international finance in 1948, a position from which he helped fashion the accord.

Martin clearly recognized the dilemma in which the Fed found itself. The Fed's purpose, he explained, was to insure that the money supply was "neither so large as to induce destructive inflationary forces nor so small as to stifle our great and growing economy."[2] His monetary philosophy was a pragmatic one that relied on discretionary control of the money supply. In Martin's view, the economy was hard to judge and predict, while the Fed faced constant pressures to balance strong economic growth with low inflation. The Fed's job was that of a dam master, to keep the supply of money at a healthy level. "We want the flow of money and credit to be like a stream," Martin explained in a 1955 interview. "This stream or river is flowing through the fields of business and commerce. We don't want the water to overflow the banks of the stream, flooding and drowning what is in the fields. Neither do we want the stream to dry up, and leave the fields parched."[3]

This metaphor led in turn to another one, Martin's famous declaration of the Fed's job: "Our purpose is to lean against the winds of deflation or inflation, whichever way they are blowing."[4] "Leaning against the wind" was fundamentally a justification for discretionary policy making, since the Fed would have to determine which way the wind was blowing, when to move, and how far to lean against it. If the Fed was to lean against the wind, it must be free from political pressures like the Treasury's crippling peg. The declaration thus also implied that the Fed must maintain its operating independence.

Martin, however, was always very careful to frame his arguments in terms of independence from the executive branch, not from Congress. "It is clear to me," he told a Senate committee, "that it was intended the Federal Reserve should be independent and not responsible directly to the executive branch of the Government but should be accountable to the Congress." He continued, "I like to think of a trustee relationship to see that the Treasury does not engage in the natural temptation to depreciate the currency or engage in practices which would harm" the general welfare. Instead, he

2. William McChesney Martin, "The Transition to Free Markets," *Federal Reserve Bulletin* 39 (April 1953): 331.

3. Interview in *U.S. News and World Report*, February 11, 1955, 56.

4. Martin's testimony in U.S. Senate, Committee on Banking and Currency, *Nomination of William McChesney Martin, Jr.*, hearings, 84th Cong., 2d sess., 1956, 5.

argued that the Fed and the Treasury "must be partners in promoting the welfare of the Government securities market."[5]

Martin's formulation was a masterpiece of ambiguity. The Treasury would not be allowed control over the Fed's operations, but neither would the Fed simply abandon the Treasury. In an interview, Martin explained: "Now, we have no obligation to finance the Government at just any rate, arbitrarily chosen. But we do have the obligation to see that the Government can get the money needed to pay for expenditures which are authorized by the Congress."[6] So long as the Treasury conducted its financing to fund programs created by Congress, the Fed would support the Treasury, but it would not keep an arbitrarily low rate simply for the Treasury's convenience.

All of this required, Martin told members of Congress, that the Fed have "a reasonable opportunity to make its decisions, insulated from direct political pressures." Key members of Congress, though, were determined not to allow Martin to take this argument too far. At one hearing, when Senator Douglas worried that Martin was taking the rhetoric of independence too seriously, he told the chairman, "I have had typed out this little sentence which is a quotation from you: 'The Federal Reserve Board is an agency of the Congress.' I will furnish you with scotch tape and ask you to place it on your mirror where you can see it as you shave each morning."[7] If the accord was a triumph for the Fed, it was also a victory for the Congress over the administration, and members of Congress were insistent on reminding Martin just whose creature he was.

Martin trod through these conflicts with a style unique in the Fed. Although a nominal Democrat, he remained scrupulously nonpartisan in monetary policy and refused to venture into other policy areas. Before coming to the Fed, Martin had a lifelong devotion to its operations and principles. He was a man of deep sincerity and strong personal charm, a warm man whom his colleagues genuinely liked. The contrast with Eccles, the presidential counselor, New Deal cheerleader, and energetic administration spokesman, could not have been greater. Most of Eccles's associates had found him irascible and hard to work with. Martin thus gave a much different personality to the board.[8]

Unlike the authoritarian Eccles and the weak McCabe, Martin ran the board and the FOMC in a collegial spirit. One Fed official said Martin was

5. Martin's testimony in U.S. Senate, Committee on Banking and Currency, *Nomination of William McChesney Martin, Jr.*, hearings, 82d Cong., 1st sess., 1951, 5.

6. Martin interview, *U.S. News and World Report*, 124–25.

7. Senate Banking Committee, *Nomination* (1956 hearings), 24–25.

8. Maisel, *Managing the Dollar*, 117; C. R. Whittlesey, "Power and Influence in the Federal Reserve System," *Economica* 30 (February 1963): 34–35.

"responsive, fair, and ready to compromise."[9] Meetings revolved around a long series of "go-rounds" in which every member freely spoke in a predetermined order. Martin's role was not like Eccles's, who decided what the Fed's policy ought to be and forcefully argued for it. Martin was never known as a top economist, and he did not have the training to lead the system's policies intellectually. His role, rather, was that of a consensus builder. He always spoke last and then tried to articulate a position on which nearly everyone could agree. His technique typically produced unanimous (or nearly so) votes, and he was willing to delay issues for one or two meetings until a clear consensus had emerged.

Under Martin's chairmanship, therefore, the Fed usually spoke to the outside world with one voice. Following the conflict of the preaccord days, this was an important foundation for rebuilding the Fed's power. Martin's consensus-building approach helped as well to accommodate the Fed's procedures to changing Fed operations. Before 1955, the FOMC met only four times per year and usually did little more than ratify decisions made earlier by a small working subcommittee led by the chairman. By the 1950s, the rapid development of air travel made more frequent meetings possible. In 1955, the Fed abolished the subcommittee and the full FOMC began meeting about every three weeks. With a larger group participating more regularly in making decisions, the consensus approach proved a way to match FOMC policy to the disparate views of the committee's members.[10]

The consensus-building strategy was also important in strengthening Martin's personal position, especially against his principal rival, Allan Sproul of the New York Federal Reserve Bank. Sproul had been with the system since his graduation from college in 1919 and had served as president of the New York bank for ten years. Ever since the days of Benjamin Strong that post had been a powerful one within the system, and Sproul had used it to become the preeminent force, intellectual and political, within the Federal Reserve System. His arguments for independence from the Treasury had been among the most powerful and influential, and members of Congress regularly called upon him during hearings. When Martin assumed the chairmanship, Sproul was thus a powerful rival for influence within the agency. Martin's approach helped him outflank Sproul by developing a broad coalition behind whatever policy the FOMC adopted. As Martin explained later: "I decided right from the start that the only way to handle this situation was to ask every member of the FOMC to state his views about the economy and the policy to be adopted. When the go-round was completed, I then

9. Interview with the author.
10. See Whittlesey, "Power and Influence in the Federal Reserve System," 36.

said, 'As I understand it, this is the consensus of what we want for policy and we will vote on it.' Of course, I stated what I wanted—taking into account what I had heard expressed at the meeting—and that was what became policy."[11] Sometimes this meant that policy emerged slowly, but it also meant that no one FOMC member could dominate.

Soon after he assumed the chairmanship, Martin faced an important challenge from Sproul. To help the Fed determine how to deal with the post-accord world, he had established an Ad Hoc Subcommittee of the FOMC to study the Fed's policies and procedures. The subcommittee, composed of Martin, newly appointed board member Abbot L. Mills, Jr., and President Malcom Bryan of the Atlanta reserve bank, concluded that the Fed ought to aim for a government securities market "characterized by great depth, breadth, and resiliency."[12] This guideline became the Fed's watchword in a not-so-subtle slap at the Treasury, whose insistence on the peg had made the market shallow, narrow, and stale. To produce such a market, the subcommittee concluded, the FOMC should "confine its operations to bills"—Treasury obligations maturing in a year or less. The subcommittee also recommended that the FOMC change its directive for open-market operations from "maintenance of orderly conditions"—the watchword for low rates—to "correction of disorderly conditions."[13]

These recommendations had several important implications. The Fed would intervene only rarely in the government securities market, instead of constantly as had previously been the case. In fact, the Fed would attempt to support the Treasury's prices only when the market became "disorderly," with the definition of just what was disorderly as well as the timing and scope of the Fed's actions determined by the Fed itself. Furthermore, by limiting the FOMC's actions to bills—short-term obligations—it would keep the Fed away from longer-term bonds and thus far away from the pegging issue that had dominated the previous decade.

The recommendation of this "bills only" policy was thus a clear slap at the Treasury. Less clear was the fact that it would lessen the role of the Federal Reserve Bank of New York, which managed the system's open-market account: it conducted the buying and selling of government securities to accomplish the FOMC's objectives. If the FOMC decided to limit its operations to bills, the New York reserve bank would have far less discretion in carrying out Fed policies. (Prior to the "bills only" policy it could,

11. Quoted in *Forbes*, September 17, 1979, 98.
12. Described in U.S. Congress, Joint Economic Committee, Subcommittee on Economic Stabilization, *United States Monetary Policy: Recent Thinking and Experience*, hearings, 83d Cong., 2d sess., 1954, 260.
13. Ibid., 268.

for example, deal in longer-term securities at its discretion to produce the same degree of "tightness" or "easiness" of the money supply.)

In addition to distancing the Fed from the Treasury, the new policy was thus also aimed at reducing Sproul's influence. The subcommittee's report suggested that he came to FOMC meetings with an inevitable conflict of interest: he attended "not only as a contributor" to discussions but also "as a protagonist for the actual day to day operation of the account." In fact, the report concluded, management of the account ought to be taken out of the hands of the New York reserve bank. The account manager, instead, ought to be an employee of the FOMC rather than the New York bank. Sproul countered that operation of the account by an FOMC employee might result in a less effective, "remote control" administration. Even more important, Sproul argued, the "bills only" policy might handicap the agency by unnecessarily limiting the range of its tools. Sometimes, he suggested, "the System might better be able to effectuate its policies by operating in other sectors of the market."[14]

Despite Sproul's protests, Martin won a consensus to adopt the "bills only" policy in the FOMC on March 4 and 5, 1953. At the next meeting, however, Martin lost his advantage. Two board members were absent, another seat was vacant, and the bank presidents held a 5–4 voting edge. Sproul argued that the market had not demonstrated "breadth, depth, and resiliency" since the March decision. The country's booming economy made making FOMC decisions like walking a tightrope, and Sproul did not think the committee could "walk the tightrope successfully" if the "bills only" policy remained in effect—"We should reserve for ourselves maximum freedom to operate."[15] Sproul's arguments won the support of the other bank presidents, and with a 5 to 4 vote they reversed the "bills only" policy.

At the next meeting, though, the tables turned once again. The two absent board members returned and Martin had a 6–5 margin over the bank presidents to reinstate the "bills only" policy. When some presidents worried that the policy might limit the Fed's flexibility in the future, Martin reassured them that "no tablets of stone were being written."[16] Martin won the votes of all six board members present as well as three bank presidents to defeat Sproul, 9–2. Sproul continued to raise the issue and Martin continued to preserve a consensus in favor of "bills only," which became the Fed's guiding principle throughout the 1950s.

14. Comments by the New York Federal Reserve Bank, in Joint Economic Committee, *United States Monetary Policy*, 326, 311.
15. Federal Open Market Committee, Memoranda of Discussion, June 11, 1953, 14–15.
16. Ibid., September 24, 1953, 29.

"Bills only" was an unmistakable declaration of operating independence from the Treasury. It was also the final battle in the long struggle for primacy in the system between the New York Federal Reserve Bank and the board. Most importantly, though, "bills only" was an important part of the Fed's shift from a narrow concern for money and credit policy to a much broader concern for governing economic growth and prices. For the first time, the Fed aggressively took a strong role in stabilizing the economy, "a near-revolutionary change," according to Friedman and Schwartz.[17] In his first two years in office, Martin thus transformed the Fed and its relations with the administration. It remained to be seen, however, just how Martin would use the new power he had built.

NEW TIES WITH THE WHITE HOUSE

Monetary policy got off on a cooperative footing in the Eisenhower years. When the Treasury received few bids for its securities in mid–1953, the Fed increased the money supply and thus made it easier for the Treasury to market its obligations. A recession, meanwhile, was beginning, and within a few months Eisenhower wanted even easier money. "I talked to the secretary of the Treasury," he wrote in his diary on April 8, 1954, "in order to develop real pressure on the Federal Reserve Board for loosening credit still further." Treasury Secretary Humphrey, the president wrote, "agreed with me and promised to put the utmost pressure on Chairman Martin of the Federal Reserve Board in order to get a greater money supply throughout the country."[18] The Fed predictably resisted such pressure so soon after the accord—but only to the point of refusing to conduct open-market operations to ease the money supply; instead the board lowered reserve requirements. As Fed officials had frankly testified earlier, they could not buck a direct plea from the White House. To prove their argument on independence, though, Martin used a different tool to produce the result Eisenhower wanted.

In 1955, however, Martin began worrying more about inflation than recession. Fed officials were concerned that the economy was starting to overheat, and the board increased the discount rate to try to slow it. With an election approaching, however, administration officials were worrying that the Fed's action would weaken the economy too much. Arthur Burns, Eisenhower's chairman of the Council of Economic Advisers, pressed Martin

17. Friedman and Schwartz, *A Monetary History of the United States*, 628, 631.
18. In Robert H. Ferrell, ed., *The Eisenhower Diaries* (New York: W. W. Norton, 1981), 178.

in January 1956 to ease Fed policies and to avoid further changes in the discount rate.[19] The board raised the discount rate in April anyway, and administration officials began a public attack. Commerce Secretary Sinclair Weeks argued that the decision "may prove to be a handicap" to the economy, while Labor Secretary James Paul Mitchell contended, "I don't happen to believe there is an inflationary trend right now."[20] Congressman Wright Patman, always concerned that Fed policy was too restrictive, held hearings and called Martin and Humphrey to testify about the conflict.[21]

The battle created a difficult problem for Eisenhower. He certainly did not want the economy to weaken as he sought reelection. On the other hand, in the wake of Truman's public squabbles, he did not want to appear to be putting public pressure on the Fed. When reporters questioned him about the issue at a press conference, Eisenhower admitted the dispute but said: "Well, I think the only comment I can logically make is this: the Federal Reserve Board is set up as a separate agency of the Government. It is not under the authority of the President, and I really personally believe it would be a mistake to make it definitely and directly responsible to the political head of state." Furthermore, he continued: "Certain individuals had viewpoints on the opposite sides of the fence. But . . . I do have this confidence in the Federal Reserve Board: they are watching this situation day by day."[22] When pressed again during three different news conferences later in the campaign, Eisenhower each time repeated his endorsement of the Fed's independence.[23] If not a ringing endorsement of the Fed's policy, the president's careful answer was at least an acknowledgment that he would not interfere publicly as Truman had done.

Eisenhower's statements in the face of obvious differences with the Fed on monetary policy strengthened the agency's young postaccord independence. The episode established an important principle: administration officials reserved the right to lobby Fed officials privately for policies they preferred, but to take the Fed on publicly risked making presidential advisers look like apologists for inflation and Fed officials champions of tough if unpopular policies. The Fed could not afford to be far out of step with what the administration wanted, but administration officials could not risk

19. Telephone calls log, January 24, 1956, Whitman Papers, Dwight D. Eisenhower Library.

20. *Wall Street Journal*, May 4, 1956, 4.

21. U.S. Congress, Joint Committee on the Economic Report, Subcommittee on Economic Stabilization, *Conflicting Official Views on Monetary Policy*, hearings, 84th Cong., 2d sess., 1956.

22. *Public Papers of the Presidents: Dwight D. Eisenhower*, 1956, 438–39.

23. The press conferences were on May 4, October 5, and October 11, 1956.

too strong and too public an attack on Fed officials. Compared with the close cooperation of the Eccles years and the confrontation of the McCabe years, Martin relied on behind-the-scenes discussion and negotiation with the president on the conduct of monetary policy.

That approach suited Eisenhower. He resented public criticism that held him personally responsible for everything that happened. The president believed his powers, especially in economic affairs, were limited, and he was only too happy to allow the Fed to take responsibility for economic stabilization—especially in an election year.[24] Eisenhower's public comments solidified the Fed's position as the guardian against inflation, a role that had emerged as a result of the accord. Even if the administration might not favor its actions, the Fed stood ready to combat rising prices when the winds seemed to be blowing that way. Indeed, the London *Economist* suggested, the Fed "seemed to relish its role of grumpy sobriety at a time of exuberance almost everywhere else."[25]

Such talk masked a far more important trend. Freed from the constraints of wartime finance and the peg, Martin was establishing for the Fed not only operating independence from the Treasury but also greater importance in steering the economy. Since its founding, the Fed had played mainly a supporting role for the president's budget. By the end of Eisenhower's administration, however, the prestigious national Commission on Money and Credit concluded, "Monetary and fiscal policy are to a degree substitutes for each other." Along with the Fed's maturity as an institution came the assertion that its policy tools were on a par with the budget. That, the commission noted, required much closer coordination between the Fed and the White House. "The real ability of the System to influence national economic policy might well be increased rather than diminished if its ties to the President were closer," the commission argued.[26]

The commission made four proposals for strengthening these ties, proposals that were remarkably similar to the ones Eccles had put forward thirty years earlier. First, the commission suggested, the chairman and vice-chairman of the Federal Reserve Board should serve four-year terms coterminous with the president's term. That would give an incoming president the right to name his own chairman. Second, the commission proposed reducing the board from seven to five members, with overlapping terms of

24. See Sherman Adams, *Firsthand Report: The Story of the Eisenhower Administration* (Westport, Conn.: Greenwood Press, 1974), 296.

25. "Supplement: A Survey of International Banking," *Economist*, November 17, 1956, 9–10.

26. Commission on Money and Credit, *Money and Credit* (Englewood Cliffs, N.J.: Prentice-Hall, 1961), 251, 44, 77.

ten (instead of fourteen) years at higher salaries. A smaller, better-paid board, the commission believed, would make the Fed easier to manage and would attract better board members. Third, the commission contended that open-market policy should be shifted from the FOMC to the board. Finally, the commission said that Congress should draft a new legislative mandate to define the Fed's responsibilities more crisply.[27]

Martin and Eisenhower favored many of the recommendations, as did President John F. Kennedy and his economic advisers. Martin, in fact, had tried almost since he had become chairman to reduce the board to five members.[28] Neither president ever made the proposals a top priority, however, and Congress never took action on any of the commission's major recommendations. Although the report failed to change the Fed's structure, it demonstrated that monetary policy had become an important force with which presidents had to deal. The Fed's critical relationship was no longer with the Treasury but with the president. Presidential attention naturally turned to strategies for insuring the Fed's cooperation.

THE QUADRIAD

Before the Eisenhower administration, there had been several temporary arrangements for Fed–White House cooperation. During the Roosevelt administration the president established an informal group, including Eccles, for "high economic thinking."[29] In 1938, Roosevelt created a more formal economic advisory body, the Monetary and Fiscal Advisory Board, composed of the secretary of the Treasury as chairman, the chairman of the Fed, the director of the budget, and the chairman of the Advisory Commission on Natural Resources. The board atrophied during the war, but it was the precursor of postwar strategies for continuing presidential-Fed relations.[30] During the 1953 congressional investigation of the accord, in fact, new proposals surfaced for a permanent group composed of the secretary of the Treasury, chairman of the Fed, director of the budget, chairman of the Federal Deposit Insurance Corporation, and the comptroller of the cur-

27. Ibid., 86–90.

28. Memo, J. K. Vardaman, Jr., to Gen. Walter B. Persons, Assistant to the President, October 10, 1958, WHCF/GF, File No. 14, "Federal Reserve System (3)," Eisenhower Library; *Economic Report of the President, 1962*, 22. The report, however, was silent on the other recommendations; and memo, Walter Heller for the Files, December 14, 1961, WHCF FG233, Federal Reserve System, John F. Kennedy Library.

29. Harold L. Ickes, *The Secret Diaries of Harold L. Ickes*, vol. 2: *The Inside Struggle, 1936–1939* (New York: Simon and Schuster, 1954), 114–15.

30. Stein, *The Fiscal Revolution in America*, 129–30.

rency.[31] Senator Douglas feared that such close relations might provide an arena in which the Fed might continually be subjected to arm-twisting by the Treasury, but the accord made some kind of continuing Fed–White House consultation essential.

CEA Chairman Burns relied on his Advisory Board on Economic Growth and Stabilization to get a fix on the Fed's policies, but it was a large, staff-level group that did not provide direct consultation among the principals. To remedy this, Martin began meeting with Treasury Secretary Humphrey at the Treasury Department, and on Wednesdays Treasury officials visited the Fed. And when Raymond J. Saulnier succeeded Burns as CEA chairman, he lunched every two weeks at the Fed with Martin and Vice-Chairman C. Canby Balderston.[32] Fed officials tended to be aloof during these sessions and never tipped their hand about future policies, but they did establish the principle of consultation among equals that was the core of the accord.

Crises tend to beget new organizational strategies, and the 1956 discount rate dispute led Eisenhower to suggest that Treasury Secretary Anderson, Saulnier, and Martin meet regularly with the president to discuss the economy. Regular meetings, he believed, would minimize public suspicion that major changes were brewing when the top economic officials met.[33] The group had no special name, but it met often in 1958 and more irregularly afterward. The agenda was wide-ranging, Saulnier later recalled, and the participants had "the frankest, most down-to-earth discussions imaginable."[34]

Following the 1960 election, Secretary of the Treasury designate C. Douglas Dillon urged Kennedy to continue Eisenhower's group, for without it meetings with Martin would be impossible "without attracting undue attention."[35] Kennedy agreed. To the chairman of the Council of Economic Advisers, secretary of the Treasury, and chairman of the Board of Governors, he added the director of the budget. The group met about every two months at the call of CEA chairman Walter Heller. When it was time to call a meeting, though, White House officials stumbled awkwardly in christening the group. They called it the "Financial Summit Meeting"

31. U.S. Congress, Joint Committee on the Economic Report, Subcommittee on Monetary, Credit, and Fiscal Policies, *Monetary, Credit, and Fiscal Policies*, report, 81st Cong., 2d sess., 1950, 4.

32. Raymond J. Saulnier oral history, 12–13, Eisenhower Library.

33. Meeting notes, October 14, 1957, Whitman Diary, "Staff Notes, October 1957," Eisenhower Library.

34. Saulnier oral history, 14.

35. Memo, C. Douglas Dillon to Kennedy, January 17, 1961, POF, "Treasury," Kennedy Library.

for a while, but that proved too long and stuffy. Heller solved the problem by searching Webster's dictionary, in which he found *Quadriad*: " 'A union or group of four. *Rare.*' That's us!" he joked.[36] The name stuck.

During the Kennedy administration, the Quadriad was nearly the sole contact between the president and Martin. (See table 1.) Heller wrote frequent memos to the president about Martin suggesting the need "to stiffen his back" if Fed support of administration policies seemed to be lagging.[37] In June 1961, for example, Heller warned Kennedy that Martin's "foot is poised nervously above the anti-inflationary brake pedal. The time may come to step on the brakes to stop a boom from becoming an inflation. But that time isn't at hand now," he concluded, and he urged the president to keep the pressure on Martin at an upcoming Quadriad meeting.[38]

Heller found the meetings produced the desired effect. The president was particularly eager for the Fed to maintain purchases of long-term bonds as part of the administration's balance of payments program. Heller monitored the Fed's activities closely, and when purchases lagged he would suggest a meeting. Just calling the meeting, Heller discovered, would improve the Fed's compliance. Martin would increase the system's purchases to be able to come to the meeting and report he was doing just what the president wanted him to do. The prospect of face-to-face confrontation with the president seemed to improve the Fed's performance, Heller decided.[39]

At first, President Lyndon Johnson decreased the number of Quadriad meetings and instead relied on the famous "Johnson treatment" to work with Martin as it had so successfully with others. The CEA rejoiced at Johnson's first attempt, which took place in May 1964 during a walk with Martin around the White House's South Grounds. After an application of the "treatment" by Johnson, Martin made a statement that there was no need for tighter money, a statement that helped firm the government securities market. Heller wrote Johnson afterward, "You may well wish that your words had as much impact on prices of goods and services as Bill Martin's words have on the price of money." Heller hailed the "treatment" as "a new secret weapon in the arsenal of government economic policy."[40]

36. Memo, Heller to Kenneth O'Donnell, August 7, 1961, Heller Papers, "Monetary Policy," Kennedy Library.

37. Memo, Heller to Kennedy, May 27, 1961, Heller Papers, "Monetary Policy"; and memo, Heller to Kennedy, November 12, 1961, WHCF FG233, "Federal Reserve System," Kennedy Library.

38. Memo, Heller to Kennedy, June 12, 1961, POF, "Council of Economic Advisers," Kennedy Library.

39. Heller oral history in Erwin C. Hargrove and Samuel A. Morley, eds., *The President and the Council of Economic Advisers: Interviews with CEA Chairmen* (Boulder, Colo.: Westview Press, 1984), 190–91.

40. Memo, Heller to Johnson, May 13, 1964, WHCF EX FI8, Lyndon B. Johnson Library.

Table 1: Chairman Martin's Meetings with the President, 1953–1968

Year	Number of meetings	Quadriad meetings*	Meetings alone
1953	3	0	1
1954	4	0	0
1955	2	0	1
1956	2	0	0
1957	2	1	0
1958	12	7	0
1959	4	1	0
1960	5	0	0
1961	7	7	0
1962	8	7	1
1963	7	5	1
1964	4	3	1
1965	14	9	0
1966	10	6	1
1967	13	5	3
1968	12	5	1

Source: Logs in presidential libraries. Social meetings and official events, like bill signings, are excluded.

*Not until the Kennedy administration was the "Quadriad" formally christened, although its members met irregularly under different names in earlier administrations. It consisted of the chairman of the Board of Governors of the Federal Reserve, the chairman of the Council of Economic Advisers, the secretary of the Treasury, and the director of the budget. Not all members attended all meetings, and the group was sometimes expanded to include other participants.

Heller's glee soon turned to disappointment, however, as Martin proved immune to further applications. As Heller's successor, Gardner Ackley, put it, Johnson "had worked him over on more than one occasion without appreciable results."[41]

With his most potent weapon neutralized, Johnson reverted to the Quadriad. Heller, and then Ackley, continued to call meetings when tighter money threatened. In 1964, for example, Heller warned Johnson that Martin had an "itchy trigger finger on interest rates," and he suggested that " 'gentle reminders' are very much in order" at an upcoming Quadriad meeting.[42] The administration also used the Quadriad meetings to soothe feelings after conflicts arose. After one episode, Ackley reported to Johnson: "[Martin] wants to be a 'team player,' and to work out a unified position with you on all issues. And it is clear that he doesn't expect to win them

41. Ackley oral history, Johnson Library, 2:3.
42. Memo, Heller to Johnson, March 2, 1964, WHCF CF F18, Johnson Library; and memo, Heller to Johnson, March 17, 1964, WHCF EX FI, Johnson Library.

all."[43] What was just as clear was that the administration could not hope to win them all. The Quadriad was the centerpiece of Fed-administration bargaining.

During the Kennedy and Johnson administrations, the Quadriad thus emerged as an important institution, but one that depended on the personal relationship between the president and the Fed chairman. Kennedy initially was suspicious of Martin, but he eventually came to have great appreciation for the Fed and Martin. He and his staff relied heavily on the Quadriad for sending signals to the Fed. Lyndon Johnson, on the other hand, was far less attuned to economic issues than was Kennedy. He had populist Texan blood in his veins that rebelled against high interest rates, and he was naturally suspicious of Martin. Formal Quadriad meetings, furthermore, did not fit LBJ's more informal style, and there were few meetings during his first year in office.[44] Close relations between the president and the Federal Reserve were essential, Eisenhower's CEA Chairman Saulnier contended, so that the Fed "would never act in ignorance or in misunderstanding of our views." It was not so much the case of telling the Fed what to do, he said. Rather, the relationship depended on "full information, full understanding, full disclosure."[45] Disclosure did not necessarily mean revealing the details of future Fed policy decisions, for Martin and other board members resisted tipping their hands or receiving lectures. Martin was leery about both political pressure and leaks affecting the bond market. For their part, however, administration officials wanted to make sure that Fed announcements did not take them by surprise.

A pattern of cooperation overcame these biases. Typical of Quadriad meetings were long conversations, pledges of cooperation, and general Fed support for administration policy. The meetings, however, followed one important pattern: they became more frequent and more meaningful after major Fed-administration disputes. The Quadriad thus typically served less as a way of coordinating policies in advance than as a means of insuring that past problems, and sometimes public controversies, did not recur. Eisenhower's version of the Quadriad, in fact, emerged only after the 1956 discount rate dispute. During the Kennedy years, Quadriad meetings were most important in defining the uneasy relationship between the administration and the Fed and in keeping the Fed attentive to the administration's balance of payments strategy. During the Johnson years, the Quadriad

43. Memo, Ackley to Johnson, February 15, 1965, WHCF EX FG11-3, Johnson Library.
44. For a discussion of this point, see Bach, *Making Monetary and Fiscal Policy*, 121; and Flash, *Economic Advice and Presidential Leadership*, 214-15.
45. Saulnier oral history, 12, Eisenhower Library.

emerged as an important institution only after the Fed increased the discount rate in December 1965, a break with administration policy that produced large headlines and great concern within the White House. The Quadriad thus tended to follow, rather than lead, events.

The Fed had gone through a remarkable metamorphosis. Eccles had transformed it into a more centralized and powerful institution, and his close ties to Roosevelt solidified the Fed's new status. McCabe tried and failed to bargain the Fed's way out of the peg; his failure immobilized monetary policy and produced the sharpest crisis in the Fed's history. Martin reinvigorated the Fed. As Treasury assistant secretary, he helped craft the accord, and then as Fed chairman he helped to bring it to life. Central to the Fed's new role was renewed stature but also a more complicated environment. Martin dealt with that environment as a skilled politician, guiding the Fed through political pressures. It was a style of leadership the Fed had not seen before.

KENNEDY AND THE BALANCE OF PAYMENTS

As Kennedy aides planned the 1960 presidential campaign, Paul H. Nitze warned, the balance of payments deficit created "a serious basic problem." The situation, he worried, threatened the nation's economic health and might create a crisis as the administration neared the beginning of a second term.[46] Kennedy himself, however, did not take the issue too seriously during the campaign but concentrated instead on the domestic economy's slow growth. Shortly after taking office, however, the balance of payments problem preoccupied him. He often told his advisers that the payments deficit and nuclear war were the two things he worried about most. "He had acquired somewhere," Arthur Schlesinger remembered, "perhaps from his father, the belief that a nation was only as strong as the value of its currency," and Kennedy became determined to keep the currency solid.[47] Some of his advisers, in fact, thought him even "excessively concerned about the problem."[48]

In part the problem arose because Kennedy had only a slight grasp on economics. He had trouble remembering the difference between monetary

46. Nitze memo, November 24, 1959, Pre–Presidential Papers, "Balance of Payments," Kennedy Library.
47. Arthur M. Schlesinger, Jr., *A Thousand Days: John F. Kennedy in the White House* (Boston: Houghton Mifflin, 1965), 654.
48. Theodore C. Sorensen, *Kennedy* (New York: Harper and Row, 1965), 408.

and fiscal policy. At an early meeting with his economic advisers, he asked CEA Chairman Walter Heller, "Now tell me again, how do I distinguish between monetary and fiscal policy?" Heller replied, "Well, monetary, M, that's Martin." (Heller hesitated to bring up as well the fact that the Fed began with F—and that Martin might not stay in the job forever.[49]) To remedy the problem Heller and the Council of Economic Advisers began a regular seminar through memoranda to educate Kennedy on Keynesian economics, the need for a tax cut, the balance of payments problems, and other economic issues. Heller estimated that in the thirty-four months of the Kennedy presidency the council produced more than three hundred memos.[50] At least in Heller's view, the seminar proved a success. The council converted Kennedy to Keynesianism and sold him on the tax cut. When Roy Harrod, a leading British economist, wrote that the Kennedy administration seemed wrongly obsessed with the need for a balanced budget, Heller wryly wrote the president that Harrod thought that both of them "need to become convinced Keynesians—as if we weren't!"[51]

Kennedy's early views on economic policy included a deep distrust of the Fed. He had campaigned in 1960 on the need to rescue the country from the slow growth induced by the Fed's policies. The Democratic platform promised that a "Democratic President will put an end to the present high-interest, tight-money policy" that had produced "two recessions within five years" and had "bankrupted many of our families."[52] During the campaign Kennedy confidently promised, "I have no doubt that any new Democratic President will find the Federal Reserve pursuing a somewhat different policy." He concluded, "The President has great influence."[53] Kennedy seemed to believe that bankers personally determined interest rates, and he constantly wondered why Martin could not get his friends in New York to cooperate by lowering them.[54] He even suggested during the campaign that he might replace Martin when he took office.

After the election, Heller visited Martin, who had been stung by the president-elect's campaign remarks. "I'm not going to give up the independence of the Fed," Martin told him. Heller replied, "Well, I'm sure that's

49. Heller in Council of Economic Advisers oral history, 195–96, Kennedy Library.

50. Walter W. Heller, *New Dimensions of Political Economy* (New York: W. W. Norton, 1966), 29.

51. Memo, Heller to Kennedy, May 26, 1962, POF, "Council of Economic Advisers," Kennedy Library.

52. New York *Times*, July 13, 1960, 21.

53. Quoted in *Banking* 53 (September 1960): 90.

54. Heller and Tobin in Council of Economic Advisers oral history, 33, Kennedy Library.

not what the President's going to ask you to do." Martin added, "There's plenty of room here for cooperation."[55] Administration officials were unsure, however, about just what cooperative action they wanted from the Fed.

The administration and the Fed had sharply different views on the problem of stimulating economic growth. Heller's Council of Economic Advisers believed that the nation's unemployment problem was cyclical and that the economy required government stimulus to get it moving again. Martin and the Fed, however, argued that the problem was structural, fundamentally rooted in the makeup of the economy. Only by modernization of factories and retraining of workers could the economy be rejuvenated. Moreover, pumping out money through stimulative fiscal policy would only be inflationary, since more money would not cure the underlying structural problems.[56] The Kennedy administration thus began with great skepticism on both sides of the Fed–White House relationship.

The administration's "Operation Nudge" quickly brought that skepticism to a head. The plan aimed to reverse the flow of capital abroad and induce the investment of foreign currency in the United States by "nudging" short-term interest rates up. Meanwhile, long-term interest rates would be kept low so that manufacturers could borrow cheaply to improve their factories. To make the "nudge" work, both the Treasury and the Fed would have to behave in uncharacteristic ways. The Treasury would have to sell more short-term debt and accept higher interest rates, although it typically preferred to finance the debt with the longest term and lowest rates possible. The Fed, meanwhile, would have to abandon its decade-old "bills only" policy and buy long-term bonds to "nudge" their prices up.[57]

Administration officials worked hard to win Martin and the Fed over, and less than one month after the inauguration they agreed. "This is an historic reversal of policy," Heller told Kennedy, "for which Chairman Martin deserves our appreciation."[58] Almost immediately, however, Heller began fretting that the Fed would stray from the game plan. In pressing for the president's plan, Martin had fought against strong opposition from other board members and the reserve bank presidents. Of the nineteen members of the FOMC (seven board members and twelve bank presidents, only five

55. Heller oral history in Hargrove and Morley, eds., *The President and the Council of Economic Advisers*, 189.
56. Schlesinger, *A Thousand Days*, 627; and James L. Sundquist, *Politics and Policy: The Eisenhower, Kennedy, and Johnson Years* (Washington, D.C.: Brookings Institution, 1968), 57.
57. David P. Calleo, *The Imperious Economy* (Cambridge: Harvard University Press, 1982), 225n.
58. Memo, Council of Economic Advisers to Kennedy, February 16, 1961, Heller Papers, "Monetary Policy," Kennedy Library.

of whom voted at any given time), seven were strongly opposed to the end of "bills only."[59] For the opponents of the "nudge," the end of "bills only" was a step back toward political interference in monetary policy and a pegged bond market. Martin tried to convince them by saying, "A man isn't a drunk just because he takes a couple of drinks."[60] Martin's support of the president's "nudge" rested on very fragile support within the system, but he worked hard to keep a majority of FOMC members in favor of the plan.

Heller recognized Martin's problem as a need to save face, but he argued, "We need to be watchful that the face-saving doesn't become a half-hearted effort."[61] Heller kept up a drumbeat for the "nudge" and complained to Kennedy about the "timid moves of the Fed." Rarely shy about pressing a clever turn of phrase, he told the president: "The evidence is clear that it takes more than a nudge to budge the market." In fact, he said, Martin should be persuaded to pursue an even stronger, "aggressively expansionist policy," operating with a "twist" instead of a nudge.[62] Once again a Quadriad meeting produced the desired result, and Operation Nudge became a more vigorous Operation Twist.

Kennedy's actions, orchestrated by Heller to "stiffen Martin's back," finally took effect in July. George Mitchell, a Kennedy appointee to the board, reported to Heller that "the President has had a remarkable influence on the board" and that Operation Twist had become firmly established.[63] Martin told Heller a few months later, "I want you to consider me a member of the team." Whenever his team spirit seemed to lag, Heller scheduled a Quadriad meeting. Faced with heavy White House pressure for buying bonds and resistance within the Fed to the White House plan, Martin carefully maneuvered his way. His style was bargaining, for as Heller explained, "It was not just a one-way street with Martin." Instead, "basically there was give and take."[64]

Martin's allegiance to Operation Twist played an important part in Kennedy's decision in January 1963 to redesignate him chairman. Since the beginning of the administration, the president's advisers had considered

59. Memo from Tobin for the files, May 30, 1961, Heller Papers, "Monetary Policy," Kennedy Library.

60. Memo, Bart Rowen to Heller, advance text of *Newsweek* story, February 24, 1961, POF, "Council of Economic Advisers," Kennedy Library.

61. Memo, Heller to Frederick G. Dutton, February 23, 1961, POF, "Heller," Kennedy Library.

62. Memo, Council of Economic Advisers to Kennedy, April 6, 1961, POF, "Council of Economic Advisers," Kennedy Library.

63. Memo, Heller to Kennedy, July 13, 1961, WHCF FI8, Kennedy Library.

64. Heller oral history in Hargrove and Morley, eds., *The President and the Council of Economic Advisers*, 191.

replacing him. They discovered, however, that Martin had a formidable reputation in the domestic business community, and internationally he was a symbol of the fight to maintain the dollar's value. "He can be a tower of strength," Treasury Secretary C. Douglas Dillon wrote Kennedy. Reappointing him would strengthen foreign confidence in the dollar.[65] Heller, however, always saw Martin's support for the administration's plan as tenuous. The Fed, he feared, might "tire of the twist before the dawn" and not "twist with enough vigor."[66] When Martin argued the need to increase the discount rate from 3 to 3½ percent, Heller in a Quadriad meeting extracted a promise that the Fed would try hard to prevent a rise in long-term interest rates, which would counteract the "twist." Kennedy concluded the meeting by reminding everyone—but especially Martin—of the importance of shielding the economy from the impact of the increase.[67]

A few days later, during congressional testimony, Martin made no mention of the need to keep down long-term rates. Heller was furious because Martin had let slip an opportunity to embrace low interest rates and he feared that the Fed might slip into a "posture of passive resistance." One member of Heller's staff said, "It's true he didn't hit into many double plays, but is striking out with men on base real support?"[68] To make things worse, Heller worried that the Treasury was developing financing plans that would untie the "twist" as well.[69] Heller wondered "whether we're getting the twist or the screw."[70]

To tackle both problems, Heller arranged another Quadriad meeting, at which Kennedy activated a tape recorder he had previously had installed in the Oval Office. Treasury Secretary Dillon affirmed his own support for Operation Twist by telling the president, "So far, I think we've generally been very successful." For his part, Martin knew precisely why he was there: a leak in the New York *Times* had suggested the Fed was backing away from the twist. He reassured Kennedy that he had not made the leak and said, "Mr. President, at the time of our meeting in July, at the end you joked with me about this operation and I told you that despite some reser-

65. Memo, Dillon to Kennedy, January 16, 1963, POF, "Treasury," Kennedy Library.

66. Memo, Heller to Kennedy, July 8, 1963, POF, "Council of Economic Advisers," Kennedy Library.

67. Memo, Heller to Kennedy, July 18, 1963, Ackley Papers, Box 5, "Monetary Policy 1963," Bentley Historical Library, University of Michigan.

68. Memo, Heller to Kennedy, July 24, 1963, POF, "Council of Economic Advisers," Kennedy Library.

69. Memo, Heller to Dillon and Roosa, August 30, 1963, Heller Papers, "Monetary Policy," Kennedy Library.

70. Memo, Heller to Kennedy, September 9, 1963, Heller Papers, "Monetary Policy," Kennedy Library.

vations within the system, I assured you we'd do our best with it, and I think we've done fairly well." The market people, he told Kennedy, "are very surprised with the degree of success that we've had" with the operation. "By and large, they accept the fact" that Fed officials "*have* minimized pressures on long-term interest rates and helped move the short-term interest rate up."

Heller wanted to make sure everyone clearly got the message, and he pointedly raised the issue of Martin's refusal to publicly embrace the administration's term *twist*: "Mr. President," he argued, "I think we're all agreed that this twist—if you'll pardon the expression, Bill [Martin]—is off to a very good start." It was important, he continued, "that we sort of keep up the *talk*" that the program was successful. Before the meeting ended, he concluded, "I think we have a much better chance to influence the long-term market by purchases of long-term securities that inject funds into the market. And I think that's the operational thing that has to be done very vigorously."[71] Martin could not have missed the point.

Relations between the White House and the Fed (and for that matter, between the White House and the Treasury) were not always smooth during Kennedy's thousand days. Heller worried about both the twist and the economy's growth. Dillon was concerned about the Treasury's borrowing costs and the international position of the dollar, while Martin was leery about setting off inflation with low interest rates. Within the Fed, furthermore, Martin had to fight a constant rearguard action against those who worried about the specter of pegging. The Quadriad helped jog Martin's support, and the Fed rarely strayed far from the administration's position. Even the most threatening Fed decision—to boost the discount rate in the summer of 1963—was bargained to an acceptable consensus during a Quadriad meeting.

Martin and other Fed officials never lost a chance to assert their independence and to renounce pegging. Martin studiously avoided, either in public or in private meetings at the White House, an official endorsement of the "nudge" or the "twist." Instead, he simply presented changes in the Fed's buying habits as shifts in operating policy rather than explicit coordination with the administration. That helped win support within the Fed, for an embrace of the administration's policy would have recalled for many Fed officials the preaccord nightmare and would surely have sunk the plan. The White House, meanwhile, contented itself by following weekly figures on the Fed's bond purchases and scheduling Quadriad meetings when the

71. Transcript, meeting of September 12, 1963, POF, Audiotape 110, item 3, Kennedy Library.

purchases seemed to slip. In the end, Martin accommodated the president's demands, but he did so through a fluid, dynamic process.

MONETARY POLICY AT THE CROSSROADS

Despite Kennedy's conversion to Keynesianism, he could not convince a more conservative Congress to buy his economists' plans for a stimulative tax cut. When Johnson succeeded to the presidency, Kennedy's advisers were unsure whether the new president would support the tax cut, or even if he understood its theoretical underpinnings. On the evening of Kennedy's burial, however, Lyndon Johnson stunned his inherited counselors by enthusiastically embracing the tax cut. To insure its passage, he also pledged to keep the federal budget to less than $100 billion. Kennedy's economists protested that the budget ceiling would reduce the cut's stimulus and thus counteract its basic purpose. For Johnson, though, the tax cut served other purposes: he intended a quick and dramatic action to demonstrate who was in charge of the country and a congressional success to show he would be master of a domain that had frustrated his predecessor. The strategy worked. Within three months of the assassination, Johnson signed the tax cut into law and won the symbolic victory he intended.[72]

In the midst of Johnson's initial emphasis on fiscal policy, the Fed took a back seat. Fed officials, in fact, remained unconvinced that the tax cut was needed and continued to argue that unemployment was caused by the underlying structure of the economy. Their reservations, however, mattered little to Johnson. Engaged in consolidating his power, running for reelection, and basking in the success of the tax cut, Johnson largely ignored Martin and the Fed for his first year in office. Quadriad meetings lapsed and the Fed became only a bit player in the administration's economic policy. When the economy jumped resoundingly after the tax cut, Martin in fact confided to Walter Heller that he had been wrong. Economic developments, the Fed chairman concluded, were "just right—a good strong advance without exceeding economic speed limits."[73]

Martin, however, was worried that tighter money would eventually be needed to slow the boom. He gave a speech on June 1, 1965, that shocked both the administration and the financial community. Martin warned about

72. See Rowland Evans and Robert Novak, *Lyndon B. Johnson: The Exercise of Power* (New York: New American Library, 1966), 368–76. Secretary of the Treasury Douglas Dillon urged Johnson to take this move for similar reasons. See memo, Dillon to Johnson, November 25, 1963, WHCF EX FI11-4.

73. Memo, Heller to Johnson, July 17, 1964, WHCF EX FG233, Johnson Library.

"the threat of another Great Depression," and concluded, "We find disquieting similarities between our present prosperity and the fabulous twenties."[74] Martin's worries rocked the stock market and puzzled administration officials. Gardner Ackley, who succeeded Walter Heller as CEA chairman, complained to the president that Martin seemed not to recognize that economists and economic policymakers had made enormous progress in the preceding thirty years. Although White House officials recognized the value of Martin's high standing in the financial community, they thought little of his abilities as an economist. "It is hard to know what Bill was really driving at in his speech," Ackley told the president.[75]

In fact Martin had three important ideas embedded in his speech. First, he told his audience, the nation needed to be "continuously on the alert to prevent a recurrence of maladjustments." Put more simply, Martin was suggesting that runaway inflation had triggered the Depression and ought not to be allowed to begin again. His speech was a warning to administration officials not to forget the dangers of a boom in their eagerness to promote economic growth. Second, he argued the need for "prompt antirecession measures," if the economy slowed in the future, to prevent recessions from becoming Depressions. Finally, he argued for an "understanding of the international implications of national events and policies."

Martin's triple message was a classic statement of traditional Federal Reserve worries: the ever-present danger of inflation in good times; the need for flexible countermeasures to balance adverse economic trends; and a recognition of the interdependence of nations within the international economy. White House officials had long recognized that the Fed was preoccupied with "the [price] stability objective," and former CEA chairman Heller had characterized Martin in the first months of the administration as the "in-fighter against inflation."[76] Both Ackley and Treasury Secretary Henry Fowler worried, though, that Martin's choice of language would unnecessarily weaken business confidence in the president's policies. A Quadriad meeting a few days later resolved the differences, at least for a while.

In the meantime, however, the Vietnam buildup that began in June 1965 made Martin even more nervous. After fourteen years in the Fed, Martin had developed an elaborate network of contacts, including some in the Defense Department, and from them he learned that Vietnam expenditures

74. New York *Times*, June 2, 1965, 69.
75. Memo, Ackley to Johnson, June 3, 1965, WHCF EX FG11-3, Johnson Library.
76. Memo, Seymour E. Harris to Roosa, April 14, 1964, Heller Papers, "Monetary Policy," Kennedy Library; and memo, Heller to Johnson, January 10, 1964, Heller Papers, "Monetary Policy," Kennedy Library.

would prove larger than the administration was publicly admitting.[77] War spending always brings the danger of inflation, and by September, pressures were building within the Federal Reserve System for an increase in the discount rate to restrain the economy. Ackley reported to Johnson that "monetary policy stands at the crossroads." The administration's position was that the Fed should avoid any policy change until January, when the full implications of the new budget would be clear and monetary and fiscal policies could be coordinated.[78]

Martin and the Fed, however, refused to follow this strategy. By early October, Martin was signaling at Federal Reserve Board meetings that he favored a tighter monetary policy, and he wrote a terse memo to Johnson arguing for an immediate increase in interest rates. The board, however, was divided evenly on the question. At the meeting of November 23, however, Martin signaled he was ready to change policy by announcing that he would vote for a rise in the discount rate at a subsequent meeting if one of twelve reserve banks proposed such a change. (By Fed rules, the board does not set the discount rate but instead approves applications by reserve banks for discount rate changes.) On December 5, the swing vote on the board, J. Dewey Daane, joined with Martin and two other governors to approve the application of the reserve banks of New York and Chicago to raise the discount rate from 4 to 4½ percent.

Johnson was furious. He and his advisers believed that the decision was precipitous, and they claimed to have been caught by surprise. Furthermore, they believed they had an agreement with Martin and other Fed officials to wait until January to develop a coordinated monetary-fiscal approach to Vietnam spending. "The Federal Reserve Board is an independent agency," Johnson said curtly in a prepared statement. "Its decision is an independent decision," and he regretted that the board had acted before the new budget could be developed.[79] The press pictured the move as a sharp break in White House–Fed relations, while Senator Russell Long (D-La.) called the decision "Dickens's Christmas Carol in reverse."[80]

Johnson's advisers, however, could not have been surprised by the decision, even if the timing upset them. For months, Martin had been sending unmistakable signals that the Fed would soon raise the discount rate. Ackley warned Johnson in September, "It is clear that the upward pressure on interest rates is intensifying every week." He added, "If there is to be a

77. Interview with Andrew Brimmer, June 22, 1984; see also Hargrove and Morley, eds., *The President and the Council of Economic Advisers*, 249.

78. Memo, Ackley to Johnson, October 5, 1965, WHCF EX FI, Johnson Library.

79. Statement, December 5, 1965, WHCF EX FI6, Johnson Library.

80. Bach, *Making Monetary and Fiscal Policy*, 123.

showdown with the Fed on monetary policy, it probably cannot be delayed much longer."[81] Treasury Secretary Fowler agreed with Martin that the case for a rate increase might be growing, but he said the case was not yet conclusive and he urged Martin to wait.[82]

Martin had told the president in October that the level of interest rates itself was not important. It *was* important, he said, that rates be allowed "to respond to market forces" (that is, to move upward) to avoid excessively increasing demand for money.[83] White House officials countered by lobbying board members Dewey Daane, a Kennedy administration appointee who provided the crucial vote for the increase, and Sherman J. Maisel, a Johnson administration appointee who opposed it. Meanwhile, the CEA staff worked with members of the Fed's staff to produce a memo urging no change from the status quo until the gross national product increased substantially. The CEA hoped that such a joint effort would forestall the Fed's action, but Martin pocketed the memo and never showed it to the other members of the board.[84] As late as December 1, the president's key economic advisers concluded, "The case for monetary action *now* is not persuasive."[85] On December 3, Martin warned Secretary Fowler that he soon expected a discount rate increase. Fowler did not realize just how soon.[86]

Johnson never had fully trusted Martin, and this episode only made things worse. Believing that Martin could keep the rate down if he wanted to, the president saw the discount rate increase as a personally vindictive act. Furthermore, a Quadriad meeting was scheduled for the LBJ Ranch only a few days later, and Johnson was annoyed that Martin had moved preemptively. To some administration officials, however, the upcoming meeting explained the timing of the Fed's action. Martin, they speculated, feared that the Quadriad meeting would provide Johnson with a chance to apply the "treatment," ranch-style, and extract from Martin a promise to forestall future restrictive action.[87]

As the Federal Reserve Board was deciding on an increased discount rate, administration officials were puzzling over the need for a tax increase. To Ackley, the case for slowing the economy was clear, and he put the argument

81. Memo, Ackley to Johnson, September 16, 1965, Ackley Papers, Box 13.

82. Memo, Fowler to Johnson, October 6, 1965, WHCF CF FI, Johnson Library.

83. Memo, Martin to Johnson, October 6, 1965, Diary Backup, Johnson Library.

84. Arthur Okun oral history, vol. 1, 23–25, Johnson Library.

85. Memo, Fowler, Schultze, and Ackley to Johnson, December 1, 1965, WHCF CF FI9, Johnson Library (emphasis in the original).

86. Bach, *Making Monetary and Fiscal Policy*, 122–23.

87. Ibid., 125; Lyndon Baines Johnson, *The Vantage Point: Perspectives on the Presidency, 1963–1969* (New York: Holt, Rinehart and Winston, 1971), 445; and Charles J. Zwick oral history, vol. 1, 27, Johnson Library.

twice to Johnson. The president's conversations with Wilbur Mills, however, convinced him that Congress would never approve a tax increase. Budget Director Charles Schultze, therefore, developed a two-pronged plan. First, the administration would budget for a war ending by June 30, 1967, the end of the fiscal year. Since nobody knew how much the war would cost in the end, this device would imply more money would be needed later. Second, the administration planned to request a supplemental appropriation, accompanied by a tax increase, later in 1966 when the war's financial implications were clearer.[88]

Johnson's advisers agreed with Martin that the economy would eventually need to be slowed. They contended that the Fed should not have acted unilaterally but should have waited for the administration's budget in January. Martin and his colleagues, however, were more worried than were Johnson's economists about inflation, and they feared that the administration, if it acted at all, would move too late.

Martin and his colleagues turned out to be right, and Johnson's advisers came to be relieved that the Fed had done the dirty work for them. Ackley later admitted that he "had a certain amount of sympathy for what the Fed was doing, although we didn't always express that sympathy very strongly or clearly in the President's presence."[89] Even in January 1966, however, Ackley hinted to Johnson that money "may have to get still tighter to help keep things from boiling over."[90] But Johnson was obviously in no mood to slow the economy. He had been won over on the benefits of stimulative federal spending, and even with the Vietnam war building he did not want to put his Great Society programs on the line. They were his "children," his "babies," as he used to describe them.[91] The Fed's preemptive action met the immediate need for cooling an economy that was overheated from defense spending, without the necessity of taking on a politically explosive battle over increasing taxes.

At a December meeting at the LBJ Ranch, Martin and Johnson patched up their differences. Martin and Ackley resumed speaking during the retreat, and the president ordered closer contact to prevent any future surprises. The CEA started regular lunches with the whole Federal Reserve

88. For an exploration of these issues, see Donald F. Kettl, "The Economic Education of Lyndon Johnson: Guns, Butter, and Taxes," in Robert A. Divine, ed., *Remembering the Sixties* (Chapel Hill: University of North Carolina Press, forthcoming).

89. Ackley oral history, vol. 3, 4, Johnson Library.

90. Memo, Ackley to Johnson, January 18, 1966, WHCF EX FI6, Johnson Library.

91. Ackley oral history in Hargrove and Morley, eds., *The President and the Council of Economic Advisers*, 247.

Board every two weeks, while staff-level contacts increased.[92] As had often been the case throughout the Fed's history, crises produced closer Fed–White House ties.

Moving in close contact with the administration, the Fed continued to tighten credit during the spring and summer of 1966. Although the administration for the most part kept publicly silent about the Fed's squeeze, the president's advisers quietly supported the strategy. Ackley wrote Johnson in July 1966, "We cannot fault them for their general policy position."[93] The president's economic advisers told him that "monetary policy has done more than some of us expected it would or could." It was a "major contribution" to slowing the economy "to a healthy pace."[94] Arthur Okun, a member of the CEA and later its chairman, contended that the Fed's policies were "outstanding" through 1966, and that the Fed's independence had "proved to be a valuable national asset."[95]

The Fed's policy of tight money did have serious effects on some segments of the economy, especially home building and municipal bonds. For a few days in late August and early September, in fact, there was almost no market for municipal securities, and the crises threatened two bond houses with collapse.[96] The Fed eased up enough to prevent a crisis, but Martin also kept up a drumbeat for increasing taxes. The chairman told Johnson in March, "To the extent that such fiscal action is taken, the burden on monetary policy would be lightened and the upward pressures on interest rates diminished."[97] He stressed that "the rise in prices has to be slowed down *this* year" and repeated his call throughout the year.[98] To Ackley, Martin's campaign was a clear signal. He told Johnson, "Perhaps it's a means of telling us that—if we do move on taxes, the Fed is ready to move on money."[99] A tax increase proposal, Ackley speculated, would produce easier money from the Fed.

The Fed started to ease off the brakes in September, when Johnson an-

92. Okun oral history, vol. 1, 26, Johnson Library; and Bach, *Making Monetary and Fiscal Policy*, 132.

93. Memo, Ackley to Johnson, July 29, 1966, WHCF CF FG233, Johnson Library.

94. Memo, Fowler, Schultze, and Ackley to Johnson, November 11, 1966, WHCF EX BE5, Johnson Library.

95. Arthur M. Okun, *The Political Economy of Prosperity* (Washington, D.C.: Brookings Institution, 1970), 81.

96. Bach, *Making Monetary and Fiscal Policy*, 127–28.

97. Memo, Martin to Johnson, March 15, 1966, WHCF EX FI6, Johnson Library.

98. Memo, Martin to Califano, June 6, 1966, WHCF CF FI11–4 (emphasis in original); memo, Martin to Johnson, March 15, 1966, WHCF EX FI6; memo, Martin to Johnson, April 8, 1966, WHCF EX BE; and Martin to Johnson, December 13, 1966, WHCF EX FI11–4, Johnson Library.

99. Memo, Ackley to Johnson, November 23, 1966, WHCF EX FG233, Johnson Library.

nounced that he would reduce federal spending and would request a suspension of tax incentives for corporate investment. In the State of the Union address in January 1967, furthermore, Johnson announced he would request a 10 percent income tax surcharge. Because there were signs that the economy was starting to soften, administration economists decided to delay submitting the tax increase plan until the economy began moving ahead again. The combination of the president's proposal and the economy's softness convinced the Fed it could safely continue the monetary expansion of late 1966 into 1967.[100] In the eyes of at least some administration officials, there was an implicit bargain between the Fed and the administration: the Fed would ease the monetary brakes in return for action on the tax front.[101]

Through most of 1967, the Fed kept money relatively easy. When the economy started strengthening rapidly in late spring, Ackley and Okun met with all seven members of the Federal Reserve Board to urge them to keep interest rates low. They were surprised to find that the Fed had been buying long-term bonds and considering a discount rate cut to do just that. The board members told the CEA officials, however, that they were not sure that they could hold the line on interest rates unless Johnson—and Johnson personally—showed "that he still means business about taxes."[102] Martin joined Johnson's economic advisers with a plea in July for a tax increase, and Johnson finally agreed. On August 3, he requested a 10 percent surcharge on personal and corporate income taxes.

Congress in general and Wilbur Mills in particular were reluctant to act on the tax increase. Mills did not trust economists, and he was not willing to push for an *immediate* tax increase on the basis of projections of *future* inflation. Okun argued later that both administration and Fed officials believed that "you had to let the economy take on somewhat of a booming mood before the Congress would take you seriously." The Fed continued monetary ease through most of 1967, even after the economy began to grow rapidly, to let "the economy have enough rope to make clear the danger that it would hang itself" without a tax increase, as Okun put it.[103] In private policy discussions, Fed officials suggested that tighter money was needed, but they feared that if they acted unilaterally, it would take the pressure off Congress to produce the needed tax increase and would unsettle the

100. Philip Cagan, "Monetary Policy," in Philip Cagan, Marten Estey, William Fellner, Charles E. McLure, Jr., and Thomas Gale Moore, *Economic Policy and Inflation in the Sixties* (Washington, D.C.: American Enterprise Institute, 1972), 101.
101. Okun, *The Political Economy of Prosperity,* 85.
102. Memo, Ackley to Johnson, May 26, 1967, WHCF EX FI8, Johnson Library.
103. Okun oral history in Hargrove and Morley, eds., *The President and the Council of Economic Advisers,* 305.

financial markets.[104] Therefore, to keep the heat on Congress, the Fed kept money looser than it otherwise would have, and Martin joined administration officials on Capitol Hill to lobby for the tax bill.[105]

When Congress finally passed the tax bill in June 1968, the Fed relaxed, confident that monetary policy would no longer have to carry the burden alone. Fed officials expected, as did most administration economists, that the surcharge would provide all the restraint necessary. Martin and his colleagues soon discovered that "this fiscal bomb was a dud," as economist Philip Cagan explained it.[106] The surcharge proved to brake the economy far less than anyone anticipated, and in December 1968 the Fed regretfully moved to tighten money again.

Economists and politicians criticized the Fed for its stop-go policies. Heavy restraint had seriously damaged interest-rate-sensitive industries, especially housing, while easier money unloosed inflation and inflationary expectations. Many members of Congress complained that the Fed had driven interest rates too high, while monetarist economists like Milton Friedman reasoned that the Fed ought to adopt a steady policy "to prevent money itself from being a major source of disturbance."[107] Throughout the difficult years of the Johnson administration, however, the Fed had acted on two principles: to compensate for delays, by both the president and the Congress, in changing fiscal policy; and to pressure for such action by demonstrating the costs of a failure to act. The Fed's tightening in 1966, ease in 1967 through 1968, and renewed tightening in 1969 were thus the product of an elaborate political minuet in which Martin struggled to accommodate the Fed to a turbulent environment.

WHICH WIND, WHICH WAY?

During Martin's tenure as chairman, the Fed had a remarkable renaissance. He took over the agency at a time when many observers wondered if it would ever regain its operating freedom, a time when nearly everyone relegated monetary policy to a supporting role, at best, in national economic policy. By the end of Martin's tenure in 1970, the Fed had demonstrated not only that it could—and would—act independently of the wishes of the president and Congress but also that monetary policy could compensate for

104. Federal Open Market Committee, Memoranda of Discussion, October 3, 1967, 86; and February 2, 1968, 108.
105. Memo, Fowler to Johnson, March 22, 1968, WHCF CF LE/F111-4.
106. Cagan, "Monetary Policy," 102.
107. Friedman, "The Role of Monetary Policy," 14–16.

mistakes or delays in changing fiscal policy. From a weak and dispirited organization playing a supporting role in 1951, the Fed by the end of the 1960s was a powerful organization recognized as an economic policymaker in its own right.

Martin transformed the Fed by institutionalizing the base of its power. He established the principle of the Fed's nonpartisanship and demonstrated that it would not cater to the demands of any political party or the short-term needs of any candidate. He also built the Fed's staff so he could firmly root monetary policy in technical competence, which not only helped minimize mistakes but also covered monetary policy with the mantle of great expertise. This technical competence, in fact, was the corollary of and strong support for the agency's political neutrality. Finally, Martin strove constantly to maintain the Fed's flexibility. He refused to commit the Fed in advance to any president's strategy. To avoid being tied to the White House's programs, he carefully avoided using their names. During his tenure, Martin tacitly cooperated with most presidential policies, but always in a way that avoided a public embrace of them. That strategy helped protect the Fed's neutrality and gave Martin maneuvering room when, as in 1965, he wanted to move in a different direction from the president. This constellation of strategies established the institutional base for ongoing cooperation with the president in a way that did not diminish (and even enhanced) the Fed's power. These strategies lasted long after Martin's term was over.

At the same time, though, Martin was very careful about claiming too much credit for monetary policy. In the first months of the Johnson administration, he wrote the president, "We cannot produce, *through monetary policy alone,* high or low interest rates, balance of payments surpluses or deficits, rising or falling prices, more or less employment, or a sound or unsound financial structure."[108] Accompanying the Fed's new mission thus was also a new interdependence with the rest of the Washington community. Martin's leadership built a new vision for the Fed that, remarkably, lasted through five presidencies: Truman, Eisenhower, Kennedy, Johnson, and finally Nixon.

This is not to say, of course, that the Fed's relationship with the executive branch did not vary with Martin's personal ties with each president. Each president had his own way of dealing with the Fed and his own expectations about what monetary policy should contribute to his plans. Martin's great political skill was in flexibly adapting himself and the agency to these changes.

108. Memo, Martin to Johnson, January 10, 1964, WHCF EX LE/FI11, Johnson Library.

At the same time, presidents came to rely more on the Fed. Martin's tenure marked the synthesis of several trends that had been evolving for decades: the doctrines of economic stabilization, which held that the government had a positive role in steering the economy; and the public embrace by elected officials, especially the president, of these doctrines. This meant that there needed to be new cooperation between the Fed and the White House, and especially between the chairman and the president. The Quadriad became an important feature, but just as important was the network of staff contacts among the Fed, Treasury, CEA, and Bureau of the Budget. The Fed's maturity thus also meant a new place in the bureaucratic scene.

The looseness of presidential influence over Martin and the Fed nagged Eisenhower, Kennedy, and Johnson. In 1968, Johnson was so concerned that the reserve banks were undermining his policy that he appointed a task force to consider basic changes to the Fed.[109] For the administration, it was bad enough to worry about Martin's sensitivity to the president's policies. It was worse worrying constantly that Martin's position would be eroded by his need to accommodate pressure from the reserve banks.

Martin firmly cemented the Fed's independence. He not only established the rhetoric of operating flexibility, but he also demonstrated that the Fed reserved the right to take independent action when the economy threatened to overheat. Despite occasional disputes, however, the presidents during Martin's tenure usually got what they wanted; monetary policy typically was one of accommodation. Martin rarely strayed far from presidential policy, and on those occasions when he did, it was for a common reason: inflationary pressures were mounting and the reserve banks were pressing for tighter money. The overall pattern of Fed–presidential relations, therefore, was accommodation, with an anti-inflationary spin. "Leaning against the wind" was the metaphor that guided Martin's actions.

It was sometimes difficult, though, to determine which way the wind was blowing, which way to lean, when, and how far. Johnson, furthermore, made serious fiscal policy mistakes that complicated the Fed's problems. As a result, monetary policy in the late 1960s went through rapid starts and stops that created alternately fears about inflation and credit crunches. Some sectors of the economy—housing in particular—especially suffered. These problems emerged in part because the Fed was attempting to deliver what the administration wanted—or was acting in the place of presidential de-

109. Memo, Warren L. Smith to Califano, September 9, 1968, WHCF EX FG233; memo, Okun to Califano, September 3, 1968, and report, November 4, 1968, "Task Force on Reorganizing the Federal Reserve System," in "1968 Interagency Task Forces," Johnson Library.

cisions. In part, however, these problems stemmed from the difficulty of judging which way the wind was blowing and which way to lean.

Because of the president's pragmatic needs, the Fed and the White House became inseparable if sometimes reluctant partners. As a key player in this partnership, Martin proved a consummate politician. He built a stronger foundation for the Fed's policymaking, and he institutionalized the Fed's power in the chairmanship so it would live past his tenure. That was to prove crucial in the chairmanship of Martin's successor, Arthur Burns, and the difficult economic problems he faced: simultaneous high inflation and high unemployment that defied economic theory and conventional policy prescriptions.

As the symbol of the Fed's guardianship of the country's currency a seal adorns the floor leading into the Fed's Board Room. Courtesy of Board of Governors of the Federal Reserve System

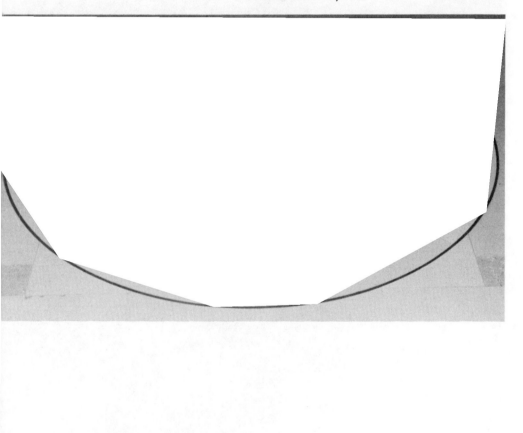

Members of the first Federal Reserve Board in 1914 (seated clockwise around the table, left to right): H. Parker Willis, secretary, W. P. G. Harding, P. M. Warburg, William G. McAdoo, chairman and secretary of the Treasury, Charles S. Hamlin, governor, John Skelton Williams, comptroller of the currency, Adolph C. Miller, and F. A. Delano, vice-governor. Courtesy of Board of Governors of the Federal Reserve System

Dedication of the Board's building in 1937 by President Franklin D. Roosevelt. Courtesy of Board of Governors of the Federal Reserve System

CARTER GLASS
DEFENDER
OF THE FEDERAL RESERVE SYSTEM

IN THE FEDERAL RESERVE ACT WE INSTITUTED
A GREAT AND VITAL BANKING SYSTEM
NOT MERELY TO CORRECT AND CURE
PERIODICAL FINANCIAL DEBAUCHES
NOT SIMPLY INDEED TO AID
THE BANKING COMMUNITY ALONE BUT TO GIVE
VISION AND SCOPE AND SECURITY TO COMMERCE
AND AMPLIFY THE OPPORTUNITIES
AS WELL AS TO INCREASE
THE CAPABILITIES OF OUR INDUSTRIAL LIFE
AT HOME AND AMONG FOREIGN NATIONS

AN ADVENTURE IN CONSTRUCTIVE FINANCE
CARTER GLASS

On December 23, 1938, the twenty-fifth anniversary of the signing of the Federal Reserve Act, Fed officials unveiled a bas-relief of former congressman and later Senator Carter Glass, who had played a major role in drafting the act. The bas-relief portrait of Glass is accompanied by a quotation from his account of the creation of the Fed. Courtesy of Board of Governors of the Federal Reserve System

Although he neither attended college nor received any formal training in economics, Marriner S. Eccles became the intellectual force who led the Fed through financial crises during the Depression and World War II. Courtesy of Special Collection, University of Utah Library

William McChesney Martin, left, chairman of the Federal Reserve Board, discusses the Board's action on raising the discount rate at a news briefing. President Lyndon B. Johnson, right, had criticized the Board's action. AP/Wide World Photo

Arthur F. Burns, who served as Fed chairman during the Nixon, Ford, and part of the Carter administrations, at the table in the Fed's Board Room. AP/Wide World Photo

Paul Volcker, chairman of the Federal Reserve Board, appears on Capitol Hill at a hearing of the House Ways and Means Committee concerning economic conditions in the United States. AP/Wide World Photo

The securities trading room—commonly called the Open Market Desk—of the Federal Reserve Bank of New York is the control center of the Federal Reserve System's open-market operations. To carry out monetary policy set by the Federal Open Market Committee, the System buys and sells government securities in the open market. Courtesy of Federal Reserve Bank of New York

Federal Reserve Board Chairman Paul Volcker speaks to a gathering of protestors against high interest rates outside the Fed in Washington. AP/Wide World Photo

The Board Room, which serves as the meeting place for the seven-member Federal Reserve Board as well as for the twelve-member Federal Open Market Committee. Courtesy of Board of Governors of the Federal Reserve System

An imposing marble portal leads to the Fed Board Room, where the Federal Reserve Board and the Federal Open Market Committee meet to set monetary policy. Courtesy of Board of Governors of the Federal Reserve System

CHAPTER FIVE

STAGFLATION AND PRESIDENTIAL POLITICS

William McChesney Martin maintained a studied political neutrality throughout his years with the Fed. In contrast, Arthur Burns was often an unabashed partisan. Martin limited his discussions with White House officials to narrow monetary policy issues, while Burns never hesitated to deliver advice on a very wide range of issues. It would be hard to imagine two chairmen with more different styles. And at a time when old economic tools no longer seemed to be working, the Fed chairman's style had never before been more important.

So strong and partisan was Burns in his arguments, in fact, that a rich lore has developed that he had become an accomplice in Richard Nixon's attempts to manage the economy to insure his reelection in 1972. The charge is important for understanding both Burns's tenure as chairman and the Fed's evolving role in American government. To this point in the Fed's history, its nonpartisanship had been a source of strength. With the exception of Marriner Eccles, Fed chairmen had scrupulously avoided even the appearance of taking sides in partisan battles. William McChesney Martin, in fact, had made nonpartisanship a veritable house religion, and it was the religion on which the Fed built its power after the accord.

A story by Sanford Rose in the July 1974 issue of *Fortune* argued that Burns used the Fed to help Richard Nixon win reelection in 1972. While no evidence has ever emerged to substantiate the story, it has acquired a life of its own, a legend representing the financial community's worst fears about a central bank under the control of politicians. Rose alleges that a majority of the FOMC called for tight money, while Burns countered that the economic recovery in 1972 was very fragile and needed easier money to keep it going. When in the midst of a heated meeting he was unable to convince the FOMC, Burns left angrily only to return an hour later to announce, "I have just talked with the White House." The statement electrified the meeting, Rose wrote, and convinced the FOMC to ease the money supply. The money supply increased, the economy grew, and Nixon was reelected. In the process, though, the Fed unloosed a frightful inflation.[1]

The story about the 1972 election hit a basic chord: many observers believed that politicians' self-interest led them to try to manipulate the economy to help their reelection chances.[2] Since then, the story has persuaded many others of the Fed's complicity in this political-business cycle. In 1983, the *Wall Street Journal* reported that President Ronald Reagan's aides were asking, "If good old Arthur Burns could flood the nation with liquidity and reelect Richard Nixon in 1972, why couldn't this chairman [Paul Volcker] at least have cut the discount rate" in 1982 to prevent a slide in the stock market that they blamed for the loss of Republican seats in the House.[3] (The president's party, of course, typically loses seats in mid-term elections, but Reagan's advisers preferred to remember the Nixon story.)

Fed officials at the time vehemently denied Rose's account. Burns wrote *Fortune*, "There is not one grain of truth in his report," and Andrew Brimmer, who often locked horns with Burns, claimed, "These assertions are false—both in general and in particular."[4] Every other Fed official interviewed about it has denied the charge. Furthermore, careful statistical work by political scientists shows no convincing link between Fed policy and presidential elections.[5]

The money supply did in fact grow more rapidly from 1970 to 1973 than for any other three-year period since the end of World War II. The supply of cash and checking accounts—M1, the narrowest measure of money— grew 6.9 percent in the twelve months ending October 1971, and in the next twelve months ending just before the election, M1 grew an additional 7.4 percent. The reasons for this money growth, however, have very little to do with Burns's efforts to reelect Nixon and a great deal to do with the

    1. Rose, "The Agony of the Federal Reserve," 186–88.
    2. See Nordhaus, "The Political Business Cycle"; and Tufte, *Political Control of the Economy.*
    3. *Wall Street Journal*, April 21, 1983, 32.
    4. *Fortune* 90 (August 1974): 113.
    5. On support for the Rose story: my own interviews with Fed officials; and John T. Woolley, *Monetary Politics: The Federal Reserve and the Politics of Monetary Policy* (Cambridge: Cambridge University Press, 1984), 161–62. On the connection between Fed policy and presidential elections, see Nathaniel Beck, "Domestic Sources of American Monetary Policy: 1955–82," *The Journal of Politics* 46 (1984): 786–817.

difficulty of making monetary policy in an environment full of sharp political pressures and enormous technical uncertainties.

Part of that environment was the new era of puzzling high unemployment and high inflation that began in the late 1960s. Part of it as well was the grudge Nixon bore against the Fed since the 1960 presidential election. Early in the campaign, Burns, then chairman of Eisenhower's Council of Economic Advisers, called Nixon to warn him that the economy was sagging and that, unless the federal government took decisive action, economic growth would dip noticeably just before the election. He strongly urged Nixon to encourage the administration to loosen credit and increase federal spending to spur the economy. Nixon took the matter up with Eisenhower, he writes in his memoir, but he could not convince the president. Federal spending stayed on course, Fed policy remained tight, and the recession developed as Burns forecast. Nixon, in fact, attributed his loss in the 1960 election principally to two things: the shooting down of Francis Gary Powers in a U-2 spy plane over the Soviet Union and the slowdown of the economy.[6] Eisenhower's advisers since have denied that Nixon ever made a strong case for stimulating the economy, but Nixon was convinced that poor economic performance—especially a recalcitrant Fed—had cost him the presidency.[7]

Burns's warning, however, impressed Nixon, and throughout the 1960s they kept in close touch. It was scarcely surprising, therefore, that when Nixon finally won the presidency in 1968 he created a special post, special counselor, for Burns. After Burns came to the White House, however, it was unclear just what he was to do. Nixon had a Council of Economic Advisers for economic advice, and Daniel Patrick Moynihan was Nixon's principal domestic adviser. Moynihan and Burns tangled constantly over their turf, and Nixon quickly began looking for a better way to use Burns.

The opportunity came in late 1969, as Martin's term was expiring. To Nixon, Martin was "a stereotypical tennis-playing Easterner, Ivy League banker who considered himself wholly independent of the Nixon administration," as presidential adviser John Ehrlichman put it.[8] Furthermore, Nixon "always feared that the Federal Reserve was about to put the economy through the wringer," Nixon economic adviser Herbert Stein explained.[9] The end of Martin's term thus gave Nixon a chance to put someone he viewed as a loyalist in the job. The decision to name Burns chairman sur-

6. Richard M. Nixon, *Six Crises* (Garden City, N.Y.: Doubleday and Co., 1962), 309–11.
7. Saulnier oral history in Hargrove and Morley, eds., *The President and the Council of Economic Advisers*, 155.
8. Interview with the author.
9. Herbert Stein, *Presidential Economics: The Making of Economic Policy from Roosevelt to Reagan and Beyond* (New York: Simon and Schuster, 1984), 138.

prised few Washington observers; indeed, some reporters had speculated that the counselor's position was a holding action until the chairmanship opened for Burns.

On the day Burns, at the age of 65, took office in January 1970, Nixon left little doubt about the relationship he expected. He joked: "I respect [Burns's] independence. However, I hope that independently he will conclude that my views are the ones that should be followed."[10] Members of the Federal Reserve Board, including Burns, thought the joke dangerous, but its meaning was inescapable. Nixon had no intention of risking uncooperative Fed policies when he sought reelection to a second term, and to insure the Fed's cooperation he placed a trusted associate in its chairmanship. Nixon viewed Burns as his "own man" at the Fed, as Ehrlichman put it.[11] However, a careful look at the Fed's policies during those fateful years, in which the Fed helped unloose an inflation that took the rest of the decade to bring under control, reveals a much more complicated tale of cross-pressures and uncertainty. Burns and the Fed were much less Nixon's accomplices than participants in a desperate struggle to develop new answers to problems for which the old remedies no longer worked.

BURNS AT THE FED

At the beginning of the Nixon administration, there was surprising unanimity among economists about the economy. Johnson's Council of Economic Advisers thought that tight monetary and fiscal policies would take about six months to check the inflation that Vietnam had sparked; Nixon's CEA thought it would take twelve months.[12] Both guesses quickly proved far off the mark. Unemployment rose from 3.5 percent in 1969 to 4.9 percent in 1970, and the consumer price index unexpectedly rose as well, from a 5 percent increase in 1969 to a 6 percent increase in 1970. Such statistics befuddled economists, who for years had theorized that unemployment and inflation moved in opposite directions. (Economic theories had hypothesized that as more workers lose their jobs, the economy slows and there will be less pressure on prices. On the other hand, the higher inflation is, the more demand there is for goods as consumers seek to buy before prices rise even higher, and thus the lower unemployment will be.) Now economists agreed

10. *Public Papers of the Presidents, 1970* (Washington, D.C.: U.S. Government Printing Office, 1971), 45–46.

11. John Ehrlichman, *Witness to Power: The Nixon Years* (New York: Pocket Books, 1982), 221.

12. Stein, *Presidential Economics*, 151.

only on a name for the new phenomenon: *stagflation*, for stagnant economic growth and high inflation.

Burns thus came to the Fed at a time of great uncertainty. For an era of turmoil in the business cycles, however, there were few more obvious choices. When early in Eisenhower's administration the CEA was in shambles and his counselors recommended that it be replaced by a single adviser, the president sent his advisers on a search to find "the best man in the country on the ups and downs of business."[13] They returned with the name of Arthur Burns, a professor of economics at Columbia University, the director of research at the National Bureau of Economic Research, and a leading student of business cycles. Burns had been born in Stanislau, Austria, in 1904, and as a boy he had moved with his family to Bayonne, New Jersey. After working his way through Columbia to earn a Ph.D. in economics, he championed the school of inductive economics, a pragmatic approach based on empirical evidence rather than ideology. He was thus neither a Keynesian nor a monetarist. Instead, Burns believed that economic policies had to be shaped with one eye on history and one eye on the unique situation of the present.

Burns convinced Eisenhower that the president needed continual economic advice and that the advice would be best produced if the president were served by a deliberative body instead of a single adviser with one viewpoint. Burns urged that the CEA be reconstituted, and Eisenhower made him chairman of the new CEA. Burns was successful beyond Eisenhower's hopes and fears. In contrast with his predecessors—Edwin G. Nourse, who advocated a scientific and independent CEA, and Leon Keyserling, who became a public proponent for a stronger government role in managing the economy—Burns saw his role as a personal consultant to the president.[14] He ruled the CEA with tight control over the staff and high analytical standards. He forced the CEA's staff to filter policy judgments from their analyses; the judgments would be his job. He duplicated assignments to cross-check the staff's work, and with his grasp of economics he rejected any work he considered second-rate. It was a style he would take with him to the Fed.

When he assumed the chairmanship, two competing views on the economy's problems faced him. Many conventional economists suspected that the old theories were still working, but that the Kennedy and Johnson administrations had underestimated the level of "full employment," the

13. Hugh S. Norton, *The Employment Act and the Council of Economic Advisers, 1946–1976* (Columbia: University of South Carolina Press, 1977), 138.
14. See Flash, *Economic Advice and Presidential Leadership*, 4.

level of employment at which everyone who wanted to work was working—
only those persons between jobs or not in the work force would be unemployed. Economists in these administrations believed that government
could—and should—stimulate the economy to reach full employment. For
Johnson's CEA, the magic number was 4 percent unemployment, and the
economy briefly flirted with that level before becoming dangerously unbalanced toward the end of the decade.

An important corollary of this theory was that attempts to push unemployment lower than "full employment" would trigger inflation. The emergence of a vigorous inflation with unemployment hovering in 1971 around
6 percent suggested to Keynesian economists that the level of full employment had drifted upward from 4 percent and that they might therefore have
to accept higher levels of unemployment in return for stable prices. Curing
stagflation thus meant bringing the economy in for a soft landing at a new,
higher equilibrium between unemployment and inflation.

Monetarist economists, on the other hand, argued that the Fed was a
prime culprit in the combined high inflation and economic sluggishness. By
attempting to steer the economy, to pilot its course, they believed, Fed
officials had produced wide swings in the money supply and had destabilized
the economy instead. Curing stagflation, according to Friedman and his
colleagues, thus meant keeping a stable course of money growth instead of
trying through changes in the money supply to manage the economy.

Burns rejected both of these arguments and argued instead for pragmatic
economic management through flexible monetary and fiscal policies. Burns
told a friend, "The argument between the Friedmanites and the Keynesians
is a false argument. It's an argument about how well this or that group of
economists can forecast the future. They cannot do so, and thank God they
can't."[15] Burns's views were eclectic. The federal government's growing
commitment to social welfare, high economic growth, and low unemployment, he believed, had created an inflationary bias in the economy. In days
past, the economy's natural cycles had promoted stability: downturns had
wrung inflationary forces out of the economy. The federal government's
growing self-confidence in managing the economy, however, had reduced
the severity of recent downturns. When the economy had threatened to
slow, furthermore, the federal government had established many generous
new programs, from unemployment insurance to welfare, to ease the pain.
As a result, Burns argued, the market no longer served as a natural check
on prices, and the economy had developed an inflation with "no close par-

15. Lawrence Malkin, "A Practical Politician at the Fed," *Fortune* 83 (May 1971): 260.

allel in economic history."[16] Burns believed that the Fed could tackle this new breed of problems by well-timed applications of monetary restraint. The job, he was convinced, was a double one: to slow the growth of money at proper times and to disrupt the public's expectations of future inflation.

The new chairman was a respected economist who had a firm view about the economy's problems and what to do about them. He had such confidence in his judgment, furthermore, that he had little hesitation in telling any-one—colleague, member of Congress, or president—what ought to be done. He was, as Dan Rather christened him, a "complete pedagogue" who now had the world as his classroom.[17] Burns was also an unquestionably skillful politician. No less colorful a political authority than John Connally, former Democratic governor of Texas and Nixon's Republican secretary of the Treasury, said of Burns, "He's as cagey as a tree full of owls," and Henry Kissinger called him "one of the canniest infighters in Washington."[18]

The contrast with Martin's nonpartisanship could not have been greater. Burns saw himself as much a politician and adviser as a central banker. Even after coming to the Fed Burns maintained his White House ties. Within the Fed he pushed aside Martin's consensus-based approach and, as one Fed governor explained, he "was more aggressive by far than Martin in putting forward his views. He often came in with his mind made up, and there was more effort to lead the board in the direction he decided was appropriate."[19] As Nobel laureate Paul A. Samuelson quipped, "If he were alone on a desert island, he'd be giving orders to himself, and they'd stick."[20]

At his first meeting as chairman, Burns demonstrated just how great the change would be. Martin had always relied on a series of "go rounds," in which every member of the FOMC gave his views in predetermined order. Martin always spoke last, summed up the apparent consensus, and then voted last. "Bill heard every expression of view before stating his own pref-erence for policy," one former governor explained.[21] Burns did exactly the reverse. He began his first meeting by saying that he would not be bound by the old ways and that there would be no set order for discussion. Then he argued that the Fed had slowed the economy too much by keeping

16. Speech delivered December 29, 1972, quoted in Arthur F. Burns, *Reflections of an Economic Policy Maker: Speeches and Congressional Statements, 1969–1978* (Washington, D.C.: American Enterprise Institute, 1978), 143–46.

17. Dan Rather and Gary Paul Gates, *The Palace Guard* (New York: Harper and Row, 1974), 64.

18. Quoted by Malkin, "A Practical Politician at the Fed," 264; Henry Kissinger, *Years of Upheaval* (Boston: Little, Brown, 1982), 81.

19. Governor Charles Partee, interview with the author.

20. Quoted in *Business Week*, November 21, 1977, 110.

21. Interview with the author.

money too tight. He contended that monetary policy should be looser, and after considerable debate the FOMC agreed, but on an unusual 9–3 vote. Martin would never have thus gone out in front of a policy change and never would have allowed such a split to develop, a former governor asserted. "Arthur Burns did—at the first meeting."[22] He intended to steer firmly the Fed's course, and he was willing to operate at a far lower level of internal support than was Martin. "I vote *first*," Burns explained. "I'm willing to stick my neck out. I think it's important that I make my position known. A Chairman who sits there until everyone has made his position known and then votes with the majority—what kind of leadership is that?" he asked, with a pointed reference to Martin.[23]

Burns compensated for lower consensus by seeking greater control over the board's staff. He appointed more technical experts and cultivated personal loyalty by supporting allies for key positions. Burns saw himself as the system's contact with the outside world, and he even sought to control what other board members said in speeches. The new chairman also cut board meetings from five to three times per week, a move that strengthened his own role in setting the agenda and controlling discussion at meetings.

Most of all, though, Burns came to dominate the Fed by the force of his ideas and by hard work. As he had at the CEA, he rejected any staff studies he did not find up to his standards of scholarship. He started his day with a breakfast meeting at 8:00 A.M. and often worked in his Watergate apartment until 4:00 A.M. the next morning.[24] With prodigious effort, a strong hand, and an independent intellect, he shaped the Fed's policies during a turbulent time.

CONTROLLING INFLATION, SPURRING GROWTH

Nixon's expectations about his new Fed chairman were crystal clear. At a meeting in the Oval Office soon after naming Burns chairman, Nixon told him, "You see to it: no recession," according to notes of the meeting made by presidential adviser John Ehrlichman.[25] A few weeks later, Nixon repeated this concern to Ehrlichman and Bob Haldeman. "The Fed *must* loosen—it must risk inflation."[26] A few months earlier, administration offi-

22. Interview with the author.
23. Quoted by Malkin, "A Practical Politician at the Fed," 151; emphasis in the original.
24. Hobart Rowen, "Keeping Secrets at the Fed," *Columbia Journalism Review* 14 (July/August 1975): 53.
25. Notes taken by John Ehrlichman on White House meeting between Burns and Nixon, October 29, 1969, Ehrlichman Papers, Fenn Gallery, Santa Fe, New Mexico.
26. Ehrlichman notes, December 19, 1969; emphasis in the original.

cials had supported the Fed's tight money policies. In March 1969, CEA Chairman Paul McCracken wrote Ehrlichman, "The first requirement" was "to arrest inflation."[27] The tax surcharge had been late in coming and, when finally passed, it proved to apply far less restraint than Johnson's economists had hoped. The job therefore fell to the Fed, and in the Nixon administration's first months, his advisers strongly supported the policy.

They soon began worrying, however, that the Fed might keep the screws too tight for too long and that "a soft economic situation" might develop.[28] McCracken therefore developed a new two-part strategy: "a stringent fiscal policy" to keep down inflation and to avoid the Johnson administration's mistake of recurring large deficits; and "an easier monetary policy" from the Fed to keep interest rates down and to lower unemployment. Where fine-tuning was needed, it would come through monetary policy because, McCracken believed, there was "too much viscosity in fiscal policy for short-term maneuvers."[29] By June 1970, McCracken told Nixon that "a rapid rate of monetary expansion is urgently desirable."[30]

Nixon focused single-mindedly on economic growth high enough to bring unemployment down by the 1972 election, even if that meant higher inflation.[31] The administration's targets, as McCracken framed them in November 1970, were "to regain the zone of full employment by mid-1972," to reduce unemployment to 4.5 percent and inflation to 3.5 percent. To get there, he concluded, "Monetary policy will need to be more expansive" than it had been through the early months of Burns's tenure. Because of the long lag between changes in the Fed's policies and changes in the economy, McCracken said the need for a policy change was urgent. "Time is pressing on this," he warned the president.[32]

Nixon quickly discovered, however, that Burns was not to be the president's operative at the Fed. After Burns assumed the chairmanship, Ehrlichman explained that Nixon felt he could not count on him in the same way he could when he was around him. Nixon often talked about scolding Burns, and he regularly used Ehrlichman to send messages to the Fed about

27. Memo, Paul McCracken to John Ehrlichman, March 18, 1969, Box 19, "Memos to the White House, March 1969," McCracken Papers, Bentley Historical Library, University of Michigan.

28. Memo, McCracken to Nixon, April 26, 1969, Box 19, "Memos to the White House, April 1969," McCracken Papers. See also Stein, *Presidential Economics*, 151–52.

29. Memo, McCracken to Nixon, November 15, 1969, Box 19, "Memos to the White House, November 1969," McCracken Papers.

30. Memo, McCracken to Nixon, June 13, 1970, Box 19, "Memos to the White House, June 1970," McCracken Papers.

31. Nixon phone call to Ehrlichman, December 19, 1969, Ehrlichman notes.

32. Memo, McCracken to Nixon, November 16, 1970, Box 19, "Memos to the White House, November 1970," McCracken Papers.

the policies he desired. In March 1970, for example, Nixon sent him to warn Burns that the economy was in a very tight situation and that it would be the Fed's responsibility if a recession occurred. He urged that the Fed free up money to help the construction industry before it was too late. Burns, in such situations, invariably replied, "Well, I guess I'd better come over and talk to the President."[33]

Burns resented Nixon's meddling and he complained later, "Nixon tried to tell me what the Federal Reserve ought to be doing."[34] The chairman often took advantage of the White House meetings to deliver lectures of his own. He argued that the White House ought to try harder to balance the budget instead of pressing the Fed to ease money. Burns usually added a rebuke about interfering with the Fed's independence. Quadriad meetings were held regularly, but as McCracken's successor as CEA chairman, Herbert Stein, explained, they "were more often occasions for Arthur to lecture the president than for the president to lecture Arthur."[35] CEA officials complained that the regular Fed-CEA lunches turned out to be occasions when the CEA staff shared their hopes about the gross national product and Fed officials shared their tennis scores.[36]

Burns was also a master of the artful dodge. After one scolding from Ehrlichman, he replied with a message that Ehrlichman found so deliciously ambiguous that he recorded it: "You know," Burns said, "the idea that I would ever let a conflict arise between what I think is right and my loyalty to Dick Nixon is outrageous."[37] Fed officials—especially Burns—proved inscrutable, to the administration's frustration.

Of greatest concern to Nixon and administration officials was Burns's ongoing campaign for an incomes policy. The chairman had diagnosed the economy's problem in the early 1970s as a cost-push inflation, in which rising costs, especially wages, pushed prices continually upward. The Fed's usual answer to inflation—tight money—would, he reasoned, have little effect on such a problem. It would only further slow economic growth and drive up unemployment without having much effect on wages. Members of Congress, furthermore, were worried that money already was too tight and interest rates too high. Proposals were circulating on Capitol Hill for legislative control of interest rates. These proposals represented a real threat

33. Ehrlichman notes, March 16, 1970; Ehrlichman, *Witness to Power*, 223.
34. Interview with the author.
35. Interview with the author; and Hargrove and Morley, eds., *The President and the Council of Economic Advisers*, 378.
36. Stein oral history in Hargrove and Morley, eds., *The President and the Council of Economic Advisers*, 376.
37. Ehrlichman, *Witness to Power*, 228.

to the Fed, for Burns feared that they would limit the Fed's ability to tighten money and thus would make inflation even worse. He hoped that a short-term incomes policy, in which the federal government held down wage increases, would help break the back of inflation while protecting the Fed from the demands for interest rate controls.

Starting in May 1970 he began a series of speeches warning that inflation was the nation's fundamental challenge. Inflation had become ingrained in the economy, he claimed, and the Fed's tight money campaign had only increased unemployment without producing a significant effect on inflation. The only way to deal effectively with inflation, Burns contended, was to adopt government controls on wages. Burns foresaw a long and painful transition to more stable economic growth that only strong government action could bring. He acknowledged the problems of government controls, but he argued they could play an important role "in shortening the period between suppression of excess demand and restoration of reasonable price stability."[38] Burns certainly was not the only advocate of wage and price controls, for the stubborn inflation of the preceding years had converted many business leaders, but his support was crucial. Arguments from such a well-informed, well-positioned official, who had impeccable conservative credentials, added great weight to the campaign. Anyone who wanted to press the idea could say that "'even' Arthur Burns" favored it.[39]

Nixon was infuriated. He saw Burns's campaign as an attack on his economic policy, an act of personal disloyalty, and an attempt to evade the Fed's responsibility. "The Fed wants others to act," he complained to his advisers; "it won't do the right thing itself."[40] He fumed, "Burns will get it right in the chops!"[41] Some of Nixon's advisers saw Burns's campaign as an implicit bargain: the administration's imposition of wage and price controls as the chairman's price for easier money. CEA member Stein warned administration officials to "prepare . . . for battle" if the Fed could not be moved.[42]

After the 1970 mid-term elections, Nixon's economists worried that the economy was starting to stall and needed more stimulus, especially from a more vigorous monetary policy. The Fed had set a meager 5 percent target for growth in the money supply, McCracken told Nixon, but could not seem

38. Speech, May 18, 1970, in Burns, *Reflections of an Economic Policy Maker*, 100.
39. Stein, *Presidential Economics*, 156.
40. Ehrlichman notes, November 30, 1970.
41. Ehrlichman, *Witness to Power*, 223–24.
42. Memo, Stein to [Treasury Secretary] Kennedy, McCracken, and Shultz, December 21, 1970, Box B23, "Council of Economic Advisers, 1970," Burns Papers, Gerald R. Ford Presidential Library.

even to accomplish that. If the administration was to meet its full employment target, he concluded, the Fed would have to supply easier money quickly. Nixon and his advisers decided, therefore, to press Burns directly about whether he shared the president's objective of full employment by mid-1972.[43]

Burns came to the White House on November 20, 1970, and countered that the money supply was already growing adequately. Interest rates were coming down across the board while, he warned, prices were rapidly increasing. Inflation was not under control, and easier money would only feed it while worsening international attacks on the dollar. The basic problem, Burns argued, was confidence, both of American consumers and of international financiers, that the value of the dollar would hold.[44] When the meeting ended Nixon had achieved neither of his goals: a pledge of easier money from Burns and an end to his campaign for an incomes policy.

Nixon did agree that the problem was a lack of confidence—and he thought Burns's statements were a prime cause. He and his advisers worried that the constant talk about an incomes policy undermined the economy and that a "psychological recession" might result.[45] The president decided to try to counter this danger with a speech on December 4, 1970, to the National Association of Manufacturers. In the speech, Nixon announced a series of strategies to jawbone against price increases—inflation alerts, a national commission on productivity to study ways of cutting costs, and a construction industry collective bargaining commission to help hold down wages. He told his audience, "Now this is the moment for business and labor to make a special effort to exercise restraint in price and wage decisions." He had also consulted with Burns, Nixon continued, and he assured them that the Fed would supply enough money for stable growth.[46] Burns quickly struck back to insure that the speech did not commit him to the administration's plan. Three days later he resumed his calls for an incomes policy. He warned that "once an economy becomes engulfed by inflation, economic policy makers no longer have any good choices."[47]

Nixon saw Burns's campaign as a personal vendetta, but the chairman had the Fed and its staff behind him. The administration's policy posed a special threat to the Fed. Burns and his staff worried that inflation was not under control and that fiscal policy was completely inflexible. Nixon's budget faced heavy pressures from Vietnam war spending, high costs for programs

43. Ehrlichman notes, November 19, 1970.
44. Ehrlichman notes, November 20, 1970.
45. Ehrlichman notes, December 15, 1970.
46. *Public Papers of the Presidents, 1970,* 1093.
47. Speech, December 7, 1970, in Burns, *Reflections of an Economic Policy Maker,* 103.

for the unemployed, and constant pressure from a Democratic Congress that wanted to continue the growth of the Great Society. The president thus had little chance of balancing the budget. After having eased the money supply on the promise of fiscal action just a few years before—and after being forced to take up the slack when the surcharge proved ineffective—there was no support in the Fed for complying with Nixon's strategy. If money was to be easier, Burns and the Fed wanted the assurance of a wage and price board to keep the economy from quickly overheating again. The Fed felt victimized by the ups and downs of fiscal policy during the Johnson years, and that shadow still hung over the agency.

The Fed's staff blamed the economy's muddle on the administration which, one Fed staff member argued, "has created, in the economic policy area, a credibility gap in the public mind as great as the one confronting the previous administration over its Vietnam policy in the spring of 1968." That "credibility gap," he argued, came from "widespread public recognition that economic policies are not working." Moreover, he charged, administration officials were chronically guilty of interpreting economic data in ways "that suggest failure to appreciate the seriousness of the situation, lack of candor, lack of concern, or some combination of all three."[48] After having been trapped in Johnson's maneuverings over wartime finance, Fed officials and staff members were determined not to be ensnared by the White House once again.

For Nixon, however, the issue was a personal one. The president considered taking on Burns publicly and even threatened, "I'll unload on him like he's never had."[49] Some of these complaints, Ehrlichman explained later, were an "off-with-their-heads" reaction, an expression of the president's anger but not meant to be taken seriously. He talked constantly about getting tough with Burns, but he rarely followed through.[50] Nixon's anger, though, reflected a deeper fear that the Fed would again sabotage his election campaign. At a December 15, 1970, meeting, he told Ehrlichman and adviser George Shultz, "we'll take inflation if necessary" but, according to Ehrlichman's notes, "we can't take unemployment."[51] A week later, he insisted to Haldeman, Ehrlichman, and Shultz, "The trend must be *improving* in '72."[52] The third year of his administration was to be the big year for economic improvement, and the president worried about how to get Burns

48. Memo, Lyle G. Gramley to J. Charles Partee, August 11, 1971, Box B60, "Incomes Policy, 1971," Burns Papers.
49. Ehrlichman notes, December 15, 1970.
50. Interview with the author.
51. Ehrlichman notes, December 15, 1970.
52. Ehrlichman notes, December 23, 1970.

"off this wage and price board thing."[53] Nixon proved unable to silence Burns, however, and around Washington wags clucked, "Nixon fiddles while Burns roams."[54]

As interest rates and unemployment stayed high, there was strong public support for the federal government to do something about rising prices and interest rates. To most people, that meant wage and price controls coupled with easier money from the Fed. From the left, the Fed faced attack from Walter Heller, who told the Joint Economic Committee that to lower the unemployment rate someone would have to "wheedle an aggressively expansionary monetary policy out of the Federal Reserve."[55] Treasury Secretary–designate John Connally, meanwhile, maintained at his confirmation hearing that he was confident he could work with Burns toward an "easy money policy."[56] Office of Management and Budget Director Shultz testified before the Joint Economic Committee that the president's budget would provide a strong fiscal stimulus. The rest of the job, he implied, would be the job of the Fed. Congressman Henry Reuss (D-Wis.) agreed that "monetary policy would have to be the culprit" if the economy failed to expand rapidly.[57]

Board members unmistakably got the message: administration officials and members of Congress, as well as liberal and conservative economists, expected easier money to combat the increase in unemployment, which had grown from 4.9 percent in 1970 to 5.9 percent in 1971. The high unemployment, pressure from the White House and Congress, complaints from outsiders like Heller, and serious talk of credit controls convinced Burns and his colleagues to push their fears about worsening inflation to the background and to ease the money supply. The Fed started to ease off the brakes in early 1971, and from January to August 1971 the money supply (M1) grew at a very rapid 10.8 percent.

The administration's jawboning, however, failed in the meantime to slow either the growth in prices or erosion in the dollar's international value. In March 1971, the administration began wage controls for the construction industry, but wages continued to gallop ahead. Average hourly earnings increased 7.2 percent in the first six months of 1971. By late summer, the

53. Ehrlichman notes, March 23, 1971.

54. William Safire, *Before the Fall: An Inside View of the Pre-Watergate White House* (New York: Belmont Towers, 1975), 491.

55. Summary of Joint Economic Committee Testimony, February 1, 1971, Burns Papers.

56. U.S. Congress, Senate, Committee on Finance, nomination of John B. Connally, hearings, January 28, 1971.

57. Reported in memo, John S. Ripley to Board of Governors, February 9, 1971, Box B76, "Joint Economic Committee, 1971," Burns Papers.

dollar's problems finally forced the administration to take decisive action. Burns joined a small group of administration officials who met in complete isolation in Camp David over the weekend of August 13–15. Nixon came down from the mountain to give a Sunday evening speech in which he said the United States would devalue the dollar, impose a 10 percent import surcharge, reduce taxes to stimulate the slow business recovery, suspend the convertability of the dollar into gold, and impose a wage and price freeze. Nixon's advisers had quietly been working on wage and price controls for months, and Burns finally won his point under the heavy pressure of the international crisis.

Burns still was not convinced that Nixon's strategy was wise. He publicly worried that the administration's economic growth targets were too high and therefore risked making inflation worse. Nixon countered by sending Ehrlichman to scold Burns about stirring up uncertainty by publicly disagreeing with the administration, to ask for his loyalty, and to warn him that the president would hold him personally responsible for the money supply.[58] Burns responded by publicly complaining about the administration's continuing pressure.[59] The growth of the money supply began to fall and Nixon's advisers worried that they would lose what little progress they thought they had gained.[60]

In pressing his campaign, Nixon found unusual allies in the Democratically controlled Congress and in liberal economists. The Joint Economic Committee's 1972 report stated that "fairly rapid money growth will be needed if recovery is not to be choked off by rising long-term interest rates."[61] Respected liberal economists like Walter Heller and Paul Samuelson warned against repeating the mistakes of the Eisenhower administration by repressing economic recovery with tight money.[62] There was remarkably uniform judgment, in fact, that the Fed was too tight, and that tight money risked causing the economy's fragile recovery serious damage. "We shared a common error that there was a lot of room for expansion without reviving inflation," Stein recalled later.[63]

Complicating Burns's problem was a second hat he wore as chairman of the Committee on Interest and Dividends (CID), an interagency watchdog

58. Ehrlichman notes, conversation on Air Force One, February 13, 1972.

59. *Business Week*, April 15, 1972, 82.

60. Memo, McCracken to Nixon, October 27, 1971, Box 20, "Memos to the White House, October 1971," McCracken Papers.

61. U.S. Congress, Joint Economic Committee, *Report of the Joint Committee on the 1972 Economic Report of the President*, 92d Cong., 2d sess., 1972, 18.

62. Woolley, *Monetary Politics*, 168–69; Stein, *Presidential Economics*, 184; and James L. Pierce, "The Political Economy of Arthur Burns," *Journal of Finance* 34 (1979): 489.

63. Interview with the author.

established in October 1971 after the imposition of wage and price controls. The CID's mission was to keep interest rates and corporate dividends from rising too high and adding to the cost of goods. Some board members argued that the job would pose a conflict of interest for Burns, since the CID would try to keep interest rates and dividends low while inflation-fighting might mean the Fed would have to work for higher rates. Burns, however, felt he had little choice, since he believed the job would go to Treasury Secretary Connally if he did not accept it. That risked leading the Fed back to the era of the Treasury's peg, and Burns found that completely unacceptable.[64]

Burns used his position on the CID to oppose mandatory interest rate ceilings, especially the plan being developed by Democrats on the House Banking Committee. His approach was to use instead the committee's moral suasion on banks and corporations that threatened to increase their rates and dividends. The main problem, as he saw it, was that interest rates tended to lag behind as market rates came down. The CID would try to speed up the adjustment process by "a nudging exercise" that would "reduce the time lag between movements in market rates and the stickier conventional rates."[65] In fact, as the election approached in 1972, there was considerable pressure within the Fed for tighter money. Board member Andrew Brimmer argued for an increase in the discount rate in September 1972, but Burns vigorously opposed it. "He told us," Brimmer remembered later, "that to enhance the prospect of extending the controls program, labor's support was needed. To gain it, in Burns's view, we had to keep interest rates down."[66]

In 1972, therefore, Burns found himself at the center of conflict. The White House was incessantly pressuring for easier money, while members of Congress threatened interest rate controls if the Fed did not loosen the money supply. To keep political support for the controls program alive, furthermore, Burns had to keep interest rates from rising higher, and that meant easy money as well. On the other side, however, bankers were skeptical that inflation was licked and some FOMC members wanted to make sure it would not reemerge through a too-easy monetary policy. Burns did not align himself with either camp, and thus was not an accomplice in Nixon's reelection campaign. Rather, he gingerly guided the Fed through

64. Interview with the author; Woolley, *Monetary Politics*, 170; and *Dun's Review* 106 (November 1975): 42.
65. Burns statement, Minutes of CID Meeting, February 9, 1972, Box B16, "CID Minutes, 1972," Burns Papers.
66. Quoted in *Dun's Review* 106 (November 1975): 42; see also Pierce, "The Political Economy of Arthur Burns," 490–91.

these pressures by promoting easier money coupled with wage and price controls to try to keep inflation under control.

By the end of 1972, Nixon was pleased with the results of his program. He had easily won reelection and had avoided a recession. The economy seemed to be growing nicely. The CID believed its programs had been a success, and the committee agreed on an inflation goal of 3 percent for 1973, a goal which a consensus believed realistic. Administration economists hoped even more optimistically to reduce it to 2½ percent.[67] Inflation seemed at last under control, and administration planners began thinking about the best way to relax controls without signaling a return to old-style behavior.

The honeymoon lasted only weeks. By early 1973, one of the strongest bursts of peacetime inflation in American history ignited. The ease in the money supply combined with other forces in the world economy—crop failures, especially in the Soviet Union, and the Arab oil embargo—to push prices rapidly higher. In March several banks increased their prime rate by one-half of one percent, from 6¼ to 6¾ percent. Burns sent telegrams to the banks that had announced rate increases, asking them to submit justification for their actions to the CID. The CID's pressure was the first strong move the committee had made against rising rates, since in its first eighteen months its job had been to nudge rates downward rather than to restrain their increase. The CID had little effect on the upward course, and the rising inflation caused new problems for Burns. The inflation problem seemed to have shifted from a cost-push inflation, in which costs of production like wages and interest rates pushed prices higher, to a demand-pull inflation, where a large supply of money fueled demand and pushed prices higher. One solution was to restrain the growth of money, but that ran against the CID's mission of keeping interest rates down. Burns and his CID colleagues continued to jawbone against rate increases, but the bizarre combination of his two hats, uncertainty over the state and direction of the economy, and rapidly changing problems like the oil embargo made it difficult to judge just what action the Fed should take.

By September 1973 the prime rate at some banks had risen to 10 percent while the Fed tried to rein in the inflation it had helped to create. A New York *Times* poll of 415 business economists showed that 41.2 percent rated the Fed's policy in the previous year "poor" and another 38.8 percent rated it "fair."[68] By that time, inflation was out of control. The consumer price

67. Stein to Burns, December 23, 1972, Box B23, "Council of Economic Advisers, 1972," Burns Papers; Minutes, December 20, 1972, Box B15, "CID Minutes, Sep.–Dec., 1972," Burns Papers.
68. New York *Times*, September 17, 1973, 49.

index, which had moderated to a 3.3 percent increase in 1972 from a 4.3 increase in 1971, exploded into a 6.2 percent increase in 1973 and then an 11 percent increase in 1974, the highest levels of the postwar economy.

Fed officials, however, did not realize just how much they had eased the money supply. Throughout much of 1972, in fact, they had been trying to moderate the growth of money, and they had succeeded. Money supply figures at the time indicated that M1 had slowed from 6.9 percent in 1969 to 6.5 percent in 1972. Like all money supply statistics, these figures were only estimates subject to later revision, and those revisions showed that the money supply had in fact grown by nearly 7.5 percent. (In hindsight, former reserve bank governor Robert C. Holland wished that the Fed had been firmer, but, he argued, the Fed's policies "were reasonable in light of the economic situation at the time."[69] The Fed thus did in fact rapidly increase the money supply in 1972. Its policy, however, was the result of a complex constellation of pressures and problems: substantial conflicts between the White House and Burns; pressures from members of Congress for easier money; criticism by many economists that the Fed had been too tight; and technical problems that made it hard for the Fed to determine just how "easy" its policies were.

Despite his constant squabbles, however, Burns's policy was rarely far out of step with the Nixon administration. He largely delivered the expansive policies the president and his advisers wanted (even if somewhat belatedly, not quite in the measure they intended, and only after heavy pressure), and his relationship with the White House was close if sometimes tense. He was far more likely to give than to receive advice, to lecture the president and his advisers than to accept their counsel. Burns consistently leaned toward restraint rather than expansion and he vigorously insisted on the Fed's independence when he thought Nixon was leaning on him too hard.

The tension with White House officials, in fact, earned Burns a share of the administration's "dirty tricks." In one meeting during 1971, a staff member opposed to Burns told Nixon that the Fed chairman had proposed, in the midst of his public campaign for wage and price controls, an increase in the chairman's salary to the level of cabinet members. "Do you mean Arthur is preaching wage-and-price controls and he wants a pay raise?" Nixon asked. "Well how do you like that?" Nixon then turned to Charles Colson and said, "Get that out, Chuck. Get that into the papers." Colson arranged through a staff assistant to leak the story to the *Wall Street Jour-*

69. Letter, Robert C. Holland to Robert L. Bartley, editor, *Wall Street Journal*, June 2, 1983, 31.

nal.[70] At the same time administration officials also leaked a story that they were considering "packing" the Fed board by increasing its size to make it more responsive.

The leaks greatly embarrassed the administration. Reporters found out that Colson had been the source of the first leak, and the discovery led to speculation that the administration was out to get Burns. Burns, further-more, had not in fact proposed a raise for himself but for his successor; the chairman was simply reviving a sore issue that had circulated within the system since its earliest days. Administration officials dispatched presiden-tial speechwriter William Safire to soothe Burns. Burns told Safire that the board-packing plan was stupid and that the pay raise leak was vicious and mean. At a news conference soon afterward, Nixon tried to make up by calling the salary increase charge "a very unfair shot." Burns replied later through Safire that Nixon's public support had "warmed my heart." He promised, "We have to work more closely together now."[71]

Nixon tolerated Burns's disputes because he needed the Fed. It was much easier to gain leverage on the economy through monetary policy than through the federal budget. He also found in the Fed chairman a counselor on a wide range of issues. Burns advised the administration on topics from Mideast diplomacy to plans for the "southern strategy" to win the support of the South during the 1972 presidential campaign.[72] From Burns's point of view, he had a sound relationship with the president because they agreed on the fundamental issue: the need to support economic growth without taking undue inflationary risks. Nixon and his CEA usually leaned more toward stimulating economic growth, especially as the 1972 election ap-proached, while Burns and the Fed consistently pressed for harnessing in-flation. The debate was largely one of degree and relative emphasis, but both Burns and Nixon in the end traveled along a common, if often rocky, course.

PRESIDENTIAL ADVISER

When Gerald Ford came to the presidency in 1974, the economy was en-tering the worst recession since the 1930s. Unemployment jumped from 5 percent in May to 7.2 percent in December, while inflation grew even more rapidly. The consumer price index rose 12.2 percent for the year, while the wholesale price index jumped an even more rapid 20.9 percent.

70. Charles W. Colson, *Born Again* (Old Tappan, N.J.: Chosen Books, 1976), 62–63.
71. Safire, *Before the Fall*, 492–96.
72. See, for example, Kissinger, *Years of Upheaval*, 906.

To make matters worse, the prime rate hit 12 percent in mid-year, the highest rate to that point in history.

In the midst of such a troubled economy, Ford and Burns depended on each other. Ford became president on the heels of a scandal and needed to rebuild public trust in the presidency as well as to build legitimacy for his own leadership. Economic shocks posed fundamental problems: an energy crisis that forced car owners to wait in long lines for gasoline; inflation that reached crisis proportions; and economic growth that remained sluggish in spite of Washington's efforts to nudge it higher. Ford's continuing confrontations with Congress made compromise on the budget all but impossible. The president thus deeply needed the Fed's cooperation to gain leverage on the economy, his biggest policy problem.

For his part, Burns keenly enjoyed the challenge of battle, whether with those who disagreed with him or with an intransigent economy. He also enjoyed access to the levers of power, so Ford's need for Burns's cooperation fed the chairman's desire for wide influence. The two used this interdependence to build the closest relationship between a president and a Fed chairman in history. Not only did they closely coordinate monetary and fiscal policies, but they also exchanged views on an extraordinary range of other issues. As Alan Greenspan, Ford's CEA chairman, recalled later, "Burns was very influential and extraordinarily useful."[73] Compared with the close but often tempestuous White House–Fed ties during the Nixon years, the relationship during the Ford years was closer, warmer, and even more wide-ranging.[74] Burns later commented, "Ford was the only president who really understood me."[75]

The contrast with Nixon could not have been greater. While Ford and Burns had known each other only slightly before Ford assumed office, the president discovered that their "economic philosophies were in tune."[76] Nixon, Burns complained, "tried to interfere with the Federal Reserve, and he did it repeatedly. He did it in ways that were fair and in ways that by almost any standard were unfair." Ford, by contrast, respected the Fed's independence from the White House. "Every president I have known has made remarks about the independence of the Federal Reserve. Gerry Ford believed it." It was, Burns said, "part of his political religion."[77] It was also, undoubtedly, a pragmatic matter of mutual advantage. The Fed's legal in-

73. Greenspan oral history in Hargrove and Morley, eds., *The President and the Council of Economic Advisers*, 433.

74. See Gerald R. Ford, *A Time to Heal* (New York: Harper and Row, 1979), 153.

75. Interview with the author.

76. Ford, *A Time to Heal*, 153.

77. Interview with the author.

dependence was a political fig leaf behind which Ford could hide unpleasant economic policies. The president's embrace of the Fed's independence gave Burns greater operating flexibility and influence over a very broad range of administration policies, economic and even political. A close relationship grew from such mutual advantage.

During the Ford administration the Quadriad met infrequently and was not a major policy forum.[78] Instead, Burns and Ford relied on one-on-one sessions and other meetings in which Burns advised the president. These sessions began very tentatively. In November 1974 and again in March 1975, Burns met with the president, but Ford's staff was very careful to keep the meetings secret from the press for fear of stirring speculation about presidential pressure on the Fed. Following the March meeting, however, Ford left a note for his staff saying that he wanted to see Burns monthly from then on. In August, Ford left another emphatic note saying that he wanted the next meeting to be a full hour, for he found that he had too much to discuss in a shorter session. By the end of the year, the meetings had become so routine that the White House photographer began to record them as a regular part of the president's day.[79] Over the first year of the Ford administration Burns moved into the small circle of the president's closest advisers.

From Burns's point of view, the nation's economic problems had now become far more difficult. The inflation of the 1960s had lingered through the first half of the 1970s, and the nation had begun to lose confidence that the problem could be licked. Business and citizens alike planned with a bias toward inflation, as did government itself. Burns believed that by pushing too hard to bring unemployment down too far, the federal government had made inflation worse. A successful war on inflation thus had to include two elements: a scaling back of the public's expectations of the federal government's ability to ease the pain of economic cycles; and a wringing out of the inflationary expectations that so deeply permeated the economy.

Burns put his philosophy to work in developing with Ford administration officials a closely coordinated strategy for breaking the 1974 recession without rekindling inflation. It was to come through an application of Republican "old time religion": fiscal restraint that would move toward a balanced budget and tight monetary policies that would bring down inflation. This path

78. Roger B. Porter, *Presidential Decision Making: The Economic Policy Board* (Cambridge: Cambridge University Press, 1980), 37.
79. Memo, Dick Cheney to Jim Connor, March 11, 1975, WHCF EX FG 131, Gerald R. Ford Library; Memo, Jim Connor to Jerry Jones, WHCF EX FG 131, Ford Library; and Memo, William W. Nicholson to William Seidman, December 12, 1975, WHCF EX FG 131, Ford Library.

unquestionably would bring a great deal of pain, economic and political, but Burns and administration officials alike believed that there was no other path to recovery. On October 8, 1974, Ford announced his "whip inflation now" program: a tighter federal budget, including a 5 percent tax surcharge, coupled with aid for hard-pressed industries and individuals. Congress, however, ignored most of the plan. The Democrats adopted the administration's plans to aid the poor, including a public service employment idea, and added several additional programs, but they left the painful parts of the president's program untouched. The "whip inflation now"—WIN—lapel button quickly became a joke, and the burden of restraint therefore fell more heavily than the administration had planned on Burns and the Fed. The Fed tightened money and interest rates increased sharply, and critics called Burns the "architect of the worst recession in 40 years."[80]

Within the administration, though, Burns's unflinching tight money policy won quiet applause. Ford's CEA told the president that the Fed was dealing well with the "exceedingly difficult problem of balancing objectives." The Fed's "unwillingness to 'accommodate' the steep rates of inflation of 1974 has played a very major role in getting us on the road to price-deceleration which had been a prerequisite of a healthy and sustainable recovery," the CEA concluded.[81] In fact, the administration's principal worry, in January 1975, was that the Fed might ease off too soon. Easier money, Treasury Secretary William Simon warned, would be "a formula for still higher inflation rates when the recovery goes into full swing."[82] By early spring, however, administration officials were less confident and they worried that the Fed might have been too tight for too long.[83] For his part, however, Burns promised not to precipitate a credit crunch and added that the Fed would increase the money supply in the coming months.[84]

The Fed's inflation-fighting exacted high costs. The economy's decline finally ended in April 1975 only after a nearly 10 percent annual rate of decline in the economy's output during the first quarter. Unemployment peaked at about 9 percent while interest rates hovered near historic highs. The depth of the recession raised on Capitol Hill an unusually sharp attack against the Fed (as we shall see in the next chapter). Despite these complaints, however, Burns continued to work closely with the administration

80. *Business Week*, April 21, 1975, 106.

81. Memo, Greenspan and Fellner to Ford, March 22, 1975, WHCF EX FI, Ford Library.

82. Memo, Simon to Ford, January 27, 1975, WHCF EX FI, Ford Library.

83. Talking points for Ford meeting with Burns, March 10, 1975, WHCF EX FG 131, Ford Library.

84. Economic and Energy Minutes, March 28, 1975, WHCF, Confidential File Oversize Attachment #49, Ford Library.

to engineer the recovery. Burns tried to ease off the brakes very slowly, with very moderate money growth, a strategy that had the administration's full support despite the obvious political problems it posed for the approaching presidential reelection campaign.[85]

Burns met with Ford more often and over a broader range of issues than had any other chairman in the Fed's history, with the possible exception of Eccles. In 1975 alone, he attended forty-eight meetings with the president, an average of nearly one per week. Over the nearly two and one-half years of the Ford administration, he met with Ford sixty-nine times.[86] His discussions ranged from an assessment of the proposed public service employment program to the international economic situation.[87] Burns also attended the meetings of the administration's Economic Policy Board, which coordinated economic policy. He was a member of the EPB's executive committee and he attended its meetings when the committee was to discuss something of interest to him. In all these meetings, he was a respected and valued participant.[88] Burns advised Ford on his 1975 State of the Union address and on welfare reform, and he played a key role in devising the administration's hard-line position on the New York City financial crisis.

Burns and Ford thus had a truly unique relationship. Theirs was a relationship of unmatched harmony, harmony that stood in sharp contrast with the Nixon-Burns squabbles. Monetary and fiscal policies were unusually integrated to frame a consistent view: tight money, fiscal restraint, and narrowly targeted relief for those most suffering from the recession. And despite constant complaints from Congress, they kept to their course. Congressional pressure had made the deficits larger than Ford had planned, and that put a heavier burden on the Fed. Nevertheless, at each step the Fed and the White House closely integrated monetary and fiscal policies. The Burns-Ford years were a time of close Federal Reserve–White House ties unrivaled by any but the Eccles-FDR era, and perhaps unmatched in the agency's history.

THE FED AND PRESIDENTIAL POLITICS

In close succession Burns and the Fed had moved through two very different eras. Nixon had clear expectations about the Fed. He would publicly preach fiscal conservatism and balanced budgets, but he would not countenance a

85. Memo, Greenspan to Ford, May 2, 1975, WHCF EX FI, Ford Library.
86. Presidential appointment index, Ford Library.
87. Porter, *Presidential Decision Making*, 33.
88. Ibid., 43.

recession as he faced reelection. He relied completely on the Fed, therefore, to stimulate the economy, and he expected, on the basis of his past relationship with Burns and the fact that he had appointed him chairman, loyalty from "his" chairman. Nixon largely got the policies he wanted, but he discovered that he could not expect to get his way by giving orders. Relations with Burns, while close, were always enmeshed in rancor and wrangling, in bargaining and cajoling. Burns faced other pressures, especially within the Fed, that resisted easier money, and he had his own worries about loosening money too soon.

Legends to the contrary, Burns established that monetary policy would not become a tool of electoral politics. Nixon did get an easier money supply as the 1972 presidential election approached, but almost in spite (rather than because) of his pointed demands. The Fed eased up because political support for tight money was rapidly eroding. Members of Congress and economists, liberals and conservatives, were remarkably unanimous in calling for easier money, and Burns was forced to suppress his inflation worries to maintain support. When the Fed did ease, furthermore, the technical difficulties of managing the money supply led the Fed to overshoot its intended targets. The product was a disastrous inflation and the appearance of complicity in Nixon's campaign. The reality was quite different and emphasized all the more strongly the tremendous political danger to the Fed of even the appearance of partisanship. Any president who believed that the Fed backed his electoral opponent would certainly not long tolerate the agency's legal independence.

Burns's relations with Ford could not have been more different. They established a pattern of close collaboration and easy working relations that was doubly remarkable: first, because they had no previous personal ties on which to base their relationship; and second, because the tight money policy on which they embarked together was politically dangerous. Nevertheless they developed an extraordinarily close relationship and worked together to try to break the inflation strangling the American economy. The Fed and the administration had rarely spoken so much with one voice or worked with such subtle cooperation. The 1974–75 recession, while one of the most severe in American history, was also one of the shortest, due largely to Fed–White House cooperation.

Despite the differences, however, the Nixon and Ford administrations also shared an important similarity: by the mid-1970s, monetary policy had eclipsed fiscal policy as the tool of choice for presidents. The federal budget had become too rigid for new initiatives, too enmeshed in presidential-congressional conflict to produce quick results. Monetary policy had the advantage of quick response and infinite adjustment. This is not to say that monetary policy should be used for such purposes or that the Nixon and Ford administrations used it well. Monetarist economists have strongly argued the dangers of fine-tuning, and in fact during the early 1970s the Fed made some serious errors. These objections, however, can easily disguise another fact: for presidents trying to whip new problems that defied old weapons, monetary policy was the only game in town.

At the same time, the president became the Fed's most important constituent. With the increasing complexity and centralization of economic decisions, the president took a stronger role in shaping the nation's policies. Fed officials had to take account of his preferences, for to do otherwise would be to risk public attack, loss of credibility, and ineffective policies. If the Fed had become more important to the president, the president and his advisers also became more important to the Fed.

At the presidential staff level, the pressures on the Fed have traditionally been for easier money in most circumstances. Treasury officials, who have as their primary job the financing of the government's debt, have always favored low, steady rates of interest. Eccles's complaint about the Treasury's chronic bias for cheap money in all seasons is a classic statement of the recurring Fed-Treasury tension. The administration of the public debt is a massive job, and the larger the debt the more important steady, low-interest Fed policies become for the Treasury.

The CEA has typically been an even stronger proponent of easier money. In the Kennedy administration, CEA Chairman Walter Heller labeled himself "the professional guardian of the Kennedy expansion."[89] Although other CEA officials have rarely proclaimed so boldly their devotion to economic growth, the CEA has traditionally been the primary voice within the administration for strong economic expansion. There has been a steady bias within the CEA for easier money.[90] Table 2 shows the results of an analysis of memos from the CEA to the president during the Kennedy, Johnson, Nixon (1969–71) and Ford administrations.[91] At any given state of monetary policy the president's economic advisers were likely to warn that monetary policy was too tight or that economic conditions warranted the current degree of tightness—but that monetary policy should get no tighter. I found

89. Memo, Heller to Kennedy, July 7, 1963, POF, "Council of Economic Advisers," Kennedy Library.

90. See Paul Peretz, *The Political Economy of Inflation in the United States* (Chicago: University of Chicago Press, 1983), 148.

91. Memos from the Nixon administration are drawn from Paul McCracken's Papers at the Bentley Historical Library, University of Michigan. As this book was being written, Nixon's presidential papers were closed under court order.

no document from the CEA during this fourteen-year period arguing that money was too easy.

The Nixon and Ford years thus left an important legacy for Fed-president relations. As the Fed and the president became increasingly interdependent, it became harder for the Fed to fulfill its inflation-fighting mission. In a crunch, presidents and their staffs typically worried more about promoting economic growth than reducing inflation. The Fed could scarcely ignore White House demands without risking political attack and damaging its own credibility. Rising federal deficits, furthermore, lessened the Fed's flexibility. Presidents came to rely on the Fed's monetary policy to accomplish what they could not with the budget. Yet at the same time, financiers—and, increasingly, a broader constituency as well—campaigned against rising prices. With inflation showing puzzling stubbornness, the Fed weighed the need to stimulate an already sluggish economy against the danger of fueling inflation even more.

Each president approached the Fed in his own way. Despite his budget-balancing rhetoric, Nixon demonstrated that he cared most about rapid economic growth—timed for his reelection campaign—and that he saw Fed policy as a prime instrument in producing it. On the other hand, as Ford proved, the chairman-president relationship can be very close and effective in coordinating policies. As the Fed's history constantly demonstrated and the Ford case reconfirmed, close coordination between the Fed and the White House has come more through informal ties than legal arrangements. A formal connection between the Fed and the administration, which the Fed had with the Treasury until 1935, never produced a close working relationship. On the other hand, chairmen and presidents who wanted to work together have been able to build close relations and effective policy

Table 2: CEA Advice to the President on Monetary Policy, from Kennedy to Ford

Administration	Monetary policy is—		
	Too Tight	Just Right	Too Easy
Kennedy	16	8	0
Johnson	19	29	0
Nixon*	11	4	0
Ford	1	3	0

Source: Memos from the Council of Economic Advisers to the President, in the Kennedy, Johnson, and Ford presidential libraries; and the Paul McCracken Papers, Bentley Historical Library, University of Michigan.

*1969–71 only.

coordination. The key has always been incentives for policymakers to co-operate, not legal relations.

During the 1970s the president became the most important if the most unpredictable of the Fed's constituents. However, he was only one constituent and, as the Fed painfully learned, other constituents—especially members of Congress angry at high interest rates—were determined to have their say as well.

CHAPTER SIX

CONGRESSIONAL OVERSIGHT

If critics sometimes accused Burns of being too close to Nixon, they never accused him of being too close to Congress. His confrontations with members of Congress were legendary. "Testimony under Arthur Burns was high drama," one former Fed staff member explained. "It was always a good show." Some members of Congress even rehearsed for their sessions with Burns by picking a staff member to give tough answers to their questions. "It almost became a psychological duel over who would get the upper hand," according to one Fed staffer. "When members of Congress said they disliked Burns"—which was often—"it was because he always got the upper hand." He concluded, "Burns left them frustrated."[1]

In fact, Fed officials told a story about Burns's preparation for a hearing. On his way to the committee room, the tale went, Burns was bouncing on the balls of his feet like a prizefighter, ready for battle. When asked about the story, Burns replied by remembering a confrontation he had as CEA chairman with Treasury Secretary Humphrey during the Eisenhower administration. Humphrey had challenged Burns's economic report as "no good" and "socialistic," but Burns stuck to his guns and took his case to the president. When the day came for the cabinet meeting to discuss the report, Burns came with two pipes, one in each hand. When Eisenhower noticed the extra pipe, Burns explained, "Well, Mr. President, I'm well-prepared today." He then went on to defend the report—and to win the day.[2] Burns had a taste for battle.

Conflicts between Fed chairmen and members of Congress were certainly nothing new. Eccles regularly had showdowns with Glass and Byrd, and

---

1. Interview with the author.
2. Interview with the author, June 27, 1984.

Martin's tangles with Patman were legendary. Patman, in fact, had made a career, starting in the 1930s, as the populist scourge of the Fed. He believed that Fed officials were too close to the bankers and therefore kept interest rates too high. He regularly criticized the Fed for failing to expand credit when families and small businesses needed it, and he attributed this to bankers' domination of the Fed. The Fed's legal independence thus shielded the agency from democratic control and protected the money monopoly, Patman believed. He constantly complained that the Fed acted "independently, even in defiance of the government" and condemned monetary control "in the hands of a self-appointed money trust" that "has imperiled the welfare of our citizens."[3]

So strident and predictable was Patman's barrage, in fact, that his very attacks helped defend the Fed. "He was so far out, so irrational, that other responsible members of Congress who wanted to criticize the Fed held off for fear of being associated with him," a long-time Fed staff member contended. "He was an important shield against congressional criticism."[4] In the 1970s, however, the Fed came under much broader attack, and Burns's conflicts with Congress became the sharpest in the Fed's history. In part, this was unquestionably due to the irascibility of Chairman Burns. A Fed staff member explained, "When something was coming at the Fed that he didn't like, he went to war—unremitting, unrelenting war."[5] Former board member Andrew Brimmer observed that when Burns testified, he "was running a seminar, and he had a few dull students in the class. He puffed his pipe, and took time to teach, and that gave the impression he was talking down to them. Let's face it, Arthur knew much more than the average member [of Congress], and he had been with [economic theory] for a very long time."[6]

The Fed's conflict with Congress during the 1970s, however, had deeper roots in the economic problems Burns faced. In a 1979 speech looking back over his chairmanship, which he called "The Anguish of Central Banking," Burns laid out three forces that had increased conflict over monetary policy. First, he contended, the economy had developed a fundamental bias toward inflation. Government had assumed the responsibility "to solve problems and relieve hardships—not only for society at large but also for troubled industries, regions, occupations, or social groups." Well-meaning government policy, he claimed, dampened the economy's natural adjustments to

3. U.S. Congress, Joint Economic Committee, *Standards for Guiding Monetary Action*, committee print, 90th Cong., 2d sess., 1968, 21–22.
4. Interview with the author.
5. Interview with the author.
6. Interview with the author, June 22, 1984.

change and imparted "a strong inflationary bias to the American economy."
The government's attempts to ease economic pain became cumulative and
led to ever-greater federal spending.

This process, furthermore, transferred to the monetary arena problems
that fiscal policy could not solve and that, in fact, fiscal policy decisions had
sometimes created. The federal budget was becoming less malleable, subject to longer lags before changes could be made, more entangled in presidential-congressional disputes, and subject to seemingly permanent
deficits. With the federal budget ever more stimulative, the Fed became
the guardian against inflation, a role in which "the opportunities for making
mistakes are legion." When Fed officials decided that the economy needed
restraint, furthermore, congressional pressure would often prevent the Fed
from maintaining tight money long enough to end inflation.

Finally, economic theory had ceased to provide an effective guide to
policy. Traditional theories of economics, especially about the relationship
between inflation and unemployment, had crumbled. The unexpected stubbornness of inflation had led many individuals and corporations to hedge
their investments. They looked for a premium on interest rates to protect
themselves against rising prices. Furthermore, the federal tax deduction for
interest payments lessened the pain of rising rates. The result was that the
Fed needed ever-greater restraint to slow the economy, especially higher
interest rates that in turn meant ever-greater political conflict and economic
uncertainty.[7]

These challenges led Burns zealously to defend the Fed's policy flexibility.
His earlier research had convinced him that economic control needed to be
based on discretionary management. The new reality of the 1970s only
confirmed his belief in flexible monetary policy. Money managers had to
feel their way in an uncharted world, where stagflation defied theory, where
energy crises disrupted planning, where fiscal policy was unremittingly
stimulative, and where political forces—especially members of Congress—
yelped at the thought of rising interest rates. Flexibility was Burns's watchword: to provide the Fed with maneuvering room for charting a new course
through great economic uncertainty and high political conflict.

Rising interest rates in the early 1970s brought Patman new allies. Wis-
consin populists who chaired the congressional banking committees—Senator William Proxmire and Congressman Henry Reuss—took up Patman's
agenda and determined to open up the Fed, to free it from the grip of tight-
money-minded bankers. Their reforms—to "democratize" the Fed, as they

7. Arthur Burns, *The Anguish of Central Banking* (Belgrade: Per Jacobson Foundation,
1979), 11, 16, 15.

put it, or to "politicize" the central bank, as their foes characterized the effort—concentrated on making the Fed more accountable to Congress. Their proposals were an all-out attack on the Fed's prerogatives. They argued that Fed officials ought to appear regularly before Congress to explain their decisions and that the Fed ought to be required to meet congressionally defined interest rate goals. They pressed for auditing by the General Accounting Office to reduce the Fed's budgetary independence. They held that the Fed ought to disclose its decisions immediately, to keep and release verbatim transcripts of its debates, and to open its meetings to the public and press. They argued that, since reserve bank presidents voted on the government's monetary policy, they ought to be subject to presidential nomination and senatorial confirmation; furthermore, the Senate ought to have the right to confirm the board's chairman.

Never before had the Fed faced such sweeping attacks on its autonomy. The attacks were perhaps predictable given the era's economic pain, but the political climate made Burns and his colleagues even more determined to preserve their flexibility. The result, one early reviewer raved, was the "best theater in Washington."[8] As interest rates went higher, as unemployment stayed high, and as inflation proved unpredictably stubborn, congressional restiveness rose. Burns found himself in the middle of the most intense congressional battles of the Fed's history.

MONETARY TARGETS

The Watergate crisis helped end Wright Patman's reign of the House Banking Committee. The 1974 congressional elections brought a large, reform-minded class of freshmen to Capitol Hill, and they seized on emerging plans to reform the selection of committee chairmen. Patman, who was 82, was widely viewed as eccentric and autocratic and losing control of his committee. To replace him, House Democrats elected Henry Reuss, who took up his predecessor's populist attack on the Fed from a new tack. Instead of complaining about bankers' control, he introduced a resolution to force the Fed to lower interest rates by increasing the money supply.

In the late 1960s, members of the Joint Economic Committee had been outraged by the high interest rates that the Fed's Vietnam-era policy had brought. To block stronger congressional attack, Fed officials agreed in 1968 to send an explanatory letter to the committee when monetary growth was outside a four to six percent range. The committee's staff found the letter

8. Malkin, "A Practical Politician at the Fed," 254.

of no real value, but it was the first shot in the battle to increase the Fed's reporting to Congress. In the midst of the 1974 debate over reforming the congressional budget process, staffers considered even more stringent controls. Fed officials would present their annual money targets and at a congressional hearing would lay out the targets' implications for unemployment, interest rates, and inflation. Congress would then formally approve the targets as a "monetary budget" along with the rest of the federal budget. In the heat of the reform debate, however, the proposal disappeared.[9]

The rising tide of stagflation, nevertheless, focused more congressional attention on the Fed. The Fed's independent ability to impose economic pain, even to cancel out congressional action, worried many members of Congress. Monetary economists, furthermore, argued that the Fed's penchant for fine-tuning tended to focus policy decisions on the short run, which produced unpredictable fluctuations in monetary policy and dangerous results in the long run.

These two very different complaints made strange bedfellows of populist members of Congress and monetarist economists. Both camps argued that the Fed should adopt and adhere to long-term (that is, more than six-month) monetary targets, but they agreed for very different reasons. Populists worried that the Fed was keeping rates too high. Public disclosure of its targets would allow congressional pressure for easier money. Monetarists, on the other hand, worried that fine-tuning was inherently dangerous. Monetary targets would force the Fed to keep to a more stable course, whatever the proper course. The pressure for monetary targets was not a purely American phenomenon; other western nations moved toward them at about the same time.[10] In the United States, however, the pressure for targets came from unusual allies. Recurring monetarist complaints provided intellectual support for the populists' pragmatic goal of forcing the Fed to lower interest rates. This strange union begat Congress's first concerted attempt since 1951 to assert its primacy over the Fed.

Reuss's goal was to set explicit interest rate targets for the Fed and to establish a time limit within which the Fed would be expected to meet those targets. To blunt Reuss's attack, Burns and his staff adopted a three-part strategy. First, if the Fed was to be forced to report to Congress, there had to be more than one monetary target. No one measure of money, Burns believed, was adequate to describe the condition of money and credit. Re-

9. See Weintraub, "Congressional Supervision of Monetary Policy," 343.
10. Monetary targets were adopted in Germany in 1974, France in 1976, and Britain in 1977. See Arnold J. Heidenheimer, Hugh Heclo, and Carolyn Teich Adams, *Comparative Public Policy: The Politics of Social Choice in Europe and America* (New York: St. Martin's, 1983), 148.

liance on only a single indicator would force the Fed to place inordinate weight on one measure to the exclusion of other equally important measures. That, he feared, would place the Fed in an impossible situation: pressure to meet its target, while the effort to meet the single target would create new economic problems. Burns insisted that the Fed itself define the indicators by which it would be judged.

Second, Burns wanted to insure that the Fed was not held directly responsible for the economy's performance—either over those portions it could influence or, particularly, over those portions it could not control. He wanted especially to insure that the Fed was not maneuvered into accepting responsibility for setting the level of interest rates, economic growth, or inflation. If the Fed were to be held to certain standards of performance, Burns preferred that they be measures like the money supply over which the Fed had more direct control. Finally, Burns insisted on a range instead of a precise target for each measure. He was doubtful of the Fed's ability to hit any target exactly, and he wanted to protect the agency's maneuvering room. In sum, if the Fed were to accept closer scrutiny, it would do so under Burns's terms, in ways that preserved as much flexibility as possible.[11]

Burns relied upon these principles to bargain with Proxmire in his efforts to frame a money growth resolution in the Senate Banking Committee. Proxmire pressed for the Fed to report "numerical target ranges with respect to the rates of growth of monetary and credit aggregates." Burns made a counterproposal that the Fed report instead on "general objectives and plans with respect to monetary and credit policy." Proxmire objected vigorously. "There is no reason to hold hearings about 'general objectives,'" he complained. "We already know what they are." Instead, Congress needed to know the specifics of the Fed's policy.[12]

Under the political pressure of rising rates, members of Congress were determined to increase their oversight of the Fed. Burns and his staff naturally were determined to minimize the damage. The staffs from the banking committees and from the Fed met in long negotiations and finally agreed to a much-weakened version of Reuss's original proposal. House Concurrent Resolution 133, passed on March 24, 1975, declared that Fed officials "shall consult with Congress" four times per year, twice with the banking committee of each house. Fed officials were to report on "objectives and plans

11. Interview with Arthur Broida, former secretary to the FOMC, July 16, 1984.
12. Memo, Proxmire to Senate Banking Committee members, March 10, 1975, Box B17, "Concurrent Resolution on Monetary Policy, 1975," Arthur Burns Papers, Gerald R. Ford Library.

with respect to the ranges of growth or diminution of monetary and credit aggregates in the upcoming twelve months."[13]

House Con. Res. 133 was a watershed in Fed-congressional relations, but the Fed had headed off the most threatening proposals. Instead of specific interest rate targets, Fed officials would report on their monetary growth targets, a goal one step removed from interest rates. The connection between monetary growth and interest rates would be up to the committee to divine. Instead of specific money supply targets, furthermore, the resolution required Fed officials to report on their "objectives and plans." Moreover, Congress established the reporting requirements by resolution, not by law. Fed officials could scarcely ignore it, but the resolution did not cement the procedures permanently in the statutes. However, for the first time Congress had voted to require Fed officials to testify regularly and publicly on past policies and future plans. Friedman called the resolution "the most important and the most constructive change in the structure for the formulation of monetary policy" since the Banking Act of 1935.[14]

Just what the resolution would mean depended on how Fed officials dealt with the new requirements. A confidential internal Fed staff memorandum laid out a three-pronged strategy that guided the Fed through the first hearings.[15] First, the staff recommended that Burns supply Congress with multiple targets. In framing policy, the Fed was already using M_1 and M_2 as well as a measure of bank credit. The staff suggested that the FOMC also begin incorporating even broader targets: M_3, M_4, and M_5. That would mean five different measures of money; the more targets the Fed reported, the harder the time members of Congress would have in trying to pin Burns down during testimony. Furthermore, the more targets the Fed used, the greater the odds that the Fed would hit at least one of them in the coming months. Second, the staff recommended that Burns report a relatively wide two-percent range for each money measure—the wider the targets, the easier to hit them.

Finally, in what was the memorandum's most clever tactic, the staff recommended that the Fed "roll the base." It was possible, the memorandum noted, to interpret the resolution as asking the Fed to project targets for the twelve months from the date of the hearing. Each new hearing—every four months—could thus produce a new set of targets, and Fed officials could bury any variance from earlier targets in the new base. It was thus

13. 89 Stat. 1194.
14. In U.S. Congress, Senate, Committee on Banking, Housing, and Urban Affairs, *Second Meeting on the Conduct of Monetary Policy*, hearings, 94th Cong., 1st sess., 1975, 34.
15. Memo, staff to FOMC, April 10, 1975, Box B17, "Concurrent Resolution on Monetary Policy, 1975," Burns Papers.

possible to hide mistakes in a new constellation of M's. With multiple measures of money, wide ranges, and a rolling base, the strategy was a masterpiece of obfuscation.

The strategy frustrated Reuss at the first hearing under the resolution. Burns noted the Fed's limited ability to influence interest rates and reiterated that no one measure of money was adequate. Instead, he presented five different targets for the coming year, but he also warned that velocity was more important than any of the money supply figures. *Velocity* is the technical term that describes the relationship between the money supply and the gross national product. It is based on the willingness of consumers to hold or spend money. The same dollar is spent over and over again during any year; the faster consumers spend a given dollar, the more any given level of the money supply increases economic growth. When pressed, however, Burns refused to reveal the velocity assumption the Fed had used to make the money supply projections. (Velocity is also a residual in the statistical relationship between the money supply and the gross national product. It thus stands for all other factors except the money supply that affect the GNP. Consequently, Burns's reluctance to discuss the velocity also gave him the flexibility to ascribe to these "other factors" any problems in achieving Congress's wishes on economic growth.) The committee's staff had been prepared for Burns's shadowboxing, and they had carefully rehearsed the majority Democrats to ask the chairman what the Fed's money targets would mean for the economy. Burns hedged, finally gave a "personal" view, but refused to state the Fed's official assumptions.

Reuss found both the substance and the style of Burns's testimony offensive. The chairman had cleverly avoided committing the Fed to anything. The multiple targets muddied the Fed's intentions, the argument about velocity made the relationship between the money supply and the economy uncertain, and the "personal" projections hid the Fed's official intentions. Reuss complained that the money targets seemed "too low" and would soak up extra money Congress was trying to make available through tax cuts. "Surely this way lies madness," he wrote Burns. In addition, he also pressed Burns for official, not personal, projections of the gross national product, unemployment, and inflation that the Fed expected would result from the money supply figures.[16] When Burns predictably refused, Reuss replied that he was "disappointed." The Congress, he avowed, "should not be kept in the dark about the choices now being made by the Federal Reserve."[17]

In the Senate Banking Committee, Proxmire did little better. "We don't

16. Letter, Reuss to Burns, July 31, 1975, Box O17, "Reuss 2–12, 1975," Burns Papers.
17. News release, August 27, 1975, Box O17, "Reuss 2–12, 1975," Burns Papers.

get any answer from you at all except a word description which can mean everything or nothing," he complained.[18] Burns steadfastly refused to accommodate what both committees considered the most important goal of the hearings: for the Fed to stipulate the connection between its decisions and their effects on the economy. He continued to make only personal projections. The reason, he told the committee, was that the FOMC consisted of twelve members, and "each of us reviews the evidence presented, adds to it, modifies it in his own fashion."[19]

The congressional committees were furious about the Fed's base-rolling tactic. In testifying against the practice, Milton Friedman charged that it effectively meant that the Fed was making projections for only the coming three months—until the next congressional hearing. Friedman feared that the Fed was reverting "to its old bad habit of extremely short-term planning" and abandoning "any attempt to determine its long-run course."[20] Burns, however, was pleased and he concluded that the resolution "has worked out quite well."[21] To Burns, of course, "working out well" meant that the Fed had figured out a way to keep its operating flexibility within the new regime.

The committees and their staffs, however, looked on this as but the first shot in the battle. They were not surprised that Burns had proved cagey (although they were taken aback at just how clever he had been), and they determined to continue to press Burns for more information. "There was a compelling need to get them [the Fed] to talk about their perceptions of the economy over a time period of more than three weeks," one congressional staff member explained. "It was part of the Patman tradition: to get them to divulge."[22] The real role of the hearings, in fact, was to provide an opportunity for members of Congress to lobby Burns and the Fed for the monetary policy they desired. In a delicate minuet, the questions and answers danced around fundamental economic questions. In 1977, for example, Proxmire clearly signaled Burns, "I'm very concerned about the Fed's desire to hold down interest rates." Burns replied, "I continue to hope that I can persuade you that we have been on a fairly sound track and that, if anything, our monetary policy has been excessively liberal." "Excessively liberal?" Proxmire shot back. "Well, you must have some—I don't know

18. U.S. Congress, Senate, Committee on Banking, Housing, and Urban Affairs, *First Meeting on the Conduct of Monetary Policy,* hearings, 94th Cong., 1st sess., 1975, 178.

19. In U.S. Congress, Senate, Committee on Banking, Housing, and Urban Affairs, *Third Meeting on the Conduct of Monetary Policy,* hearings, 94th Cong., 2d sess., 1976, 11.

20. In Senate Banking Committee, *Second Meeting,* 48.

21. In U.S. Congress, Senate, Committee on Banking, Housing, and Urban Affairs, *Fourth Meeting on the Conduct of Monetary Policy,* hearings, 94th Cong., 2d sess., 1976, 11.

22. Interview with the author.

what they are, but some good independent spirits on that Board of yours."[23] With his question, Proxmire told Burns that he would find little support for tighter money. In his reply, Burns intimated that easier money would have dangerous consequences. These passing signals helped define the politically acceptable boundaries on monetary policy.

In the next round, members of the House and Senate banking committees determined to pry more out of the Fed. They had three goals. First, they wanted Burns to state unambiguously the Fed's policy, without a rolling base and with clear targets not muddied by wide ranges. Second, they wanted the Fed to disclose—officially—the links between its money supply goals and the expected performance of the economy. Committee members naturally were interested far less in the target for M1 or M2 than in what the Fed's policy meant for the gross national product, unemployment, and inflation. Finally, they wanted to formalize the Fed's regular appearances by placing the reporting requirements permanently into law.

With the Federal Reserve Reform Act of 1977, Reuss accomplished the last objective by having the resolution's requirements passed into law.[24] A year later, Congress took up the other issues in debate over the Humphrey-Hawkins full employment bill. By 1978, the Fed's role in governing the economy, especially in influencing interest rates and creating jobs, was irrefutable and the Fed's critics were determined that the Fed be included in the bill.

As finally passed, Humphrey-Hawkins required Fed officials to explain how monetary goals fit the president's economic policy. In addition to the regular hearings required by the 1977 act, Humphrey-Hawkins mandated that, within thirty days of the president's transmission of his *Economic Report* to Congress, the Fed send Congress its own monetary policy goals and an explanation of how those goals related to the short-term objectives laid out in the *Economic Report*.[25] In semiannual reports, furthermore, the Fed was required to lay out the FOMC's "consensus" projection of the gross national product, inflation, and unemployment for the coming year. (Staff members from both sides worked out an understanding that the center of each range marked the Fed's official "best guess," not the chairman's "personal" projections.) The legislation also ended the Fed's more mischievous dodges, like rolling the base. These provisions were little noticed in the heated debate over the government's responsibility to insure full employ-

23. U.S. Congress, Senate, Committee on Banking, Housing, and Urban Affairs, *Fifth Meeting on the Conduct of Monetary Policy*, hearings, 95th Cong., 1st sess., 1977, 172.

24. 91 Stat. 1387.

25. "Full Employment and Balanced Growth Act of 1978," 92 Stat. 1887.

ment, but ironically they have had the most lasting impact. For the first time, Fed officials faced regular and permanent congressional oversight on the substance of monetary policy, how that policy matched fiscal policy, and what economic effects Fed officials expected these policies to produce.

Burns's fuzziness in testifying under these new requirements, however, quickly ended the marriage of convenience between populist congressmen and monetarist economists that had produced the legislation. The economists found the Fed's reports unconscionably mushy, "a disgraceful sham" and a smoke screen that "has not altered the conduct of monetary policy."[26] Monetarists were deeply disappointed that Congress had not forced the Fed to define and stick with more narrow monetary targets. Even though they had not won all that they had wanted, members of Congress were pleased that they had gained greater leverage over the Fed. The monetarists dejectedly countered that Congress had lost a golden opportunity to force the Fed away from its preoccupation with the short run.

In the face of congressional demands that the Fed show its hand on future monetary policy, Burns and his colleagues demonstrated great success in pruning away the proposals that most threatened the Fed's flexibility. Burns developed defensive maneuvers to blunt the most threatening congressional tactics. He deployed shields like multiple measures of money, with broad ranges for each, and technical jargon, like velocity and $M1$ and $M2$, that befuddled most members of Congress. His constant battles diluted the reforms that Reuss and Proxmire originally had in mind. Congress gained more information and the right to subject the chairman to regular harangues on the Fed's mistakes, but Burns protected the Fed from the most serious attacks. The Fed's opponents did not give up the battle over targeting, however. They also moved to force the Fed to disclose its debate and to open its books to congressional audit.

SUNSHINE AND AUDITS

During Patman's long vendetta against the Fed, he had argued that the Fed was a secret club operated for the benefit of bankers. When Reuss and Proxmire took up the campaign to open up the Fed, they found support from the growing post-Watergate movement to put all of government in the sunshine. Under proposals put forward by Senator Abraham Ribicoff (D-Ct.), the Fed was to be required to open its meetings to the public (although board members could close some meetings dealing with sensitive subjects),

---

26. David R. Meiselman, quoted in *Wall Street Journal*, March 22, 1984, 30.

to keep full transcripts of its deliberations, and to release promptly its policy decisions.

The plan predictably sent Burns to the barricades once again. Free and secret debate, the chairman proclaimed, was "a fundamental precondition" for effective monetary policy. Sunshine "would tend to inhibit free discussion and to make performers out of participants. It is naive to believe agency officials will debate publicly with the same candor and sense of mutual purpose with which they will debate in private."[27] Forcing monetary debate into the open, Burns warned "could do serious, perhaps irreparable, damage to our financial system."[28] Publication of the Fed's internal monetary policy debates would encourage speculation, while disclosure of discussions about bank regulation might weaken public confidence in some financial institutions. In a final stroke, Burns again wrapped the Fed in the Supreme Court metaphor. Fed officials, he said, had sought "to model our conduct" on the court, and like the Supreme Court, the Fed must deliberate with complete freedom—and secrecy.[29]

The issue was of fundamental importance to Burns. If the Fed were forced to announce its decisions immediately after making them and to disclose through transcripts the rationale for policy changes, it would be impossible to avoid tremendous immediate political pressure to change them. From the Fed's point of view, the existing system had an overwhelming advantage: the Fed's tradition of free and open debate, secret decisions, covert implementation, and fuzzy, jargon-filled explanation months after the event muddied the trail. Just what monetary course the Fed had set usually was apparent long after the decision was made—and after the policy was a fait accompli. Under that system, the Fed might sometimes face sharp criticism but never immediate pressure for reversing an unpopular decision. Burns feared that full disclosure would tie the Fed's hands, that it would limit the Fed's options to what it could in the short run sell politically. There could be no greater anathema to the Fed's priesthood, charged with protecting the nation's currency, and nothing was more antithetical to Burns's conviction about the need for flexible monetary policy.

The chairman launched a three-fold attack on the sunshine proposal. He first contended that the definition of a "meeting" required to be open was vague. Even a hallway conversation might constitute a "meeting" that required advance notice. The problem might be solved, he suggested, by

27. U.S. Congress, House of Representatives, *Government in the Sunshine*, hearings, 94th Cong., 1st sess., 1975, 134–35.

28. Letter, Burns to Ribicoff, June 17, 1975, "Arthur F. Burns (3)," William Seidman Papers, Gerald R. Ford Library.

29. May 22, 1976 speech, in Burns, *Reflections of an Economic Policy Maker*, 382.

excluding any discussions among agency officials, formal or informal, before the Fed made a decision. That, he said, would protect the board's collegial spirit. It also, from Burns's point of view, had the advantage of reducing "meetings" (and thus the requirements for transcripts) to the few minutes in which the board or FOMC took a vote.

Even that, Burns continued, might not be enough, since the administrative burdens of closing meetings covering sensitive subjects would be enormous. The subjects for which the Fed could close its meetings were constantly debated, but regardless of the terms, the board's staff worried that the requirement would produce "a plethora of weekly vote actions."[30] Each action to close even a portion of a meeting would require advance public notice of the meeting, a recorded vote to close the meeting for discussion of topics like monetary policy and discount rate changes, and a written explanation of why Fed officials had voted to close the meeting. That cumbersome process, the staff argued, might require up to twenty votes per week, each accompanied with written explanations. Not only was this an extraordinary burden, the Fed's staff contended, but it also opened the door to speculation. Fed-watchers might see in the closing of a meeting a clear signal that the Fed was considering a major policy change and might gain advantage in speculating against the shift.[31] Fed officials had struggled since the 1920s to insulate the agency's decisions from speculators, and they worried that the sunshine requirements would create an open season for speculators.

The transcript requirement, however, was the Fed's biggest worry. Burns believed that mandatory transcripts would "inhibit candor and free exchange of views." Even though the proposals would allow the Fed to edit out sensitive material, "the mere fact of a deletion in a transcript of a closed meeting could cause speculation or reveal sensitive information."[32] Since 1936, the Fed had kept detailed but secret "memoranda of discussion," near-verbatim transcripts detailing FOMC debates. In the mid-1960s, however, two events forced the Fed to change procedures. Wright Patman launched a sustained campaign for public access to the old transcripts. Meanwhile, in 1963, Milton Friedman and Anna Jacobson Schwartz published *A Monetary History of the United States*, a monumental study of American monetary policy since 1867. Much of the book was critical of the Fed's decisions,

30. Memo, O'Connell and others to Board of Governors, June 13, 1975, Box B53, "Government in the Sunshine, June 1975," Burns Papers.

31. Memo, Winn to Burns, May 21, 1975, Box B52, "Government in the Sunshine, May 1975," Burns Papers.

32. Letter, Burns to Bolling, April 23, 1976, Burns B53, "Government in the Sunshine, January–May 1976," Burns Papers.

and Fed officials decided that public release of old memoranda would help right the historical record. In 1965, the Fed released all "memoranda" for meetings before 1960 and announced a policy of releasing all subsequent transcripts after a five-year delay.[33]

From 1967 to 1975, the Fed waited ninety days to release FOMC decisions. To deflect congressional pressure for full disclosure, in 1975 Fed officials shortened the wait to forty-five days. That scarcely satisfied critics like Patman, who continued to press for immediate release of policy decisions and the memoranda of discussion. Burns not only countered that this would make the decision process "sterile" but also hinted that continued pressure might lead the Fed to end the practice of maintaining the transcripts.[34]

In the midst of the sunshine debate in 1976 came a lawsuit filed by a Georgetown University law student, David R. Merrill. He challenged the Fed's refusal to release immediately FOMC policy directives and the memoranda of discussion as a violation of the recently passed Freedom of Information Act. In *Merrill v. FOMC*, the federal district court agreed and concluded that the FOMC's 45-day delay in releasing policy decisions "cannot be equated with 'promptness' " required by the act.[35] At the next FOMC meeting, on May 18, 1976, the committee decided to change its procedures: to release policy decisions immediately after the following FOMC meeting, usually four to five weeks later. It also voted to discontinue the memoranda of discussion because of "the Committee's judgment that the benefits derived from them did not justify their relatively high cost."[36] The "high cost," of course, was more than financial; the *Merrill* decision demonstrated the Fed's legal vulnerability. The Fed thus switched to brief and fuzzy reports of its decisions and ended its transcripts. The Fed could not be forced to release minutes that did not exist.

The Fed's course predictably redoubled the determination of its opponents to open up the agency, not only to sunshine but also to congressional auditing. Since the late 1960s, Patman had pressed vigorously for legislation allowing the U.S. General Accounting Office, the auditing arm of Congress,

33. Roger S. White, "Public Access to Records of Federal Open Maket Committee Deliberations: Evolution of Policies Preceding the Decision to Terminate Maintenance of Detailed Records," Congressional Research Service Report, May 16, 1977, in U.S. Congress, House of Representatives, Committee on Banking, Finance, and Urban Affairs, *Maintaining and Making Public Minutes of Federal Reserve Meetings*, hearings, 95th Cong., 1st sess., 1977.

34. Letter, Burns to Patman, June 3, 1975, Box O16, "Patman 1975," Burns Papers.

35. 413 F.Supp. 494 (1976); the Fed appealed but the Court of Appeals sided with the lower court. See 565 F2d. (1977).

36. Board of Governors, *Sixty-third Annual Report, 1976* (Washington, D.C.: Board of Governors of the Federal Reserve, 1976), 217.

to audit the Federal Reserve Board and the reserve banks. At the same time, the GAO had under the direction of Elmer Staats increasingly shifted from narrow auditing of accounts to broader evaluation of federal programs. Patman's determination to bring the Fed to heel thus neatly matched the GAO's growing interest in examining the actual operation of federal agencies. Patman would have preferred to subject the Fed to Congress's annual appropriations process. He knew, however, that he stood little chance of gaining control of the Fed's budget and concentrated instead on the need to audit the Fed's books. In lively hearings conducted during 1971, for example, he grilled Fed officials for spending their money to pay for parking tickets, babysitters for senior staff members, and bowling shirts.[37]

Until 1933, in fact, the Fed had been subject to government audit. When Congress created the GAO in 1921, auditing of the Board of Governors was transferred to the GAO from the Treasury Department. The Banking Act of 1933, however, provided that the board's funds "shall not be construed to be Government funds or appropriated moneys."[38] In the wake of the Depression, Congress wanted to strengthen the Fed, and the committee report on the bill noted Congress's intent to allow the Fed to set its own management policies. This clause ended GAO's audit of the Fed. Since then the board's auditors had examined the books of the reserve banks, and since 1952 outside auditors had examined the board's own accounts.[39]

Patman, however, had never been satisfied by private audits. Without governmental review, he contended, the Fed "remains free from effective criticism" and operated with "arrogance bolstered by its shroud of secrecy." There was no reason, he said, to single the Fed out for special exemption from GAO auditing, and since it held about one-fifth of the government debt the lack of a government audit was a "disgrace." Patman viewed interest payments on the public debt a subsidy to the Fed, and he pointed out, "Without an audit, we do not know how the Federal Reserve spends this largesse from the taxpayers."[40]

"This was a matter when the Fed went to war," a former top Fed official said.[41] To Fed officials, an audit of Fed policy was simply unthinkable. They

37. U.S. Congress, House of Representatives, Committee on Banking and Currency, *Congressional Oversight of the Federal Reserve System*, hearings, 92d Cong., 1st sess., 1971, 44–45.

38. "Banking Act of 1933," Public Law 73-66, Sec. 6b.

39. From 1933 to 1952, audit teams from the reserve banks audited the board's accounts. See American Enterprise Institute, *The Federal Reserve Audit Proposal* (Washington, D.C.: American Enterprise Institute, 1975), 5.

40. "Memo to Persons Interested in a Full Accounting of Public Funds by All Public Agencies," December 15, 1973, Box B51, "GAO Audit, Nov.–Dec. 1975," Burns Papers.

41. Interview with the author.

feared such an audit would hopelessly politicize monetary policy and destroy the Fed's operating flexibility. If the GAO were limited to auditing administrative expenses, they worried about how to insulate the expense of making monetary policy from monetary policy itself. The auditing process, furthermore, might lead to the leaking of sensitive material. Members of Congress with an axe to grind, some Fed officials worried, might compromise the agency. The Fed often operated as agent for the Treasury Department and sometimes conducted transactions to support the dollar and other currencies. Disclosure of these operations might jeopardize important transactions at critical times. In addition, Fed officials worried that GAO investigations might disrupt the Fed's carefully cultivated relations with government securities dealers. The conduct of monetary policy often meant that the Fed might buy securities one day and sell them the next, or vice versa. Critics might suggest that such rapid buying and selling was nothing more than "churning"—engaging in rapid buying and selling to enhance the profits of the dealers, who earned a commission on each transaction.[42]

Although the Fed argued that a GAO audit would disrupt the very foundation of its operations, the proposal won widespread support. "The Fed is too important and powerful an institution to be exempt from independent outside auditing," the New York Times editorialized.[43] Patman applauded the Times and criticized Burns in a letter to the editor. Summoning the ghost of Watergate, Patman charged that "Chairman Burns espouses the very kind of secretive, unaccountable government decision-making that has recently so shocked the American public." Patman's letter also confirmed Burns's worst fears. GAO audits, Patman wrote, would determine whether Burns was right in arguing that the Fed was not contributing to inflation.[44] If populists had their way, it was unlikely that the GAO would stop at examining administrative expenses.

To block the GAO audit proposal, the board's staff suggested the Fed begin by persuading members of Congress that GAO audits would inevitably produce leaks that would reflect badly on Congress itself. The staff wanted to convince members of Congress "that they can exercise oversight in matters of policy directly rather than through GAO."[45] The second part of the strategy was to marshal the Fed's supporters to try to defeat the entire

42. Memo from Alan Holmes, March 18, 1974, Box B51, "GAO Audit, Jan.–Apr. 1974," Burns Papers. See also "Background Paper," September 18, 1973, Box B50, "GAO Audit of the Federal Reserve, [Jan.] 1972–Sep. 1973," Burns Papers.

43. New York Times, October 26, 1973, 42.

44. New York Times, November 8, 1973, 46.

45. Memo, Cardon and Hackley to Burns, April 7, 1972, Box B50, "GAO Audit of Federal Reserve System, [Jan.] 1972–Sep. 1973," Burns Papers.

proposal or, if that failed, to support a weakening amendment by Congressman Thomas L. Ashley (D-Ohio) that excluded GAO from monetary policy.

This involved a detailed lobbying plan. Burns was to contact key members of Congress and congressional committee staff, Treasury officials, members of the Business Council, and reserve bank directors and "friends." Other members of the board and staff were assigned to enlist the help of former Fed chairmen and secretaries of the Treasury. The staff of the Fed's press office was to place background "horror stories" in the *Wall Street Journal,* the Washington *Post,* the New York *Times, Business Week,* and *American Banker.*[46] The staff of the Philadelphia Federal Reserve Bank reported it had contacted thirty members of Congress from the district, and the president and chairman of the Atlanta bank came to Washington for on-the-spot lobbying. Burns himself lobbied more than twenty-five members of the House.[47]

The Fed's campaign produced a flood of mail to members of Congress. One banker complained, for example, that a GAO audit "would be the first and irreversible step toward the destruction" of the Fed's independence from the political arena.[48] Meanwhile, Fed officials arranged joint statements from former secretaries of Treasury and Commerce as well as former chairmen of the Council of Economic Advisers. Four former Commerce secretaries, members of both parties, stated that GAO audits would amount to "Monday morning quarterbacking" that "would encroach upon the independence of Federal Reserve decision-making." They concluded, "It is essential to retain the non-partisan approach that the Federal Reserve has followed in both domestic and international monetary affairs."[49] Thus, while Fed officials pressed hard to stop the audit, they tried to keep their efforts subtle to avoid being charged with "public lobbying."[50]

When the issue came to a vote, their efforts paid off. They were forced to their fallback position—Ashley's amendment limiting GAO audits to ad-

46. "Outline of Contacts and Projects on GAO Audit Issue," October 1973, Box B50, "GAO Audit, Oct. 1–10, 1973," Burns Papers.

47. "Contact List," March 1974, Box B-51, "GAO Audit, Jan.–Apr. 1974," Burns Papers; and letter, Burns to Carl Albert, November 1, 1973, Box B51, "GAO Audit, Nov.–Dec. 1973," Burns Papers.

48. Letter, Howard F. Still to Thomas L. Ashley, October 11, 1973, Box B51, "GAO Audit, Oct. 11–31, 1973," Burns Papers.

49. Telex, John T. Connor, Alexander B. Trowbridge, C. R. Smith, and Peter G. Peterson to Congressmen Albert, Ashley, O'Neil, and Madden, October 22, 1973; see also John W. Snyder, Robert B. Anderson, C. Douglas Dillon, Henry W. Fowler, Joseph W. Barr, David M. Kennedy, and John B. Connally to Carl Albert, October 18, 1973; and letter, Paul McCracken, Raymond Saulnier, Arthur Okun, and Walter Heller to Congressmen Albert and Ford, October 1973; all in Box B51, "GAO Audit, Oct. 11–31, 1973," Burns Papers.

50. "Summary of Reserve Bank Conference Call," February 6, 1974, Box B51, "GAO Audit, Jan.–Apr. 1974," Burns Papers.

ministrative expenses—but they were able to win passage of his plan to weaken the audit bill. When the bill reached the Senate, Fed officials were able to keep it bottled up. The session ended before the Senate acted. Patman, of course, was furious that the Fed had rolled over him. He complained to Burns, "It is becoming apparent that the Federal Reserve is orchestrating a large-scale lobbying campaign." The very existence of such lobbying convinced Patman that an audit was even more necessary so that Congress "may have the unvarnished facts."[51]

The Fed stopped Patman again in 1975, this time in the House Rules Committee, but after new members of Congress deposed the aging chairman, Congressman Reuss and Senator Proxmire began a full-court press against the Fed. A 1976 congressional study of financial institutions produced a multi-part plan.[52] First, the report suggested presidential appointment and Senate confirmation of reserve bank presidents, who were currently appointed by the Federal Reserve Board. Because the reserve bank presidents, as members of the FOMC, voted on monetary policy and were thus governmental officials, they ought to be subject to the appointment process. Second, the study argued that the Fed chairman's term ought to be coterminous with the president's. That would allow the president to appoint a chairman in concert with his own plans soon after taking office. In addition, the congressional plan would have required the Fed to make projections of interest rates, subjected the Fed to GAO audits, and forced the Fed to comply with sunshine provisions.

Burns and other Fed officials viewed the new plans as an all-out assault that would "politicize" the Fed.[53] The Fed launched an even more aggressive lobbying campaign with the reserve banks and other "friends." The Fed's congressional liaison office worked especially hard with the Fed's allies in the House, especially senior members of the Banking Committee like Garry Brown (R-Mich.) and William Stanton (R-Ohio).[54] The Fed energized its effective lobbying machine, an operation that ranged from grass-roots pressure engineered by the reserve banks and their directors to Burns's personal contacts with members of Congress and the White House staff.

The lobbying campaign annoyed Reuss as it had Patman. He complained that "the Fed has gone well beyond the bounds of propriety" in developing

---

51. Letter, Patman to Burns, October 31, 1973, Box O15, "Patman, June 1972–Dec. 1973," Burns Papers.

52. See U.S. House of Representatives, Committee on Banking, Currency, and Housing, *Financial Institutions and the Nation's Economy (FINE)*, report 94-1073, 1976.

53. Memo, Guenther to Burns, April 27, 1976, Box B77, "Legislation," Burns Papers.

54. See, for example, memo, Guenther to Burns, September 8, 1977, Box B51, "GAO Audit, June 1976–June 1977," Burns Papers.

"a well-orchestrated lobbying campaign." After applying incessant pressure, Reuss wrested from the Fed copies of the minutes of reserve bank board meetings. He was enraged to find that board members had suggested that the board members campaign against the GAO audit. Worse yet, from Reuss's point of view, was a reference to a speech made by Robert W. Lawson, chairman of the Richmond reserve bank's board. "The bankers in our district and elsewhere did a tremendous job in helping to defeat the General Accounting Office bill," Lawson said, according to the minutes. "It shows what can be done when the bankers of the country get together."[55] To a populist, no statement could be more inflammatory than a suggestion that bankers were banding together to frustrate Congress. Reuss charged the Fed with "a pattern of disdain for public accountability," and "a history of behind-the-scenes manipulations to ward off legitimate investigations by the Congress."[56]

Burns was at his best in replying to the charges. It would be "presumptuous and stupid and certainly improper," he said, if the Fed attempted to apply pressure to members of Congress. However, there was nothing wrong when individuals communicated their views to Congress, especially when those individuals were directors of the reserve banks and influential members of their communities. Burns wryly added, "My impression is that the Members of Congress want to hear from their constituents."[57] The Fed's second great defense had a double effect. When Reuss discovered the pattern of the Fed's political activities through the reserve bank minutes, he became even more convinced that Congress had to subject the Fed to GAO audits. The Fed, however, mustered such strong political support that any frontal assault on the institution's autonomy was bound to fail.

In 1976, Congress finally passed the "Government in the Sunshine Act," but the Fed won exemptions from open meeting requirements that rivaled those for national security.[58] The Fed could close any meeting if the discussion covered information whose disclosure could lead to speculation or could endanger the stability of financial institutions. The danger of speculation, of course, is perhaps the oldest Fed hedge against public disclosure, and the defense served the Fed well in the sunshine act. Nearly anything discussed either at board or FOMC meetings could lead to speculation—a hint of concern about inflation that might signal tighter money to come, or worries about unemployment that might mean the Fed was poised to loosen

55. Statement in House Banking Committee, *Maintaining and Making*, 85–89, especially p. 87.
56. Ibid., 83.
57. Ibid., 58.
58. PL 94-409.

the money supply. Burns and his staff had thus fashioned a cover broad enough to hide all of the Fed's discussions.

Furthermore, the act did not require transcripts be kept for any meeting closed under the act. That saved the Fed from the other threat of sunshine, and the Fed's memoranda of discussion permanently died. Proxmire suggested that the Fed, "in the spirit of the new Sunshine law," release FOMC decisions immediately, but Burns politely refused.[59] The Fed thus succeeded in completely blocking the application of the sunshine law to its own procedures. In fact, as a result of *Merrill*, Reuss's leak of the reserve bank minutes, and continuing congressional pressure for release of records, members of Congress ended up with even less information when the Fed ended production of the FOMC memoranda.

The Fed was not quite as successful in blocking the GAO audit bill. In 1978, Congress gave GAO the right to audit the Fed, but efforts by two of the Fed's allies, Congressmen Brown and Stanton, significantly weakened Reuss's original proposal. They successfully pressed an amendment to limit the GAO to examining administrative expenses. The amendment specifically prohibited the GAO from auditing international transactions, monetary policy, and FOMC activities, and it had safeguards preventing the disclosure of information.[60] More than a decade of continuous congressional campaigning, first by Patman and then by Reuss and Proxmire, finally did produce a GAO audit bill, but the version that emerged from Congress was toothless. Congress established its right to subject the Fed to audit, but its members refused to approve an audit of the Fed's core functions.

DEFLECTING ATTACK

Never before in the Fed's history had the agency suffered such prolonged and serious congressional attack. Under Burns, the Fed had a series of close calls with interest rate ceilings, audits, sunshine, and targets. A special and largely underestimated threat was the GAO audit, which struck at the Fed's budgetary independence. Leverage over how the Fed spent its money could easily translate into leverage over monetary policy.[61] The reporting requirements were a more obvious problem for the Fed. Perhaps the Fed's greatest bureaucratic advantage was its opportunity to debate, frame, and implement

---

59. Press release, October 8, 1976, Box O16, "Proxmire, Dec. 1975–Dec. 1976," Burns Papers.

60. "Federal Banking Agency Audit Act," PL 95-320.

61. See U.S. Congressional Budget Office, *The Budgetary Status of the Federal Reserve System* (Washington, D.C.: Congressional Budget Office, 1985), 17.

policy in relative secrecy (and then of course to mask what it had done in abstruse language). Peeling back that cover would have meant a fundamental change in the Fed's organizational character.

In response to these challenges, Burns unceasingly struggled to maintain the Fed's flexibility. He argued continually, "the genius of monetary policy—its great virtue—is that it is flexible."[62] Part of his rationale was the constant criticism raised by the Fed's opponents. Like any bureaucracy, Fed officials valued their autonomy. Especially during the 1970s, however, the Fed's motives ran deeper. Fiscal policy had become hamstrung between ever-greater entitlements and presidential-congressional battles that limited its maneuverability. The economy refused to behave according to established theory, while greater burdens for stimulating economic growth as well as maintaining price stability fell on the Fed. The greater the uncertainty, the more Burns and his colleagues resisted congressional strictures. Furthermore, as the Fed's importance rose, so too did the political attention focused upon it. Burns sought a policy that provided maneuvering room for gingerly balancing competing political demands and constituencies in the midst of unprecedented uncertainty.

Although most Fed officials supported Burns's drive for flexibility, some of them feared that his aggressive and pedantic style invited congressional attack. Former governor Andrew Brimmer blamed Burns's prickliness in large part for the legislation, and he contended that "it wouldn't have happened under Bill Martin," who, he believed, could have dampened the congressional fires.[63] Burns was often provocative with members of Congress, and as Governor J. Charles Partee described Burns's congressional testimony, "He would sometimes view a question as an opportunity to have a lesson taught."[64] Burns awed both the staff and members of Congress, and even his most consistent foes acknowledged that he displayed "great skill." They also felt, however, that Burns engendered "a combination of fear and loathing on Capitol Hill. He wore his disdain for Congress on his sleeve."[65] His demeanor convinced many members of Congress that only formal congressional action would bring Burns to heel. In perhaps the harshest indictment of Burns, former Fed staff member James Pierce asserted that Burns "left the Federal Reserve a weaker institution than he found it."[66]

62. U.S. Congress, House of Representatives, Committee on Banking, Currency, and Housing, *Federal Reserve Consultations on the Conduct of Monetary Policy (Second Quarter 1976 to Second Quarter 1977)*, hearings, 94th Cong., 2d sess., 1976, 13.
63. Interview with the author, June 22, 1984.
64. Interview with the author, June 22, 1984.
65. Interview with the author.
66. Pierce, "The Political Economy of Arthur Burns," 485.

There was little question that Burns's irascible style aggravated the congressional attack on the Fed. Indeed, many members of Congress viewed the proposals as an opportunity to teach Burns a lesson and to curb the Fed. Yet in the face of unprecedented problems and enormous congressional restiveness, most of the Fed's flexibility remained intact when Burns left the chairmanship in 1978. In the midst of a sweeping movement to expose all of government to public view, he won the strongest exemption provided any agency in the Freedom of Information and Sunshine acts. Fed opposition neutered the GAO audit bill, and instead of establishing a single target with which to judge monetary policy, Congress retreated to five targets with broad ranges for each. Even one of Burns's archrivals, Henry Reuss, grudgingly admitted that the chairman "was a superb lobbyist, and he didn't want to make the Fed look foolish. He wanted to make the targets so broad that even a drunken sailor could hit them."[67]

Given the peculiar economic problems of the 1970s, any Fed chairman would unquestionably have faced harsh congressional scrutiny. Undergoing its own identity crisis, enmeshed in Watergate and reform of the budgetary process, Congress boasted many critics but few leaders with firm ideas about what to do about the economy. Monetary policy rose to high importance, and for the first time the Fed stood alone in the sustained public spotlight. In the face of great problems coupled with great uncertainty, Fed-baiting and -bashing was undeniably attractive to members of Congress.

In dealing with these pressures, Burns was a daunting figure on Capitol Hill. As a distinguished economist with substantial government experience, his voice was always one with which to be reckoned, even if his opponents did not want to hear it. His personality, furthermore, contrasted sharply with his irascible reputation. He was personally charming and an impeccable gentleman. One long-time friend, in fact, said Burns never failed to step aside to allow him to enter an elevator first, even though the chairman greatly outranked him. Burns was convincing and persuasive, especially in one-on-one lobbying, even if his self-assured economic lectures grated on his foes. He did not suffer fools gladly, however, and he had little hesitance in upbraiding anyone who questioned his judgment on the basis of what he considered to be inadequate knowledge.

The Fed's congressional relations, furthermore, were built on much more than Burns's contacts. The agency fielded an impressive lobbying organization. A full-time congressional liaison staff kept careful note of the emerging shape of legislation and maintained constant communication with

67. Interview with the author, March 9, 1984.

committee staffs. The liaison staff regularly obtained leaked copies of proposed legislation, the latest rumblings on new proposals, and box scores of likely votes, both on the floor and in committee. Its negotiations were crucial in winning the Fed extra maneuvering room in meeting the targets as well as the sunshine and audit requirements. Moreover, Burns and his staff spent a great deal of time cultivating key allies on the banking committees. In a pinch, these members could be counted on to defend the Fed, to propose weakening amendments, and to do battle with the Fed's populist adversaries. The Fed's congressional liaison officer noted in 1977 that Congressman Stanton, a key member of the House Banking Committee, "has been spending a lot of time and effort on our behalf." About another key committee member, however, he warned, "Apparently Garry Brown's nose is badly out of joint—he feels he is being cut out of the action."[68]

The Fed, furthermore, was extremely effective in marshaling its friends across the country. When the battle lines were drawn, Fed officials enlisted powerful allies like former cabinet secretaries and chairmen of the Council of Economic Advisers. They arranged for favorable stories in the financial press. And perhaps most importantly, they unleashed considerable pressure from the directors of the reserve banks, 275 of the most powerful bankers, manufacturers, and leading citizens located across the country. Fed officials learned the danger of being too aggressive in mobilizing pressure, but members of Congress learned as well the depth of the Fed's political support.

Members of Congress have never consistently demonstrated much understanding of or interest in monetary policy. The Fed has long been skillful in cloaking central banking in great mysticism, with talk of multiple M's and velocity and price deflators.[69] Since the 1951 accord, however, members of Congress have gradually recognized the increasing power over the economy that the Fed holds. As figure 1 shows, congressional interest in the Fed (as measured by bills affecting the Fed that members have introduced) has gradually risen since 1951. The relationship is strong and statistically highly significant.[70] Of even greater interest are the three sharp spikes in the figure, each one coinciding with a notable period of tight money: the Fed's campaign to keep down the inflation unleashed by the Vietnam war; its efforts

68. Memo, Guenther to Burns, April 27, 1977, Box B19, "Congressional Liaison Memos, Sep. 1977," Burns Papers.

69. See, for example, James L. Pierce, "The Myth of Congressional Supervision of Monetary Policy," *Journal of Monetary Economics* 4 (1978): 363.

70. In this times-series linear regression of the increase of Fed-related bills (and resolutions) introduced from 1951 to 1983, r-squared for the model is 0.4316. The constant is -76.227; $B = 1.485$ ($p < 0.001$). The number of bills introduced is derived from U.S. Congress, Library of Congress, *Digest of Public General Bills with Index*, various years.

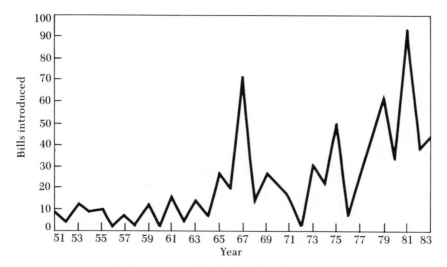

Figure 1. Congressional Interest in the Fed, 1951–1983

to rein in the economy during the Ford presidency; and the Fed's brief experiment in monetarism from 1979 to 1982 (which I will explore in the next chapter). Congressional interest in the Fed has thus been steadily rising over time.

Congressional concern has tended to be greatest when interest rates have been highest. Congress has long been a populist bastion in defense of low interest rates, and anti-inflation campaigners like Senator Paul Douglas have been rare. As figure 2 shows, congressional concern about the Fed has largely been a function of the level of interest rates. The relationship is extremely strong and statistically very significant.[71] When points on figure 2 deviate from the overall trend, furthermore, they tend to deviate on the high side—at times when interest rates increased suddenly and members of Congress demanded immediate action. In 1967, for example, the jump of interest rates to more than 5 percent, compared with less than 3 percent when the Kennedy administration took office, produced more than seventy bills dealing with the Fed. Tight money in the late 1970s produced the same effect. Congress thus has over time begun paying more attention to the Fed, but there is nothing like a sudden increase in interest rates to bring the Fed sharply to the public—and thereby to the congressional—eye.

71. Using the level of interest rates (as defined by four- to six-month prime commercial paper) to predict the number of Fed-related bills (and resolutions) introduced in Congress (from 1951 to 1983) produces an r-squared of 0.5561. The constant is -5.045; $B = 4.907$ ($p < 0.001$). The number of bills introduced is derived from U.S. Congress, Library of Congress, *Digest of Public General Bills with Index*; interest rates are compiled from *Federal Reserve Bulletin*, various years.

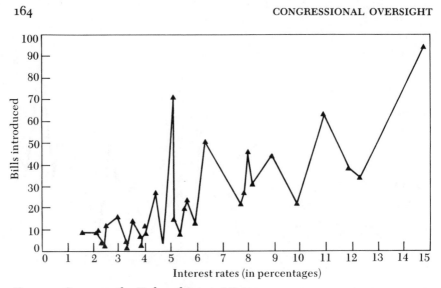

Figure 2. Congress, the Fed, and Interest Rates

Even in the midst of their deepest worries about the Fed, however, members of Congress have been unwilling to do much to rein it in. Especially during the 1960s and 1970s, members of Congress had both the motive and the opportunity to tell the Fed exactly what to do. Through all the vigorous debates, however, Congress never defined the aggregates on which the Fed was to report, narrowed the ranges within which its policy was acceptable, or specified the goals it was to seek. As James Pierce, one of the Fed's steadiest critics, reluctantly concluded, Congress "has showed little interest in providing meaningful oversight of monetary policy."[72]

Instead, former Fed congressional liaison Ken Guenther contended, Congress "preferred having the Fed there as an institution to be scapegoated."[73] Indeed, congressional action has been a strange amalgam of constant complaint punctuated by calls for the chairman's impeachment, reluctant acknowledgment of the need to restrain the economy, and a strong incentive to keep congressional fingerprints off the tools of restraint. Even when the angriest Fed-watchers launched their strongest attacks on the Fed's autonomy, they could not convince their colleagues to take a forceful stand. Just as in the original debate establishing the Fed, Congress could not bring itself to articulate clearly just what the Fed ought to do.

Members of Congress proved unable to put the Fed under final attack.

72. Pierce, "The Myth of Congressional Supervision of Monetary Policy," 364.
73. Interview with the author, June 7, 1984. Compare Edward J. Kane, "Politics and Fed Policymaking: The More Things Change the More They Remain the Same," *Journal of Monetary Economics* 6 (1980): 199–211.

The agency's principal antagonists—Patman, Reuss, and Proxmire—never had a sense for the jugular. When the Fed was on the ropes, especially when interest rates hit record highs, they never went in for the kill. In part this was due to the Fed's skill at sliding out from under the next punch, but this was also due to their inability to muster sustained, broad congressional interest in the Fed.

Congress's problems reflected the central, recurring political problem of monetary policy in the United States: the difficulty of reconciling the conflicting goals of price stability and economic growth, a difficulty aggravated by the harsh political costs of trying to define the trade-off. The inability of members of Congress to decide just how the Fed ought to conduct monetary policy, to land a powerful blow in the bout over the Fed's independence, demonstrated once again the tremendous political advantage of an independent central bank. Members of Congress could complain, criticize, and even force Fed officials to explain more clearly what they were up to. When members of Congress could not define precisely what they wanted, they left the decision once more to an "independent" agency whose job it was to balance the political pressures facing it.

This scarcely suggests, however, that the Fed ended the decade with its autonomy untouched. Congress insisted on limiting the Fed's flexibility by requiring a GAO audit and by establishing new reporting requirements. Far more important than the formal requirements, however, was the rising level of congressional attention to the Fed and the new pattern of interaction established by the reporting requirements. For the first time, the Fed chairman was required to appear regularly on Capitol Hill, to explain (even if vaguely) the Fed's intentions, and to subject himself to cross-examination.

The result was testimony rich in explicit and implicit political messages, in both directions. Members of Congress could take advantage of the chance to tell the Fed—and the wider financial audience—that they were getting nervous about tight money. The Fed chairman, on the other hand, could hint that lower interest rates might follow if Congress reduced a growing deficit. The hearings, furthermore, became a forum in which Fed officials could send powerful messages to a broader public. Financial reporters carefully probed the chairman's testimony for hints of future action, so the sessions became an important medium for affecting expectations, not only of financiers but also of consumers.

As a result, members of Congress could explore their newly acquired taste in monetary policy, a new opportunity for exercising influence. For Fed officials, the hearings provided a chance to direct a spotlight on a Congress usually reluctant to tackle hard fiscal choices. The most important product of congressional reforms in the 1970s, however, was not so much a formal change in congressional oversight but the development of a new and subtle political arena. It was an arena of which Fed officials had to take careful account in framing monetary policy, but it was also an arena in which Fed officials could communicate their position on monetary and fiscal policy to a wider audience, one that embraced the government, the financial community, and the public.

CHAPTER SEVEN
THE SHIELD OF FLEXIBILITY

Jimmy Carter came to office in 1977 committed to stimulating the economy and ending the decade's pattern of deep recessions and slow recoveries. With the help of his advisers, Carter developed a collection of spending programs, especially for jobs in public works; a tax cut, including a $50 rebate for taxpayers; and easier monetary policy to keep interest rates down. The Fed's cooperation in the strategy was crucial. Without it, the administration could put extra money into the economy only to have the Fed soak it back up through tight money. Inflation remained high, and if Burns and his colleagues worried more about that than stimulating economic growth the president's plan would be in serious trouble. Carter's staff knew just how important it was that the president and the chairman looked on economic problems the same way. A campaign issue paper on the Fed argued, "It is important that throughout a President's term he have a chairman of the Federal Reserve whose economic views are compatible with his own."[1]

Relations between Carter and Burns got off to a bad start. Burns had been annoyed by what he called Carter's "very careless statements about the Federal Reserve during the campaign."[2] The Fed chairman also viewed the economy's problems differently. He did not agree with Carter's advisers that the economy's sluggishness could be cured by government spending. Instead, Burns believed that the slow recovery had its roots in the psychology of recession and high inflation that had been fed by the economy's wide swings during the 1970s. Businessmen were hesitant to invest for fear the economy would dip downward again or that inflation would wreck their

1. Quoted in U.S. Congress, Committee on Banking, Finance, and Urban Affairs, *Federal Reserve Reform Act of 1977*, hearings, 95th Cong., 1st sess., 1977, 2.
2. Interview with the author, June 27, 1984.

plans. Burns worried that Carter's program would make things worse by convincing businessmen that the federal government would worsen inflation by beginning a new round of stimulative programs. Burns was convinced that the president should have concentrated more on providing tax cuts to businesses to revive their confidence and to provide incentives for them to invest.

This debate soon became moot, for within a few months both Carter and the Fed were worried about different problems. The economy was gathering steam on its own, and the president decided that his $50 rebate was no longer needed. By this point, though, members of Congress had been attracted to the idea of stimulative spending programs, and they added their own plans to the president's proposal. The growing deficit made Fed officials even more concerned about inflation. Rising demand for credit to finance the business expansion, meanwhile, put even more pressure on interest rates. For the Fed to accommodate the demand for credit risked making inflation worse; for the Fed to tighten money risked lowering confidence in the president's program.

Although Burns leaned toward tightening the money supply in meetings with CEA and Treasury officials, as well as with the president, he was careful not to tip his hand. He did not have the same relationship with Carter that he had established with Gerald Ford, and Burns retreated to the style he had used during the Nixon years. He vigorously preached the gospel of flexibility and independence. At a 1977 commencement address at Jacksonville University, Burns said, "The capacity of the Federal Reserve to maintain a meaningful anti-inflationary posture is made possible by the considerable degree of independence it enjoys within the government."[3]

Carter administration officials found Burns's public pronouncements and private inscrutability frustrating. They countered with a message tacked on the bulletin board of the White House press room on October 20. Since January, the Treasury's 90-day bills had increased from 4.3 percent to 6.28 percent, the "notice to the press" said, and this had "unsettled the stock market." Furthermore, there was concern that "if short-term interest rates were to increase" further, it might "reduce the supply of funds for housing" and drive long-term interest rates up.[4] The financial press immediately took the "notice" as a direct warning to Burns. When questioned by reporters, however, the White House quickly backed off. "We goofed," one senior official said. "I can give you absolute assurances that we had no intention of sending messages to the Fed." Many observers were convinced

3. Burns, *Reflections of an Economic Policy Maker*, 419.
4. Quoted in *National Journal* 9 (October 29, 1977): 1700.

nevertheless that some administration officials had indeed intended to signal the Fed but had underestimated how their message would be received. Financial reporters concluded that the administration lacked a subtle touch and had fumbled.[5]

Administration officials suffered growing frustration with Burns. They found him inscrutable in private meetings, and his speeches were embarrassing them in public. As his term as chairman drew to an end, therefore, White House officials wanted to replace him, but they found strong support for Burns in the business community. Henry Kaufman, chief economist for the investment banking house of Salamon Brothers, argued, "The chairman has become, more than any other person in the U.S., the symbol of economic integrity and security."[6] Even his critics admitted that "monetary policy was Burns."[7] However, one White House adviser asked: "What do we want, stability or progress? If we keep him, we would be sending the wrong signal. It would mean that we are sticking with the status quo because we don't know what else to do."[8]

Carter and his advisers finally decided they could not work with Burns and could not risk keeping an unpredictable anti-inflation zealot. Early in 1978, Carter determined not to redesignate Burns as Federal Reserve Board chairman and replaced him with Textron chairman of the board G. William Miller. Compared with the thoughtful, pipe-smoking Arthur Burns, Miller was a take-charge executive who immediately sought to transform the Fed's discussions from a university-style seminar into business-style, goal-oriented decisions. He attempted to ban smoking from the board room, a sharp change from Burns's pipe-smoking habits, and he brought a three-minute egg timer to limit discussions. According to a former top Fed staff member, he saw the Fed "as a diversified conglomerate of which he was chairman of the board."[9]

The financial markets surged on the confidence Miller's business background inspired, and one influential banker said, "He's bulletproof." His initial relations with the White House were good, and his go-go management style broke a congressional roadblock on several pieces of banking legislation. By the end of the year, though, his armor started to rust. Inflation again threatened to run out of control, and apparently in response to administration pressure to keep monetary policy loose, Miller voted against a Fed decision to increase the discount rate. No one within the Fed could

5. Washington *Star*, October 22, 1977, A3.
6. Quoted in *National Journal* 9 (July 2, 1977): 1042.
7. Pierce, "The Political Economy of Arthur Burns," 485.
8. Quoted in Business Week, November 21, 1977, 108.
9. Cary Reich, "Inside the Fed," *Institutional Investor* (May 1984): 139.

remember a chairman ending up on the losing side of such a decision, and his embrace of easier money in the face of inflation worried financiers. *Fortune* tagged him "a fainthearted inflation fighter."[10]

By early 1979, in fact, even administration officials had become convinced that OPEC oil price increases made tighter money necessary. They believed Miller erred by keeping monetary policy too loose. CEA Chairman Charles Schultze and Treasury Secretary W. Michael Blumenthal in April began a calculated series of leaks and interviews to pressure the Fed to tighten. It was, as the *Wall Street Journal* christened it, the "world turned upside down": the only episode in the Fed's history in which administration officials pressured the Fed for tighter, rather than easier, money.[11] Schultze leaked a story to the Washington *Post*, while Assistant Treasury Secretary Daniel H. Brill told the New York *Times* that "with businesses scrambling for materials," the time was ripe for tightening. "This is the kind of thing," Brill said, "monetary policy can work on in the short run."[12] Blumenthal told a trade group in Dallas that the country "must take the risks entailed in maintaining and, if necessary, intensifying our anti-inflation measures."[13]

Miller laughed the stories off. "There must be some lower-echelon people who are leaking their bankrupt ideas to the papers," he told the Washington *Post*. "They're wasting their time if they think they can get the President to pressure the Fed. The President is committed to an independent Fed— he's told me so repeatedly." And, he added, "pushing interest rates up won't help bring down either food or energy prices."[14] It would be dangerous, he further contended, to tighten money because economic growth was slowing. Miller was partially right, for Carter stopped the pressure-by-leak campaign. When the president learned of it, he sent strongly worded letters to Schultze and Blumenthal ordering them to stop it. (Putting the orders in writing, of course, guaranteed still more leaks to the press and further embarrassment to the administration.)[15] Carter's letters publicly silenced his administration critics but scarcely calmed their uneasiness. Inflation was becoming the administration's deepest domestic worry.

Miller found support within the Fed waning as well. To outflank opponents who were arguing for tighter money, he took the highly unusual step of calling the press in advance to tell them how an FOMC meeting would

10. *Fortune*, December 31, 1978, 40.
11. *Wall Street Journal*, April 2, 1979, 26.
12. New York *Times*, April 12, 1979, 1. Compare the Schultze oral history in Hargrove and Morley, eds., *The President and the Council of Economic Advisers.*
13. Washington *Post*, April 11, 1979, A2.
14. Washington *Post*, April 15, 1979, F1.
15. See *Wall Street Journal*, April 17, 1979, 3; and April 27, 1979, 1.

come out. It would have been hard to find a step that ran more against the grain of the Fed's tradition of free and secret deliberation, and his tactics angered fellow board members. The egg timer became the symbol of Miller's attempt to impose a corporate model on a collegial board, and that strategy lost the support of the board and its staff. Board members complained, "He didn't seem all that interested in the details of monetary policy." In fact, a senior Fed staff member said, "He wasn't even interested in the questions."[16] Over the short run, relations with Congress improved, but Miller lost the confidence of the administration and of his colleagues at a time of ever-growing economic problems.

After cooling briefly, inflation by early summer 1979 rebounded to double-digit levels. Carter's chief domestic policy adviser, Stuart E. Eizenstat, said that the anti-inflation score was inflation 99, the administration 1 (with a weak agreement from the retail clerks' union to abide by the administration's anti-inflation guidelines the president's only tally).[17] The struggle with inflation was only one of the president's mounting problems, and in July 1979 the president went to the Camp David retreat for self-study. He came down from the mountain to proclaim a national "crisis of confidence," which reporters quickly rechristened "malaise." Carter announced that he intended to take forceful action, and to back up his words he fired three cabinet members, including Treasury Secretary Blumenthal. The president asked Miller to take the job, which simultaneously rid him of a cabinet secretary he had found difficult and a Fed chairman who had lost his base of support.

The dramatic strategy backfired. Many financiers saw Carter's game of musical chairs as a sign of weakness, not strength. Furthermore, many foreign financiers were deeply suspicious of Miller's inflation-fighting resolve, and they worried that he would be even more dangerous as Treasury secretary. Within days of the speech and cabinet shift, a major run on the dollar began in the international financial markets. Carter quickly needed to send a signal that he would not surrender to inflation, and the most obvious way to do that was with an appointment to the vacant Federal Reserve Board chairmanship. The president needed a chairman who was demonstrably not under his thumb, someone with an impeccable anti-inflation pedigree, and someone whose reputation would quickly settle the international currency markets. At the same time he naturally wanted a Fed chairman who would not be so independent that the administration would be in the dark about the Fed's intentions or that administration officials

16. Interview with the author.
17. Leonard Silk, *Economics in the Real World* (New York: Simon and Schuster, 1984), 148.

would have no influence. Carter's advisers, in short, did not want to appoint another Arthur Burns.

Some of Carter's closest confidants, furthermore, had another problem. White House adviser Hamilton Jordan and Carter's old friend Bert Lance were southern populists who believed in fiscal conservatism but easy money. That made the job of finding an acceptable Fed chairman even harder. For external consumption, he had to have a sound international reputation as an inflation-fighter, and he could not be viewed as a pushover for White House views. On the other hand, for White House purposes, he could not be too independent or too strict a believer in wringing out inflation through tight money. To make matters worse, the run on the dollar meant that Carter would have to name a new Fed chairman quickly.

On everyone's list of candidates was Paul Volcker, president of the Federal Reserve Bank of New York. Volcker had begun his career with a summer job at the Fed between college and graduate school, and after earning a master's degree in public administration at Harvard in 1951, he began to work as an economist at the New York Federal Reserve Bank. He later became vice-president at Chase Manhattan Bank and served in the Treasury under Kennedy, Johnson, and Nixon. Volcker had distinguished himself in 1971 when, as undersecretary of the Treasury for monetary affairs, he managed the delicate process of removing the system of fixed exchange rates. He was favored on all sides because of his experience in both Republican and Democratic administrations. Indeed, Henry Fowler, Treasury secretary under Lyndon Johnson, had pressed then Treasury Deputy Undersecretary Volcker for the Fed chairmanship in November 1965, near the end of one of William McChesney Martin's terms. [18] Volcker quickly became the leading candidate, and when Carter named him Fed chairman the international currency markets quickly breathed a sigh of relief and settled back down.

The new chairman was a political cartoonist's dream. He was a towering figure; indeed, he had played basketball at Princeton as an undergraduate. His balding head and large cigars made him an easy target. The image could not have been more different from his predecessor's. Indeed, Volcker "was born to be chairman of the Fed," an old friend said. "It was as though somebody had trained all his life to play the piano and now was finally allowed to play the best instrument in the world."[19]

Along the way, Volcker had developed a unique view of controlling inflation through monetary targets. The new chairman agreed with monetarist economists at least to the point that money mattered. Keeping to monetary

18. Memo, Fowler to Johnson, November 10, 1965, WHCF EX FG233, Johnson Library.
19. First Boston economist Albert Wojnilower, quoted by Reich, "Inside the Fed," 139.

targets as required by Congress, he explained in a 1977 paper written while he was still president of the Federal Reserve Bank of New York, was first of all "a useful tool of communication to the public," since it represented the Fed's expectations about inflation. To Volcker, monetary targeting was "a new, and in many ways, more sensible and comprehensible symbol of responsible policy." Monetary targets thus produced an "announcement effect" that communicated the Fed's policy plans and imposed self-discipline in the growth of the money supply.[20]

While acknowledging that the money supply and its targets were important, however, Volcker refused to embrace them as the Fed's sole guide. Many nonmonetary factors—economic, social, and political—not under the Fed's control also affected the economy, he believed: "It seems to me the essence of policy making in these circumstances is that judgments must be made in the presence of uncertainty."[21] Before coming to the chairmanship, Volcker had developed an approach he called "practical monetarism": recognizing that monetary growth mattered, that the announcement of monetary targets affected public expectations, that hitting the targets made the Fed's policy credible, but that the economy's tremendous uncertainty made it essential for the Fed to retain "the right to change the targets in the light of emerging developments."[22] This "practical monetarism" was to guide him and the Fed through years of sometimes overpowering uncertainty.

AN EXPERIMENT IN MONETARISM

Volcker had little time to learn on the job. The gasoline shortage crisis at first produced a sharp drop in business activity that rapidly slowed the economy. By the end of September, however, the economy was recovering more quickly than anyone had expected. Retail sales jumped sharply and consumers borrowed wildly to spend. Savings dropped and the gross national product jumped 2.5 percent in the third quarter of 1979. The price indexes rose into the double-digit range as the economy rapidly moved from slump to boom.

Fed officials worried that the boom had an unhealthy base: consumers were borrowing and spending from their savings to buy before inflation

20. Paul A. Volcker, "The Role of Monetary Targets in an Age of Inflation," paper presented at a panel discussion on "Congressional Supervision of Monetary Policy," Annual Meetings of the American Economic Association, December 30, 1977.

21. Ibid.

22. Paul A. Völcker, "The Contributions and Limitations of 'Monetary' Analysis," remarks before the Joint American Economic Association and the American Finance Association luncheon, September 16, 1976.

pushed prices still higher. Both businessmen and consumers were starting to behave as if inflation were inevitable as they hurried to beat the next round of price increases. The problem for the Fed—and especially for Paul Volcker as its new chairman—was how to apply the brakes: to slow the boom, to cut inflation, and restore stability to the dollar without crippling the economy. Volcker had, of course, the familiar Fed toolbox, which relied on moderating such booms by nudging interest rates upward. In conducting policy, Fed officials had traditionally set targets for interest rates and then had managed open-market operations to try to hit those targets. Studies by the Fed's staff showed Volcker and his colleagues that by moving interest rates high enough they could slow inflation.

In 1979, however, Volcker and the Fed's staff doubted that would work, for they had come to believe that there was a bias toward setting interest rate targets too low. As the economy was becoming more volatile, it was harder to predict what effect any level of interest rates would produce. There was a natural tendency, therefore, not to squeeze the economy any harder than necessary to slow inflation, and this had meant that the Fed sometimes did not squeeze hard enough.

Furthermore, as the Fed's experience since the late 1960s had demonstrated, strong attempts to slow the economy through substantially higher interest rates hit some sectors of the economy much harder than others. Some businesses, like the automobile and housing industries, are especially sensitive to the level of interest rates, and they tend to get hit first and hardest by the Fed's tight money policy. The Fed's goal, of course, was to slow the economy as a whole, not to punish a few sectors. Fed officials therefore worried about what damage a new round of high interest rates might inflict on already-troubled industries.

Fed officials had often found themselves under heavy pressure to lower interest rates before they had stayed high enough long enough to reach desired effects. Sometimes that occurred because interest-rate-sensitive industries began showing severe distress. Sometimes members of Congress campaigned against a Fed that, they believed, tended always to push interest rates too high. Sometimes presidents valued economic growth more than control of inflation. For a variety of reasons, Fed officials keenly felt the political constraints on a policy of tight money.

To make matters worse, the Fed was losing credibility. Although Congress had required the chairman to report money supply targets, the Fed conducted its day-to-day operations by focusing on interest rate targets. Over the past few years, the Fed had often missed the money supply targets badly. At the same time inflation was starting to run out of control. In late

1978 and early 1979, the Fed had done better, but after mid-1979 the money supply again spurted rapidly above the top of the target range. For the narrowest measure of money, M1, the Fed had announced a target of 3 to 6 percent growth for the year. In the third quarter of 1979, M1 was growing at an annual rate of 9.5 percent. To bring inflation under control meant bringing money growth back down to the Fed's target, and that, top Fed staff members concluded, required "a considerable slowing."[23]

Since he doubted that the Fed could effectively use interest rate targets to produce that deceleration, Volcker decided that the Fed needed a new strategy. He assigned top Fed staff members to develop a proposal: to try to control inflation by controlling the growth of money instead of by controlling interest rates. In a background memo prepared for FOMC discussion, the staff members argued the need for "containment of inflationary psychology." They expressed concern that the Fed's inability to hit its money supply targets was causing consumers to fear that the Fed would accommodate rather than fight future inflation. Switching to a money growth strategy would improve the Fed's implementation of monetary policy, the staff members reasoned. It would be easier to hit the money supply growth targets and, indeed, "announcement of such a shift in procedure may itself have a beneficial calming effect on inflationary psychology."[24]

Fed staff members had been studying such a change for a long time, and officials from the Federal Reserve Bank of St. Louis had been saying for years that a switch to the monetarist course would improve monetary policy. In the autumn of 1979, however, the time was ripe for a shift in strategy. The boom was gaining strength and inflation quickly worsened. Inflation was making investors less eager to hold the dollar and, as investors lost confidence in the dollar, there was feverish speculation in gold. In late September, shortly after taking office, Volcker met with international financiers who said that they were reluctant to take any further steps to shore up the dollar until the United States got a grip on its inflation.[25] "It seemed to me," Governor Charles Partee said later, "that we were on the border of an almost classic situation of losing confidence in the currency."[26]

Volcker decided it was time for quick action, and he summoned the FOMC to Washington for a highly unusual Saturday meeting on October 6, 1979. After the secret session, he held a news conference to announce that the Fed had decided to move with all three of its policy tools. First, the

23. Stephen H. Axilrod and Peter D. Sterlight to FOMC, October 4, 1979, 3.
24. Ibid., 1.
25. William C. Melton, *Inside the Fed: Making Monetary Policy* (Homewood, Ill.: Dow Jones-Irwin, 1985), 43.
26. Quoted by Woolley, *Monetary Politics*, 104.

Federal Reserve Board voted to allow reserve banks to increase their discount rates from 11 to 12 percent, a new record. Second, it voted to establish new reserve requirements to restrain the growth of bank credit. And
most importantly, the board decided to change its method of open-market
operations. Instead of trying to stabilize the level of interest rates, the board
decided to concentrate on controlling the supply of bank reserves. The move
was more than just a signal of tighter money. It was a historic shift in
operating procedures, a shift that appeared to embrace the prescriptions of
monetarists who for decades had criticized the Fed for its fixation on interest
rates.

In a speech to the American Bankers Association several days later,
Volcker explained that the Fed needed to change policy to break inflation
and to restore "stability of expectations." He told the bankers, "This is a
time of testing—a testing not only of our capacity collectively to reach coherent and intelligent policies, but to stick with them."[27] More than anything else, Volcker wanted to demonstrate the Fed's resolve, and at this he
succeeded. At first the financial markets concentrated on the discount rate
and reserve requirement changes, but it soon became apparent that the
shift in operating procedures was the keystone of the strategy. Volcker
shocked financial observers so deeply, in fact, that some of them speculated
that the Fed's surprise announcement was a panicked response to pressure
from Europeans at his meetings the previous week. In fact, the basic work
on the policy shift was finished before Volcker left for the continent.

Economically it was perhaps the worst time for a shift to money supply
targets, as Carter administration officials pointed out to Volcker in private
meetings. Banks had shown remarkable imagination in insulating themselves from the unprecedented crush of inflation, and investors had a wide
variety of investments—including NOW accounts (negotiable order of withdrawal accounts, which acted like interest-bearing checking accounts) and
money market mutual funds (which served a similar purpose)—to help them
deal with rising prices. Because of these new accounts, it was becoming
harder to measure what "money" was and how changes in some kinds of
money, especially checking accounts, translated into changes in economic
growth.

Politically, however, it was perhaps the best time to introduce the change.
It was a time of tremendous economic difficulties, both at home and abroad.
It was a time when these difficulties would unquestionably require higher
interest rates. It was a time when the president was strongly committed to

27. "A Time of Testing," remarks before the American Bankers Association, New Orleans,
La., October 9, 1979.

stopping inflation. And it was a time when the Fed needed to demonstrate its resolve.

Volcker's move to monetary targets was a masterpiece of political leadership. After having been sharply criticized for a decade for making inflation worse, the Fed gained intellectual capital by adopting the reforms long proposed by its most vocal critics. The Fed's October 6 decision thus bearded the monetarist lion. It was also a bold move to restore the Fed's credibility by demonstrating that the agency was serious about inflation-fighting. During the 1970s, as the economy staggered through simultaneous sluggish economic growth and persistent inflation, Chairmen Burns and Miller attempted to attack both problems. Volcker's strategy was a signal that the Fed was breaking from that balancing act and was instead making the defeat of inflation its top and unchallenged priority.

The money supply target strategy also had an important implicit advantage for Fed officials. Staff analyses had demonstrated that to end the inflationary spiral, interest rates would probably have to rise at least to 15 percent. A year before, a White House official had said that the administration would be in "duck soup" if interest rates reached only 8 percent.[28] To reach and sustain rates twice that high thus would mean enormous political risk for the Fed. (The staff's estimates greatly underestimated just how persistent inflation would be. In the end, interest rates soared to more than 20 percent.) Volcker and his colleagues knew that it would be hard to reach a consensus within the Fed for such harsh measures and to maintain enough political support long enough to produce results.

Even though they never made the case publicly, Fed officials realized that conducting monetary policy through money supply targets would allow them to raise interest rates without having to do so directly. Instead, they could slow the growth of money, hit the announced money supply targets, and allow the market to determine the level of interest rates that would result. As Governor Henry Wallich explained: "Basically, we needed higher interest rates. I doubt that they could have been achieved by decision [that is, by traditional interest rate targeting]. But by putting the decision in the hands of the market and allowing things to take their course, that was more acceptable."[29] Governor Nancy Teeters was more direct: "It was a camouflage for raising interest rates," she told a reporter.[30]

Volcker thus set a course for a dramatic increase in interest rates without stating that he was doing so. His signal contribution to the economic policy

28. *Business Week*, May 29, 1978, 22.
29. Interview with the author, August 9, 1985.
30. *Journal of Commerce*, February 28, 1984, 6A.

debate was his diagnosis—that inflation was the country's top domestic problem—and his strategy—tight money. He recognized that if inflation was to end, the Fed would have to lead the attack, and if the Fed's attack was to be successful, Volcker needed a credible plan. At a time when both Carter and the Congress were immobilized on economic policy, Volcker was one of the few Washington officials with any plan. He cleverly developed tactics to help build a consensus with the Fed for the plan and, at the same time, to deflect direct attack about high interest rates from the Fed's door.

The Fed's experiment in monetarism made Paul Volcker the most influential figure in the American economy—so much so, in fact, that the chairman often became exasperated with the conventional wisdom that he personally determined the level of interest rates. (At one congressional hearing, Senator Jim Sasser [D-Tenn.] attacked Volcker's policies and declared, "I would urge you to push the button to lower short-term interest rates."[31]) Volcker and his cigar became the symbols of economic management, and his power grew enormously in government and financial circles.

Despite the rising interest rates, Volcker enjoyed generally good relations with the Carter White House. The Quadriad met quarterly, and meetings between Volcker and the Treasury and the Council of Economic Advisers continued in the established pattern. For their part, Carter's advisers found relations with Volcker better than with Burns or Miller—not because they liked Volcker's policy, because no president likes going into an election year with rising interest rates, but because Carter and his advisers had decided they needed to control inflation even more than to support economic growth. Volcker enjoyed at least tacit White House support for his strategy and, more importantly, the White House did not subject him to public attack that would have undermined public confidence in the difficult process of wringing out inflation. The overall level of communication was high, and White House officials were not surprised by the steps Volcker took.

These relatively close relations eroded, however, as the presidential election approached and interest rates soared. The prime rate leaped from 11.5 percent in the summer of 1979 to historic highs of more than 20 percent near election day. To make things worse, the record rates produced little immediate impact on prices. The consumer price index increased from 11.3 percent in 1979 to 13.5 percent in 1980. Carter had the misfortune of running for reelection as interest rates were at their peak and inflation had not yet started to break. Under the pressure of the campaign, he lost his patience with Volcker during a question and answer session with residents

31. Washington *Post*, February 17, 1983, A1.

of Lansdowne, Pennsylvania on October 2, 1980. In answer to a query about the Fed's policy, Carter replied, "My own judgment is that the strictly monetary approach to the Fed's decision on the discount rate and other banking policies is ill-advised." He concluded, "I think they put too much of their eggs in the money supply basket."[32] When pressed later, Carter refused to back off the criticism and passed orders to his aides not to soften the language.

Given the charges about slow economic growth that Ronald Reagan leveled at Carter during the 1980 presidential campaign, Carter was remarkably subdued in discussing the Fed. In part this was because it is always tough in inflationary times for any official to attack the Fed, for such attacks only suggest that political resolve in the war against inflation is weakening. The problem is even worse for Democratic candidates, for just as Republicans remain chained to the legacy of Herbert Hoover, Democrats live in the shadow of Lyndon Johnson's inflation. In part this was also because Carter had no economic policy alternative but Volcker's tight money. Ronald Reagan's promise of new leadership and a vigorous economy fueled painlessly by tax cuts—what former CEA chairman Herbert Stein called "the economics of joy"—found an enthusiastic audience.[33]

REAGANOMICS AND VOLCKER

For newly elected President Ronald Reagan, the Fed was even more important than it had been for Carter. His economic program had two parts: a fiscal component, based on a dramatic tax cut, intended to boost economic growth; and a monetary component, based on slow and steady money growth, intended to wring out inflation. In part this emphasis on steady monetary growth was a reflection of Reagan's concerns about inflation, and in part it was a result of heavy pressure from monetarist economists who had gained key positions in the administration. Early in the administration, for example, Treasury officials wrote Reagan: "There is no way the President can carry out the main points of his administration . . . unless the Federal Reserve provides the right kind of monetary policy. The right policy is stable, moderate and predictable money growth." Such a course would reduce uncertainty about the Fed's future activities, Treasury officials advised the president, and prepare the base for economic recovery. "There is no

32. *Public Papers of the Presidents, 1980,* 2040–41.
33. Stein, *Presidential Economics,* 235.

excuse for failure," the memo concluded. "If the Fed fails, the Reagan administration fails."[34]

Even nonmonetarists within the administration argued the central importance of monetary policy to the Reagan agenda. One of the administration's strongest voices, David Stockman, who was to become director of the Office of Management and Budget (OMB), suggested in his manifesto, "Avoiding a GOP Economic Dunkirk," that the White House (in concert with Congress) provide political protection for the Fed in return for stable policies and stable prices. The Fed, he concluded, was "the critical linchpin of the whole program" for economic recovery."[35] Volcker's money supply strategy thus matched the incoming administration's goals, and the Fed enjoyed support in the president's first months.

By mid-1981, however, some officials were growing restive. "The administration had no idea," Assistant Treasury Secretary Paul Craig Roberts wrote later, "that the Federal Reserve was about to slam on the brakes and throw us all through the windshield."[36] Fed policy stayed extremely tight throughout 1981 and into 1982, and interest rates remained at more than 20 percent through most of 1981. Inflation proved stubborn; it slowed only slightly from 13.5 to 10.4 percent, while unemployment grew to near 10 percent in the worst recession since the Depression. Not until 1982 did the inflation rate convincingly head downward, to 6.1 percent for the year. Interest rates for 1982 retreated to about 11.5 percent by the end of the year, but unemployment hovered near 10 percent for the year.

Administration officials began attacking the Fed, not so much because of its tight money policy but because they believed that the Fed was applying it incompetently. Leading monetarist economists shared their criticism. Karl Brunner and Allan H. Meltzer pointed out that the Fed had badly missed its money targets—by more than 2 percentage points for one measure—and that, while the Fed's new policy had produced "tactical improvements," it had not produced more fundamental changes in Fed strategy.[37] From week to week the money supply figures were erratic, and some administration economists (especially the monetarists) feared that such instability would not convince skeptical consumers that inflation would be brought under control. It was, in their view, the worst of both worlds: tight money

34. Quoted by Paul Craig Roberts, *The Supply-Side Revolution: An Insider's Account of Policymaking in Washington* (Cambridge: Harvard University Press, 1984), 116.

35. David Stockman, "Avoiding a GOP Economic Dunkirk," Washington *Post*, December 14, 1980, C5.

36. Roberts, *The Supply-Side Revolution*, 148.

37. Karl Brunner and Allan H. Meltzer, "Strategies and Tactics for Monetary Control," in *Carnegie-Rochester Conference Series on Public Policy* 18 (Spring 1983): 97–98.

that kept interest rates high, but uneven money growth, which did not sufficiently discourage inflation.

In January 1982, President Reagan echoed their criticism in complaining that an upsurge in the money supply "sent the wrong signal to the money markets," a signal of weakening resolve against inflation that was helping keep rates higher than they otherwise would be.[38] Treasury Secretary Donald Regan followed the same theme in testifying before the Joint Economic Committee: "The erratic pattern of money growth that occurred in 1980 and 1981 contributed to the onset of the current downturn." There was almost no money growth in most of 1981, he said, but beginning in October the money supply spurted ahead. Such criticism was highly unusual from the president and his chief advisers, for rarely before had top officials complained about the *implementation* of Fed policy instead of its content. "They [the FOMC] don't seem to be able to be very precise about what they are doing," Secretary Regan elaborated.[39] Volcker replied that keeping money growth stable was a difficult job in the short run. He counterattacked, furthermore, by arguing that the huge budget deficit created by the administration's tax cuts was making inflation-fighting ever more difficult.

Members of Congress, meanwhile, were becoming restive about the high interest rates. Henry Reuss used his position as chairman of the Joint Economic Committee to urge the Fed to loosen its "super tight" monetary policy. The alternative, he threatened, might be credit controls and "political dismemberment of the Federal Reserve System."[40] House Majority Leader James C. Wright (D-Tex.) joined conservative supply-sider Jack Kemp (R-N.Y.) in calling for Volcker's resignation. That, in fact, was one of the few things that congressional Democrats and Republicans could agree on in 1982. Congressman Kemp argued that the Fed was sloppy in its management of money; the answer, he suggested, was less discretion for the Fed, less governmental involvement in fixing the supply of money, and a return to the gold standard to stabilize the dollar. Even Senator Edward Kennedy (D-Mass.) joined in the attack, for different reasons and with a different remedy. The Fed, he said, was too tight; the solution, he said, was more government involvement through credit controls and mandatory easing of tight money.

As the recession deepened in the late spring of 1982, congressional signals to the Fed became more explicit. In June, the House and Senate budget

38. Washington *Post*, January 20, 1982, A1.
39. U.S. Congress, Joint Economic Committee, *The 1982 Economic Report of the President*, hearings, 97th Cong., 2d sess., 1982, 197, 228.
40. Washington *Post*, March 16, 1982, A2.

committees agreed on a warning to be attached to the First Budget Resolution: "It is the sense of the Congress that if Congress acts to restore fiscal
responsibility and reduces projected budget deficits in a substantial and
permanent way, then the Federal Reserve Open Market Committee shall
re-evaluate its monetary targets in order to assure that they are fully com-
plementary to a new and more restrained fiscal policy."[41] It was an unprecedented congressional directive on monetary policy. Even though the Fed
scarcely needed to worry that the proviso would become effective—Congress was in no danger of demonstrating fiscal responsibility by narrowing
the budget deficit—the message was unmistakable. From both the right and
the left, members of Congress were uniting in opposition to the high interest
rates and unemployment that resulted from monetarism. If the Fed pressed
ahead, it could expect ever-growing congressional attack.

At the same time, the economic situation was proving troubling to Fed
policymakers. Forecasts had predicted that the economy would turn up in
1982, and manufacturers had begun increasing production in expectation of
higher sales. Consumers, however, were not buying. Fed officials feared
that the mounting inventories might trigger another downswing and, even
worse, greater pessimism about the economic future.

On July 19, the first signs of a crack in the wall of tight money appeared.
The Fed lowered the discount rate from 12 to 11.5 percent, and analysts
widely interpreted the decision as a signal of easier money. In the eyes of
many members of Congress, however, money was not easy enough. Even
though interest rates had started to ease downward, "real" interest rates
(the difference between interest rates banks charged and the rate of inflation)
remained at historic highs. In early August, Senate Minority Leader Robert
Byrd (D-W.Va.) called "sky-high interest rates" the nation's "public enemy
no. 1," and he introduced a bill cosponsored by thirty other Democrats to
order the Fed to bring down interest rates to within 4 percent of the inflation
rates.[42] The bill had no serious chance of passage in the few weeks before
the congressional mid-term election, but several members of Congress made
no secret that they viewed the bill as a shot across the Fed's bow. Kennedy
hoped that it might at least force the Fed to "abandon this academic, ex-
perimental monetary policy."[43]

To make matters worse, consumers were not converting their money into
goods and services as Fed officials had expected. According to the Fed's
models, certain money levels ought to produce certain levels of economic

41. Sen Con. Res. 92.
42. Washington *Post*, August 4, 1982, D7.
43. *Wall Street Journal*, August 4, 1982, 3.

growth (that relationship, as we have seen, is the "velocity" of money), but the Fed's money targets were producing lower levels of economic growth than Fed officials intended. In part this was because new kinds of money were changing the composition of the money supply. More than $100 billion had flowed into the new NOW accounts. The Fed counted these deposits as part of M1 and assumed that the money was available for immediate purchase. Many consumers, though, seemed to be using the accounts as a form of savings, so they did not fuel economic growth in the same way as did checking accounts. Furthermore, since inflation had decreased, consumers no longer seemed in the same rush to spend their money before prices rose more. As a result, they held on to money longer before spending it. The Fed's money supply strategy thus produced lower economic growth than intended.

That framed a hard choice for Volcker and his colleagues. The Fed's change in operating procedures had unquestionably helped lower inflation. To stick with the procedures past mid-1982 seemed to many Fed officials to risk plunging the nation even deeper into an already painful recession. To abandon them, however, risked igniting again the inflationary expectations that the Fed had worked so hard—and the economy had suffered so greatly—to uproot. Stephen H. Axilrod, the Fed's staff director for monetary policy, argued that the Fed's willingness to stick with the procedures despite the deep recession "greatly increased the Federal Reserve's credibility in fighting inflation."[44] Fed officials puzzled over how to ease off the brakes without unloosing inflation once again, and without damaging their painfully rebuilt credibility as well.

This puzzle was nearly as challenging as the one Volcker tackled upon taking office. In October 1979, he needed a strategy for restraint so dramatic that the public would be forced to change its expectations about the inevitability of inflation. In October 1982, he needed to find a way to ease the money supply without signaling that the Fed was returning to business as usual after three painful years of high interest rates and low economic growth. On October 7, just a month before the election, the FOMC voted to ease money growth to try to bring interest rates down. At the same time, the committee backed away from money supply targeting because the main measure of money (M1) was undergoing immediate change. More than $31 billion of special tax-free All-Savers certificates were about to come due and would suddenly pour into checking and savings accounts, and that sudden flood of money would cause the Fed to overshoot its target for M1 if it

44. Stephen H. Axilrod, "U.S. Monetary Policy in Recent Years: An Overview," *Federal Reserve Bulletin* 71 (January 1985): 18.

took the target seriously. Volcker therefore announced the Fed's action as a temporary change: it would "de-emphasize," at least temporarily, the most narrow measure of money (M1) and focus instead on broader measures (M2 and M3) that included savings accounts and certificates of deposit as well as cash and checking accounts.

FOMC members had decided that continuing to follow the M1 targets would produce interest rates that were too high and economic growth that was too slow. The maturing of the All-Savers certificates gave them a technical reason to edge away from the M1 targets. At the same time, Fed officials did not want to appear to be retreating from their war on inflation. Volcker therefore announced the shift as a purely technical maneuver that did not change the Fed's fundamental strategy. The Fed, he told corporate executives in a speech soon afterward, remained committed to holding down inflation and was "continuing to restrain the growth of money."[45] Investors nevertheless saw the shift as a harbinger of easier money to come and the stock market celebrated with a big advance. The prime rate at major banks dropped as the Fed reduced the discount rate from 10 to 9.5 percent.

Volcker used the shield of flexibility to guide the Fed through unprecedented challenges. After the Fed for decades had fought against monetarism, he embraced it when it promised protection for a dramatic increase in interest rates. When in 1982 the costs of continued allegiance to monetary targets seemed too high, Volcker pleaded once again the need for the Fed to apply its judgment to economic problems. When he testified before the Joint Economic Committee on November 24, 1979, Volcker engaged in a masterpiece of "Fedspeak." The process of strengthening the economy's growth, he said, "necessarily involves continuing judgments about just what growth . . . is appropriate in the short and longer run." He told the committee, "Unfortunately, the difficulties and complexities of the economic world in which we live do not permit us the luxury of describing policy in terms of a simple, unchanging numerical rule." The chairman told the committee that "the broad framework of monetary targeting has been retained, but greater emphasis is for the time being placed on the broader aggregates."[46] From that statement, it was hard for Fed-watchers to determine if the Fed had renounced its earlier strategy, if it had embarked on a short-term departure from it, or if it had developed a new hybrid approach. The ambiguity of Volcker's remarks quite intentionally left his listeners uncertain about what the Fed would do next. The message of easier money and lower interest rates, however, was unmistakable.

45. Washington *Post*, October 10, 1982, A1.
46. Testimony reprinted in *Federal Reserve Bulletin* 68 (December 1982): 747–50.

The Fed proved indeed to be the linchpin of the Reagan administration's economic program, although not in the way the president's advisers had planned it. The administration's tax cut did not produce the economic growth it had promised, deficits soared instead of shrank, and inflation proved far harder to break than anyone had anticipated. Throughout the heavy political barrage, administration officials for the most part resisted the lynching atmosphere that arose in Congress, and Reagan was careful not to allow any sustained attack on the chairman.

Volcker's strategy had strong supporters within the administration, particularly in the Office of Management and Budget and Council of Economic Advisers. Officials there believed that the Fed's tight money policy prevented the huge federal budget deficits from fueling an even worse recession. Volcker often found himself at loggerheads with Treasury Department officials, many of whom were monetarists who believed he had applied monetary theory badly. These opponents, however, had trouble marshaling any alternative to the Fed's policies. Reagan seemed well pleased with the drop in inflation, and he had the good fortune of running for reelection in 1984 as the economy was rebounding smartly from the painful recession at the beginning of his term.

Administration officials thus often quibbled with Volcker but had no basic policy disagreement. Volcker did not always follow the monetarist prescription with the same ideological zest some Treasury officials would have preferred, and he was subjected to constant second-guessing by officials who thought they could do the job better. Restoration of business confidence in a new economy free from inflation, however, was perhaps the central economic goal of the early Reagan years, and more than anyone else Volcker was responsible for what economic success the administration achieved in its first term.

That success occurred largely on Volcker's terms. For the first time in the Fed's history, its chairman controlled the agenda for macroeconomic policy. He had in 1979 pushed control of inflation to the keystone of economic policymaking. He followed that by developing a strategy to break inflation, and he succeeded in winning political support for it. Ronald Reagan's tax cut was perhaps the most important fiscal policy decision since the beginning of the Vietnam war, but once Congress passed it into law the federal budget no longer had any flexibility for managing the economy. That task, especially the attempt to manage economic cycles, fell instead to Volcker and the Fed. Volcker's quick success in reducing inflation, although accomplished by painful steps, gained him and the Fed invaluable credibility. Then, as Reagan and Congress tackled the deficit, Volcker's leadership role grew. The Fed had unquestionably come to dominate the making of macroeconomic policy.[47]

Throughout the difficult effort to eradicate inflation the traditional contacts continued. Volcker met with Reagan in the usual Treasury lunches, and there were weekly breakfasts with officials from the Fed, Treasury, OMB, CEA, and the Commerce and State departments. In contrast to the Carter administration, however, in the Reagan White House the Quadriad was not a regular feature. Reagan met rarely with Volcker, and apparently never met alone with him. In part this was due to press speculation about the Fed's gumption in sticking to the tight money policy; when Volcker did visit the White House, members of the press speculated that the president was applying pressure for lower interest rates.

In large part, however, the lack of regular meetings can be attributed to strong political factors. The president apparently had little interest in economics or economists and had little stomach for one-on-one meetings with the chairman. In this Reagan was much different from Nixon, Ford, and Carter, who took a keen interest in the Fed's activities. He was, instead, more like Johnson and Eisenhower, who preferred to keep their economics and Fed chairmen at arm's length. The Fed's political distance from the president, moreover, was also an important political asset for Reagan, for it meant that the president could avoid a direct link to high interest rates and the great suffering they brought.

In early 1983, as Volcker's term as chairman neared its end, the chairman's tight money policies created new debates. Some Treasury officials lobbied against his reappointment on the grounds that the Fed's stop-go policies had worsened the recession and had kept interest rates high. Supply-siders in Congress like Jack Kemp joined the Treasury side in the fray and demanded that Volcker step down. Others in the administration urged Alan Greenspan's candidacy. Greenspan had been chairman of Gerald Ford's CEA, and he had the virtue of embracing Republican orthodoxy and the old-time balanced budget religion. Appointing Greenspan, some thought, would allow the administration to dismiss the architect of high interest rates without disrupting his policies.

Many administration officials, however, strongly supported Volcker and believed that continuing his chairmanship was the key to maintaining business confidence. Wall Street financiers conducted their own quiet lobbying campaign for Volcker, and in May one investment banker published a poll of 702 Wall Street investors. In answer to an open-ended question about

47. For a similar view, see Andrew H. Bartels, "Volcker's Revolution at the Fed," *Challenge* (September–October 1985).

the person in whom they had the most confidence to do a good job as Fed chairman, Volcker received the support of 76.9 percent of those asked. The closest runner-up was Greenspan, favored by only 5.8 percent of those polled.[48]

Some White House officials groped for another alternative, but they discovered they could find no other candidate who could better the confidence that Volcker enjoyed. By mid-1983 inflation had dropped to nearly one-fourth the 1980 level—3.5 percent, a level not seen since 1972. Members of the business community tended to see it as the Fed's—and Volcker's—accomplishment, not the administration's, especially in the light of a deficit nearing $200 billion. "We didn't reappoint Volcker," one Treasury official stated. "The markets reappointed Volcker."[49] This evaluation is not completely warranted, for Volcker had many allies within the administration. He had, furthermore, gained an international constituency for his handling of a debt crisis that threatened to throw the world banking industry into turmoil. The overwhelming support from the business community, though, helped insure Volcker's reappointment at a time when Reagan might have easily been persuaded to find a new chairman.

Volcker and the Fed carefully threaded their way through one of the most complicated economic and political mazes the Fed had ever faced. A decade of inflation and inflationary expectations had unleashed a demon that Volcker knew in advance would take exceptionally harsh steps to recapture. He struggled to mount a program of monetary restraint at a time when the federal budget was unquestionably expansionary. The high interest rates that resulted stirred some of the fiercest political attacks the Fed had ever endured. In addition to complaints from the Treasury and Capitol Hill, farmers blockaded the Federal Reserve building in Washington with their tractors to protest high interest rates, and thousands of builders mailed in 10-inch lengths of 2 × 4 boards pleading for a policy change.

Despite the demanding political problems he encountered, Volcker maintained a consistent attack with the same message: the Fed intended to break inflation. The evidence is clear that the Fed knew in advance that the attack would bring substantial pain, although Volcker and his colleagues greatly underestimated just how much pain would result. The economy suffered through the worst recession in forty years as unemployment rose from 5.8 percent in 1979 to 10.8 percent in November 1982, and there was no net growth in the nation's gross national product from 1979 to 1983. Some sectors of the economy, especially housing and business investment, suf-

48. A. Becker Parabas, "Decision-Makers Poll," June 2, 1983.
49. Quoted by Reich, "Inside the Fed," 162.

fered more than others.[50] But throughout it all, Volcker not only survived but emerged as a hero to many for reducing inflation from double digits to less than 4 percent. Even those who abhorred the Fed's policy of tight money acknowledged that he had waged an effective attack.

Most of all, Volcker fundamentally changed the Fed's relations with the White House. He took advantage of a vacuum of presidential leadership on economic policy to bring monetary policy into prominence. Volcker succeeded in capturing the economic agenda by defining inflation as the nation's chief economic problem, by defining and leading a strategy for reducing it, and by winning support through relatively quick success. He generally accommodated the administration's economic goals, but administration officials also acquiesced to his economic leadership. Some of them agreed with Volcker's strategy, while others reluctantly accepted it for want of a better alternative. Volcker was one of the few officials who had a plan and could build political support. Members of Congress applauded Volcker or at least, as economist Andrew H. Bartels put it, tended to "praise him with faint damns."[51]

He planned his strategy with great skill. He used the theoretical weapons of the Fed's sharpest critics as a shield behind which to increase interest rates, and when congressional attack made continued tight money politically impossible, he skillfully backed away from the monetarist prescription while leaving everyone uncertain about just what he had done. He managed to keep Reagan's support—or at least to avoid his vocal opposition—despite harsh attacks from within the administration. Volcker's war on inflation was thus as much political as economic—the deft application of strong medicine, the cooptation of the Fed's critics, and a carefully timed retreat from monetarism when political support eroded. In retreating, Volcker made plain he was switching tactics, not strategies. Instead of embracing any theoretical guide, he made flexible response to changing and unpredictable economic events the Fed's watchword.

Volcker demonstrated that flexibility again in mid-1985. The Fed had set a 1985 target for M1 growth of 4 to 7 percent. By the end of June, however, M1 was growing at an annual rate of more than 12 percent, far outside the target range. Fed officials were confused. Such high monetary growth should have produced a rapid increase in economic growth. For the first three months of the year, however, the gross national product grew at an annual rate of only 0.3 percent, and during the second three months growth

---

50. Andrew F. Brimmer, "Monetary Policy and Economic Activity: Benefits and Costs of Monetarism," AEA *Papers and Proceedings* (May 1983): 7.
51. Bartels, "Volcker's Revolution at the Fed," 36.

was a sluggish 3.1 percent. One FOMC member frankly admitted, "There are conflicting signals [from the economy]. Money growth has been strong for some months, and we ought to be seeing more of an impact. It's hard to find signs of it."[52]

The FOMC faced a dilemma. Fed officials could try to hit the monetary target. To do so, however, would have meant a quick slowdown in monetary growth and would have risked sending the fragile economy into a recession. On the other hand, they could ignore the target range and allow money growth to continue, but that risked planting the seeds for a virulent inflation in the months to come. Simply missing the target by such a wide margin caused some analysts to speculate that Volcker was losing his anti-inflation discipline. To make matters worse, international economic problems were pulling in opposite directions. Less-developed countries were struggling to pay their debts; the economic burden on those countries would be substantially increased by a policy of tighter money to hit the Fed's targets. The American economy was also strained by the high value of the dollar abroad, which made it hard for American industries to export their products and thus kept economic growth sluggish. On the other hand, the high dollar made it an attractive investment and helped the Treasury finance the burgeoning federal deficit abroad. All these issues filled a bubbling cauldron that made prediction of future events a very risky business.

Volcker dealt with the dilemma by leading the Fed gingerly along a middle course. He insisted, "I'm as concerned about inflation as I've ever been" and maintained that the Fed would continue to peg its policies to a growth in the money supply.[53] However, since hitting the 1985 targets would have proved extremely difficult, the FOMC voted to make the target range wider—a range of 4 to 8 percent instead of 4 to 7 percent—and, more importantly, to begin measuring money growth afresh from July 1. The move, technically known as "rebasing," effectively wiped out the rapid money growth of the first half of the year and gave the Fed a fresh start.

In his testimony to Congress, Volcker argued that focusing narrowly on M1's rapid growth would be a mistake. Other measures of money had generally stayed within their target ranges. "Against the background of a high dollar, the sluggishness of manufacturing output, and relatively well-contained prices pressures [that is, inflation]," Volcker told the committees, "quick and strong action to curtail the recent burst in M1 growth has not been appropriate." M1, he suggested, was an uncertain policy guide. Interest-bearing checking accounts appeared to be affecting the economy dif-

52. Washington *Post*, July 7, 1985, K4.
53. *Wall Street Journal*, July 17, 1985, 3.

ferently from more traditional checking accounts. Furthermore, the
relationship between M1 and economic growth—velocity—itself seemed to
be undergoing fundamental changes. These conditions, he concluded, un-
derscored "the need for a considerable degree of judgment rather than
precise rules in the current conduct of monetary policy."[54]

Volcker's strategy this time was a major gamble: that the Fed could recognize in advance when money growth was so high that it would reignite,
at some point in the future, the inflation that had only recently subsided.
It was a gamble, in short, that Volcker and the Fed's staff could outguess
the economy's future course. The policy he produced was, in the words of
Washington *Post* columnist Joseph Kraft, "calculated ambiguity."[55] His goal
was to maintain enough flexibility to respond to emerging problems while
preserving enough credibility to make future policies work.

Such a strategy of flexible response to uncertain problems predictably
upset the monetarists, who had long posited that attempts to outguess the
economy were the source of most Fed mistakes. Beryl Sprinkel, Reagan's
chairman of the Council of Economic Advisers in 1985 and himself a monetarist, warned constantly that the Fed's course courted future inflation. (He
had a hard time, however, getting anyone in the White House to listen.
Most of the president's advisers were concerned that the economy was
already growing too slowly even to approach the administration's economic
projections and deficit reduction plans.) The Shadow Open Market Committee, a group of monetarist economists that had met regularly to follow
FOMC decisions, charged that the Fed—along with the administration—
had "resumed the stop and go policies that produced stagnation and inflation" in the 1970s. Its members criticized the Fed for "reopening the prospect of another round of inflation" by allowing money to grow so rapidly,
and they urged the Fed "to achieve its targets" and "to stop rebasing."[56]

This episode, like every other one during Volcker's term as chairman,
illustrated quite clearly that political as well as economic judgment guided
the chairman's leadership. He was determined not to use any one standard
to guide the Fed's policy, for to do so would narrow the Fed's flexibility
when political pressures built up. Volcker recognized that such rapid money
growth in 1985 risked fanning inflation once again. At the same time, he
also saw the danger that torpid economic growth might pose for the American economy. The world's economies, furthermore, were becoming in-

---

54. Board of Governors, "Monetary Policy Objectives for 1985," July 17, 1985, 3, 5.
55. Washington *Post*, September 5, 1985, A21.
56. "Policy Statement and Position," Shadow Open Market Committee, Graduate School of
Management, University of Rochester, September 22–23, 1985, 1, 2, 5.

creasingly interdependent. The Fed's policies powerfully influenced not only American growth but also the ability of less-developed countries to repay their debt, the value of the dollar, and the competitiveness of American industries abroad.

All these issues were interconnected in complicated and often unpredictable ways. For a variety of reasons—including the huge federal deficit that immobilized the federal budget as a policy tool and the vacuum of economic leadership elsewhere in official Washington—Volcker and the Fed had seized a growing role in steering the nation's way. Each problem was technically difficult and politically hot. Volcker relied on a flexible response to steer his way through such an uncertain and risky environment.

POLICY ON A BOUNDED PLANE

Except perhaps during the Depression and the preaccord struggles, the Fed had never experienced such crises as it had during the late 1970s and early 1980s. Members of Congress had demonstrated during Burns's tenure that they had little stomach for continued tight money and that, if the Fed persisted, they stood ready to reduce the Fed's discretion. At the same time, though, the challenge of inflation continued to build. New federal spending programs added to the deficit and further fanned inflation, while conflicts between presidents and members of Congress made sustained attack on the deficits impossible.

Meanwhile, a decade of inflation and high interest rates produced rapid innovation by financiers who sought to insulate themselves from their effects. That innovation weakened the Fed's control of the money supply and greatly increased the uncertainty about what effects its policy tools would produce. Few agencies have ever faced such daunting problems and survived, let alone emerged with their power and public respect enhanced. Yet not only did Volcker's Fed take interest rates to 20 percent—twice the level of the previous record—to break the back of a persistent inflation, but Volcker also used the strategy to build unprecedented power for the agency and its chairmanship. Even his opponents gave him grudging respect.

The foundation of Volcker's leadership was his keen ability as a politician: to diagnose problems, to develop solutions that suggested a way out of a quandary, to deliver quick results, and to keep his route of escape clear. He relied, in short, on the shield of flexibility, a strategy of policymaking unbound by economic ideology or any one political constituency. So flexible, in fact, was his approach that he could slip into a hasty embrace of monetarism, an age-old Fed aversion, and then slip away without acknowledging he was doing so.

Critics were often harsh in their judgment. The economy had suffered greatly under the burden of such high interest rates, and some observers questioned whether such severe damage had really been necessary. Monetarist economists, furthermore, argued that the damage would not have been as severe if the Fed had followed their prescriptions more closely and had managed monetary growth more steadily. The Fed had unquestionably put the economy through the wringer, but under Volcker its reasons were complicated. Rarely had the economic sea been as unsettled as it was during the Volcker years. Rarely had the federal budget offered less policy leverage. The result was that the Fed's politically acceptable choices had never been more narrow. Volcker walked a thin line of great opportunity and enormous risk, battered by high inflation and even higher inflationary expectations; by changing forms of money and banking; by shifting international currencies and debt; by congressional restiveness over high interest rates; by pressure within the Fed against continued high inflation; by presidents who wanted to regain the path to economic growth; by a federal budget that was relentlessly stimulative in the midst of high inflation.

Commenting on these challenges, economic analyst Henry Kaufman concluded, "Considering the circumstances he has operated in, Paul Volcker has been the most effective Fed chairman of the postwar era."[57] Despite the great political and economic pain of high interest rates and the worst recession since the Depression, public opinion stood remarkably behind the Fed. A 1983 poll revealed that 46 percent of citizens responding said that the Fed had made "a major contribution" to lower inflation, and 64 percent were willing to have the Fed tighten money again if it were needed to curb inflation, even if that meant slowing the economy.[58] It would be hard to imagine a greater vote of confidence in Volcker's political leadership, a style of leadership grounded in flexibility and devoted to steering the narrow course that maintained political support.

57. Quoted by Reich, "Inside the Fed," 162.
58. *National Journal* (October 8, 1983): 2084.

CHAPTER EIGHT

THE CHAIRMAN AS A POLITICAL LEADER

Throughout the Fed's history, its power over the economy has depended more on the political leadership of its chairman than on any other factor. Both the friends and enemies of the Fed focus on its unrivaled legal independence, but that independence is only a precondition for power, not power itself. The Fed's power depends on the support it can build, not on its legal status. Without political support, its credibility is low, its effectiveness is sharply limited, and its legal independence is fragile. Indeed, as the Fed's history shows, its much-vaunted legal independence is most important because it provides the flexibility for building support. And this central job—of building support, of developing credibility, of dealing with the complex and conflicting political environment in which the Fed finds itself—has been the central job of the chairman.

Over the Fed's history, its chairmen have discovered the limits to insisting on the agency's independence. When Eccles sought to tighten money in 1937 against Morgenthau's wishes, the Treasury secretary demonstrated that he could develop his own stabilization fund to outflank the chairman, and President Roosevelt supported him. Legal independence meant little in the years after World War II when Truman insisted that the Fed continue its support of the Treasury's peg, and when this cost the jobs of two Fed chairmen. In 1965, Martin clearly recognized that he could not defy Johnson for long. Burns and Volcker recognized as well that consistently bucking the president's policy would destroy their own credibility and disrupt the Fed's political support. A Fed chairman who insisted on exercising the Fed's independence, while ignoring the political consequences of his actions, would surely lose his power and flexibility.

The watchword at the Fed thus has not been independence but interdependence, especially with the president. Whether they like it or not, the chairman and the president have increasingly found that their jobs are intertwined, for four reasons.

First, economic theories about stabilizing cycles in the American economy have come over time to stress the interrelationship of monetary and fiscal policies. When Congress first established the Fed, its members based the new agency's legal independence on theories that said monetary policy *could* be set independently of the government's policies. The job was then thought to be relatively automatic: to raise or lower the money supply according to the economy's demands (and not according to the demands of politicians). While the Fed made some tentative steps away from this doctrine in the 1920s, the Depression forever destroyed it. In its place emerged two doctrines: that money mattered in making national economic policy (although economists differed drastically about just how much); and that monetary policy therefore had to be carefully integrated into an administration's economic strategy (about which monetarist economists, theorists like Simons in the 1930s and like Friedman in the 1960s, strongly disagreed). If economists fervidly contested just how much money mattered and how monetary policy ought to be set, they concurred in the underlying assumption that monetary policy affected the economy in important ways: in influencing the level of employment, the rate of economic growth, and, above all, the level of interest rates. That, in turn, meant that the Fed's decisions came to matter politically, especially to the president, much more than its founders ever envisioned.

Second, by the late 1960s the president's most important economic tool, his control over federal spending, had become an inflexible tool. During the Kennedy administration, Keynesian economists self-confidently believed they could use fiscal policy through the federal budget to steer the economy. By the end of the decade, that self-confidence was gone. Political conflicts between Lyndon Johnson and Congress, over spending issues ranging from the Vietnam war to the Great Society, immersed fiscal policy in deep struggle. Those conflicts further heated up through the Watergate era and persisted through the 1970s. Presidents and members of Congress had a hard time agreeing on what fiscal policy ought to be. The result was a deadlock that produced unrelenting deficits.

Yet even if the White House and Congress could have come to terms on fiscal policy, the federal budget itself was becoming a far less pliable tool for influencing the economy. As late as 1970, 46 percent of the federal budget was "controllable"—that is, not mandated by existing laws or obligations. By 1980, that portion of the budget had dropped to 30 percent and by 1986 it was 26.2 percent.[1] Entitlements to Social Security, Medicare, and Medicaid, as well as long-term defense contracts and an inexorably growing bill for the federal debt, took a progressively larger share of federal spending. To make things worse, the ability of the president and legislators to cut even the "controllable" portion of the budget is now sharply curtailed. There is a limit to the salary cuts that can be inflicted upon federal employees, to contracts that can be canceled, to cost savings through management improvements. About 90 to 95 percent of the federal budget is effectively beyond the immediate control of the president and Congress.[2] Only wrenching battles over long-term commitments to defense and payments to individuals, like Social Security, can produce fundamental changes.

That means that the president's ability to forge a budgetary response to changing economic conditions has been increasingly constricted. Without leverage on the budget, presidents have been forced to turn to the Fed.

Third, the public has come to expect the president to deliver on promises to provide jobs and keep interest rates low. Since Hoover, no president has believed that moral leadership on the economy was enough. Presidential candidates can scarcely resist sometimes hyperbolic pledges to strengthen the economy, and the electorate in turn holds the president responsible for providing the good life. Few electoral issues have the same appeal as economic ones.[3] Because the president now has fewer options for fiscal policy, the Fed and its monetary policy have taken on extra political importance.

Finally, the internationalization of economic issues has made the Fed and its chairman key players not only in domestic affairs but in international relations. In the 1980s, the huge debt burden of less developed countries and America's own trade deficit put great strains on the international economy. The Fed's staff had great expertise in these questions, and Volcker had the confidence of world leaders. The chairman therefore became one of the principal operatives in guiding the way through these problems.

The Fed and its chairman have thus become of inescapable importance to the president, who in turn has become of greater importance to the Fed and its chairman. The chairman can insist on his independence and the Fed can manipulate the money supply as it likes, but monetary policies are

1. U.S. Office of Management and Budget, *Budget of the United States Government, Fiscal Year 1986* (Washington, D.C.: U.S. Government Printing Office, 1985), 44, 45.

2. See Lance T. LeLoup, *Budgetary Politics*, 2d ed. (Brunswick, Ohio: King's Court Communications, 1980), 70–79.

3. See Bernard Hennessey, *Public Opinion*, 12th ed. (Monterey, Calif.: Brooks/Cole, 1981), chapter 12; George C. Edwards III, *The Public Presidency: The Pursuit of Popular Support* (New York: St. Martin's, 1981), 188–93; and D. Roderick Kiewiet, *Macroeconomics & Micropolitics: The Electoral Effects of Economic Issues* (Chicago: University of Chicago Press, 1983).

always limited by their credibility. Public confidence is central to the Fed's power. The president plays an essential role in setting the general expectations for the nation's economy, and that context is crucial for the Fed's operations. Furthermore, presidential statements of opposition to the Fed's policies (or even guerrilla campaigns conducted by presidential advisers) affect public expectations about the future course of money. The Fed and the presidency, the chairman and the president, are thus inextricably interdependent.

The special ties between the chairman and the president are ironic given the Fed's legal parentage. The agency is the creature of Congress, but congressional interest in the Fed has over the years been only intermittent. Furthermore, even when congressional interest has risen—typically when interest rates have risen—members of Congress have backed away from seizing their prerogative to redirect the Fed's policies. Congress has limited itself to reacting to monetary policies its members have considered undesirable. Apart from defining the politically acceptable boundaries on the Fed's decisions, however, members of Congress have preferred to keep their distance. Regardless of the technical and economic rationales for the Fed's independence, it serves the political interests of members of Congress first.

The Fed has had to deal with other constituencies as well. As we have seen, the Treasury has long been a jealous sibling, for the obvious reason that the Fed's policies heavily influence how much the Treasury must pay to borrow money. When the federal deficit has risen quickly—during wartime, in the post-Vietnam 1970s, and in the 1980s—the Treasury's interest in the Fed naturally has been keenest. Home builders similarly worry about the level of mortgage rates, and industrialists about the cost of money for building new plants and buying new equipment. Insurance executives and bankers hope for low inflation to make long-term plans. The Fed, furthermore, has developed an international constituency, some of whom own large shares of the American debt and some of whom owe large debts to American banks. The Fed needs their support and confidence, and they need certain policies from the Fed.

The Fed thus operates in an especially complex and uncertain environment. Some constraints come from the technical difficulties all central banks share. Other constraints, however, come from the special politics of the American system.[4] The United States has an unusual number of independent power centers. The Congress, independent of the executive branch,

<hr />

4. See Arnold J. Heidenheimer, Hugh Heclo, and Carolyn Teich Adams, *Comparative Public Policy* (New York: St. Martin's Press), 260–66.

can wage separate attack on the Fed's decisions, a problem that central banks in parliamentary systems need not face. Interest groups in the American establishment, furthermore, are unusually numerous and influential. The United States has as well a unique brand of federalism and an unusual tradition of populism, a populism that holds as its core value the easy availability of money to promote economic growth. The high visibility of economic issues, furthermore, makes conflict all the more likely (but to the Fed's great relief, American pluralism makes it unlikely that all its potential adversaries will coalesce). Compared with other central banks, the Fed has a similar technical environment but its political environment is unique. Compared with other American bureaucracies, the Fed has unique legal independence, operating flexibility, and influence on the economy. It shares with them, however, the need for political support, and it is this central fact that has made the president and the chairman interdependent.

THE FUNCTIONS OF POLICY LEADERSHIP

The Fed is thus a bureaucracy in a difficult world, a world full of conflict, uncertainties, and risks. For the Fed to survive, it must travel a politically acceptable course through irreconcilable demands. And since policy changes and shifts in the economy make it hard to keep anyone happy for long, friends can quickly become enemies and enemies friends. As one Fed staff member put it, the Fed "constantly has to walk the fine line from going too far one way or another."[5] The principal task of finding and keeping to that line has been the chairman's. Since Eccles, the chairmanship has been the unquestioned center of the Fed's power.

The Fed's history is inseparable from the history of the chairmanship, which in turn is inseparable from the story of the chairman's relationship with the president. Over the years, that relationship has shown the three different patterns I described in chapter 1: accommodation, in which the Fed and its chairman act at least in general consensus with the president's policy goals; confrontation, in which the chairman and the president stand in conflict with each other; and transformation, in which White House–Fed expectations—on the one side, of monetary policy and on the other, of presidential action—are fundamentally and permanently changed.

Accommodation   Through most of the Fed's history, the relationship between the chairman and the president has been relatively stable. In fact, despite the vast quantity of writing about the Fed's independence, the most

5. Interview with the author. For an examination of the importance of political support, see Rourke, *Bureaucracy, Politics, and Public Policy*, 101.

notable fact about the Fed is that only rarely have the president and the
chairman been far out of step. This does not mean that the relationship has
always been harmonious. McCabe complained bitterly about the Treasury's
peg during the first years of his chairmanship but maintained it nonetheless.
Before the 1972 election Nixon railed about teaching Burns a lesson even
though he eventually got almost the monetary policy he wanted. However,
over the period from 1934 to 1985—the era of the modern Federal Reserve
dating from Eccles's chairmanship—the pattern is one of overall accommodation, in which the Fed delivered policy roughly in accord with the
president's policy goals. (See table 3.)[6]

The job of the chairman during these years fundamentally was seeking to
meet the presidents' overall economic goals. This is not to say that the
chairman blindly delivered what the president wanted. Fed chairmen were
always cognizant of countervailing pressures, especially from members of

Table 3: Patterns of Chairman-President Relations, 1934–1985

	Pattern		
Chairman	Accommodation	Confrontation	Transformation
Eccles	1935–45 New Deal and World War II	1945–48 the peg controversy	1934–35 Banking Act of 1935
McCabe	1948–49 the peg controversy	1949–51 the peg controversy	
Martin	1956–65 "Operation Twist" and the tax cut	1965–66 Vietnam	1951–56 "leaning against the wind"
	1966–70 Vietnam		
Burns	1974–78 stagflation-fighting (but often in confrontational style)		
Volcker	1982–85 inflation control (but with presidential accommodation of Fed)		1979–1982 experiment in monetarism

6. The years classified as periods of accommodation total 37 of the 52 years, 71 percent of
the time. The years prior to 1934 are not analyzed here because of the relative lack of relations
between the Federal Reserve Board and the president during this time.

Congress and interest groups. They were, furthermore, always mindful of avoiding presidential encroachments on the Fed's inflation-fighting mission and of maintaining the Fed's maneuvering room. For the most part, though, presidents during these eras got largely what they wanted from the Fed.

This was scarcely surprising. Part of the period (from 1952 to 1965, for example) was a time of relative economic prosperity that, despite occasional downturns, gave the president and chairman few fundamental issues over which to fight. In wartime (from 1940–45, for example), the chairman had little choice but to support the administration. In some later periods (1974–76 and 1982–85, for example), the situation was reversed: there was little conflict because the president had few other options for economic leverage than the Fed's policies.

Although the overall pattern of these times was accommodation between the chairman and the president, accommodation took different strategies. Sometimes the accommodation was explicit. Relations between the chairman and the administration sometimes have been so close that monetary and fiscal policies were explicitly coordinated. In the 1930s, political support for Roosevelt and Eccles coincided. The president had strong backing for his New Deal. Eccles, meanwhile, recognized clearly that his power was tied to the president, both because Roosevelt appointed him and because the New Deal had captured the public's mind. Eccles enthusiastically delivered the policies that Roosevelt wanted. At other times, exactly the opposite happened: relatively weak presidents relied on strong chairmen to manage economic policy. At the height of public attack on the Vietnam war, Martin by default conducted the Johnson administration's economic policy. After the Watergate crisis, the Ford administration relied heavily on Burns and the Fed in a close relationship unmatched in the Fed's history. While there was often rhetorical distance between the chairman and the president, largely to avoid the appearance that the Fed had become the captive of the White House, explicit cooperation flourished at times of great mismatch between the chairman's and the president's political power.

On other occasions, when neither the chairman nor the president enjoyed an imbalance of power, accommodation was more implicit. For example, in the early 1960s Martin had serious doubts about Kennedy's "Operation Twist." To oppose the president for more than a short period, however, would have been politically unthinkable (since it would have weakened Martin's credibility) and economically disastrous (since it would have created conflicting expectations, both domestically and internationally, about the future course of the economy). Martin agreed that the Fed would follow the administration's strategy: to buy enough short-term securities to prevent

White House attack, but to do so with enough obvious reluctance to keep the support of many Fed officials who questioned the strategy. Furthermore, Martin forced administration officials to make continual requests to the Fed for support. He refused to embrace the policy overtly or even acknowledge its name. If Kennedy got most of what he wanted from the Fed, he did so on the Fed's terms: a continuing unspoken reminder that the Fed was under no legal obligation to go along and that its cooperation would have to be bargained for. Such implicit cooperation tended to occur at times of relative balance in the chairman-president relationship.

Confrontation Despite the predominance of accommodation in the chairman-president relationship, deep conflict has been an occasional feature. Such conflict has occurred three times: in Eccles's struggles to rid the Fed of the Treasury's peg; in McCabe's similar battle; and in Martin's much-publicized confrontation with Johnson in 1965. In each case, war had put heavy demands on the economy. The president pressured the Fed to keep interest rates low, both to lower the Treasury's financing costs and, perhaps more importantly, to try to keep the Treasury's wartime needs from interfering with domestic economic growth. The chairman and the Fed, by contrast, worried far more about the dangers of inflation that low interest rates might bring.

These occasions brought the president and the chairman into fundamental conflict, because they posed basic challenges to each institution. Wars have always posed difficult challenges for presidents, challenges for achieving foreign policy goals without sacrificing, at least for long, domestic economic growth. The Fed, of course, can scarcely balk at cooperating in wartime financing, and throughout the Fed's history that never proved a problem. Such wartime financing, however, has fed the taste of many administrations for cheap money, and that has aroused the Fed's most fundamental fear: too-low interest rates encourage excessive borrowing and a buying boom, and produce in the end a crash. The economy crashed in 1929 in part because of the Fed's mismanagement, and another such failure is the Fed's recurring nightmare. The Depression demonstrated to Fed officials the enormous danger of a boom gone wild. It also clearly showed the enormous political risks to the institution if it failed in its fundamental mission, to protect the currency.

Such confrontations have been rare and short-lived. In each case, they have been eventually resolved on the Fed's terms. The controversy over the peg ended when the Treasury abandoned its pressure on the Fed for support of its securities. The clash over Vietnam financing ended in 1966 when Johnson's advisers quietly acknowledged that Martin had done them a favor by slowing the economy without their having to ask for a tax increase. In each case, however, the Fed did not break with the president by insisting on its independence. Rather, the chairman edged away from the White House only with the political support of financiers who feared that inflation would further weaken the economy and, in the case of the peg, with the backing of strong members of Congress as well.

Serious confrontations between the chairman and the president thus emerged only when the fundamental interests of each institution were at stake. They ended, sometimes quickly, sometimes not, on the Fed's terms. However, the chairman won these battles not on the strength of his own power, but with the support of politically powerful anti-inflation forces.

Transformation   Every organization occasionally encounters crucial episodes—"critical experiences," as Selznick calls them—that shape its operations for years afterward.[7] Rather than trying to accommodate or confront presidential policies, Fed chairmen have sometimes moved to alter the basic relationship with the president. These transformations have come on the heels of fundamental challenges: the Depression, which demonstrated that the Fed had to change its structure and mission if it were to survive; the post–World War II peg, which left the Fed with no effective control over the money supply; and the stagflation of the late 1970s, which threatened to push prices and interest rates ever higher. Each of these episodes damaged the American economy and political support for the Fed.

In response to these challenges came three leaders—Eccles, Martin, and Volcker—who fundamentally redefined the Fed's mission and the chairman's relationship with the president. Eccles established that there could be a cooperative relationship between the Fed and White House. Martin showed that the president could not simply work his will on the Fed; other powerful political forces demanded to be heard, while a monetary policy set by the chief executive ran the long-cited risk of inflation. Volcker further established the Fed's independence and demonstrated that monetary policy could play an even stronger role than fiscal policy in managing the economy.

In transforming the chairman's relationship with the president, these chairmen shared a common setting: a time of high crisis, for both the economy and the Fed, when old patterns were no longer working. In dealing with these problems, the chairmen shared a similar strategy: development of a pivotal idea to guide both the Fed and their own relations with the president. As Erwin Hargrove pointed out in his study of chairmen of the Tennessee Valley Authority, another politically independent agency, lead-

7. Philip Selznick, *Leadership in Administration* (New York: Harper & Row, 1957), 36.

ership "requires the ability to clarify and define ambiguous situations for others."[8] For Eccles, it was consolidation of the Fed's power coordinated with presidential policy. For Martin, it was independence from the Treasury by "leaning against the wind." And for Volcker, it was a flexible approach to "practical monetarism." By the force of their ideas, they reduced the great confusion and ambiguity the Fed faced.[9]

The driving power of these transformations came from the chairmen themselves. Each was an aggressive but not overbearing leader. Each used his new insight in the first months of his chairmanship as a way of consolidating his control of the institution after considerable turmoil within the Fed. And each employed the new vision to build broader public support for the agency. In Eccles's case, this was less urgent because he had Roosevelt's full backing. For Martin, it was crucial because Truman had fought for keeping the peg. Volcker profited from the Carter administration's lack of any alternative strategy to the Fed's new operating procedures.

The chairmen of transformation, in short, shared rising economic problems, worsened by years of weak presidential leadership on the economy, that threatened to destroy the Fed's credibility. They developed new visions about how to handle those problems and won political support from the financial community, from legislators, and even from the president. In the process, they took the relationship between the chairman and the president to new levels.

No chairman, of course, can change the institution or its relations with the president by himself. Fed chairmen rely heavily on the support of the other six board members, of the board's staff, and of the reserve banks. In part this is because of the Fed's legal structure: the chairman has only one vote of seven on the board, one of twelve on the FOMC. In part this is also because, when the Fed speaks with the voice of its expert staff and regional base, it speaks with unmatched power. Building internal support means infusing the entire organization with a sense of mission—persuading the many centers of power within the Fed of the lasting value of the chairman's ideas. On the basis of this support, the three transformational chairmen changed not only their own relations with the president but also the Fed's role in the economy.

8. Erwin C. Hargrove, "The Task of Leadership: The Board Chairmen," in Erwin C. Hargrove and Paul K. Conkin, eds., *TVA: Fifty Years of Grass Roots Bureaucracy* (Urbana: University of Illinois Press, 1983), 118.
9. Compare Robert C. Tucker, *Politics as Leadership* (Columbia: University of Missouri Press, 1981), 15–30.

RELATIONS WITH CONGRESS

The chairman's relations with Congress have followed a much different course than those with the president. Fed-congressional politics has been much more visible, has involved far more players, and does not permit the same subtle relationships that have typified chairman-president relations. In dealing with Congress, Fed chairmen have adopted the following strategies:

1. *Foot-dragging.* Even under heavy pressure from Congress, most Fed chairmen have proven skillful in deflecting attack. The most concerted congressional campaign against the Fed's power came during the mid-1970s. Burns used the shield of the Fed's independence and technical complexity to ward off the worst—from the Fed's point of view—congressional efforts to open FOMC decisions to public scrutiny. Few Indians were more adept at hiding their tracks.

2. *Hardball.* Chairmen occasionally have resorted to hardball bargaining. The FOMC's minutes show that in 1968 the Fed's officials were willing to allow inflation to build enough to make clear to members of Congress the great dangers of refusing to pass the surcharge. During Volcker's term, his speculations about how large a deficit reduction program would need to be to reduce interest rates quickly became the target at which members of Congress aimed. Congress, of course, did not miss the message Volcker brought: lower deficits would create the opportunity for the Fed to ease the money supply. That meant as well that members of Congress sometimes played the other side of the hardball game. In 1982, congressional resolutions calling for Volcker's impeachment and for congressionally mandated lower interest rates signaled to the Fed in unmistakable terms that Congress would no longer tolerate the tight money policy. The use of this strategy has increased with the Fed's power over the economy—and as Congress has found itself more entrapped in budget deficits.

3. *Lobbying.* In bargaining, Fed chairmen sometimes strengthened their position by mustering support from the agency's unmatched field network. As Burns discovered in the 1970s, it was a risky strategy, but the influence of the Fed's directors gave Burns an important advantage in his effort to resist congressional encroachment on the Fed's prerogatives. Lobbying was most active during Burns's tenure, when the Fed was under strongest congressional attack, but throughout the Fed's history its chairmen have recognized the value of its unparalleled lobbying network.

ACCOUNTABILITY, REFORM, AND INDEPENDENCE

The Fed's great—and growing—power has predictably led over the years
to calls for reform. Even Congress's relatively modest attempts to force the
Fed chairman to inform congressional committees about the Fed's monetary
targets produced little real oversight. Presidents have complained often
enough about unresponsive monetary policy to raise constant worries that
the Fed is unresponsive to the goals of elected officials. These recurring
charges raise a central question: is the Fed politically accountable, to the
president and the Congress, for its decisions? Put differently, would the
Fed's policies be "better," in some sense, if it were subject to more traditional forms of accountability? Would its economic effects be more stable,
would its decisions better match the goals of elected officials, and would
the public interest be better served if, for example, the Fed were formally
part of the executive branch or if Congress had direct control over its budget?

The Fed's critics have long argued that the answer is yes, and that the
Fed's secrecy serves principally to shield the agency from public control.[10]
Furthermore, they say, Fed officials tend to preach a common sermon from
a prepared text: the complexity of economic problems; the limited ability
of the Fed to control the economy through monetary policy alone; and the
critical importance of a sensible fiscal policy (that is, one that does not make
monetary policy too difficult). In their monumental study of monetary policy, in fact, Friedman and Schwartz argue that the Fed's annual reports
show just such a pattern. "In years of prosperity," they write, "monetary
policy is said to be a potent instrument, the skillful handling of which deserves credit for the favorable course of events; in years of adversity, monetary policy is said to have little leeway but is largely the consequence of
other forces, and it was only the skillful handling of the exceedingly limited
powers available that prevented conditions from being even worse."[11] The
Fed has always been proud but not boastful of its successes and reserved
about its failures. And always, the Fed has renounced direct responsibility
for the state of the economy.

That has regularly made the Fed the object of everyone's frustration about
the economy. "To be criticized," explained former CEA chairman Paul
McCracken, "is their lot. They must take the heat vicariously for the an-
noying inability of our economy to provide everybody with everything they

10. See, for example, Lombra and Moran, "Policy Advice and Policymaking at the Federal
Reserve," 9–10.
11. Friedman and Schwartz, *A Monetary History of the United States*, 250–51n.

want."[12] In fact, some commentators have suspected that the Fed's independence has great advantages for elected officials, who can blame everything on the "misguided" policies of an "independent" Fed.[13] For a variety of reasons, the Fed is a lightning rod for groups unhappy with the state of the economy, and that has led to continual proposals to reform the central bank. Among the most popular suggestions for reform are the following:

1. *Politicizing the Fed.* In the eyes of many critics, the Fed's principal fault is that its legal independence insulates it from democratic control. In this variant of the old populist argument, critics suggest that the Fed pursues its own private agenda, often in cahoots with bankers, to deny the general public's need for credit. The solution is to make the Fed more politically responsive by legally linking it more closely to the president. The most common suggestions are to reinstate the secretary of the Treasury as a member of the board, or perhaps even to make the Fed an agency of the Treasury.[14] The advantage of this approach, its proponents argue, is that it creates a "single locus of authority that could be held responsible" for monetary decisions.[15]

Implicit in this proposal are two arguments. One is that the Fed is not sufficiently responsive to the administration's economic goals. Indeed, nearly every president at some time has railed privately, and sometimes publicly, against the Fed's intransigence. Fed chairmen rarely make commitments to the president (or, indeed, to anyone else) about future Fed policy, and White House officials have sometimes been surprised to learn about major policy changes only after they have been made. Nearly every president has seriously considered plans to change the Fed's structure. Since the Roosevelt administration, however, contacts among both staff members and principals have generally been close. Communication problems have been rare.

The other argument for politicizing the Fed is that tighter presidential control over the Fed would make overall political accountability for economic policy neater. The Fed would no longer be able to hide behind a collection of monetary targets. The president would no longer be able to complain about the Fed's policies and avoid responsibility for them by point-

---

12. Paul McCracken, "Beleaguered Days for the Fed," *Wall Street Journal,* March 21, 1975.

13. See Edward J. Kane, "New Congressional Restraints and Federal Reserve Independence," *Challenge* (November/December 1975): 41.

14. See, for example, the House Republican Research Committee's 1985 manifesto, *Ideas for Tomorrow, Choices for Today* (Washington, D.C.: House Republican Research Committee), 5; and Kenneth M. Dolbeare, *Democracy at Risk: The Politics of Economic Renewal* (Chatham, N.J.: Chatham House, 1984), 11, 186.

15. Milton Friedman, "The Case for Overhauling the Federal Reserve," *Challenge* (July/August 1985): 8.

ing to the Fed's independence. Politicizing the Fed would consolidate fiscal and monetary policymaking in one office. The president would then be able to steer the course he wished—and the voters would have one person to hold accountable.

While presidents have often complained about their lack of control over the Fed, they have never shown much enthusiasm for running the agency. The risks would be high and the difficulty of forming a national consensus behind both the federal budget and the supply of money would be enormous. Furthermore, there is little historical evidence that presidential control over both monetary and fiscal policies would have changed the Fed's decisions. When presidents have known what mix of monetary and fiscal policies they wanted, they usually have gotten it. The exceptions—the times of confrontational chairman-presidential relations—are notable: the dispute over the peg from 1949 to 1951 and the disagreement in 1965 over the discount rate increase. Sometimes the administration has not known what policy it wanted. From 1977 to 1981, for example, the Carter administration switched course several times and in the end left economic management to the Fed. The history of the Fed is that of an agency rarely far out of step with the president's policies.

On those few occasions when the chairman and the Fed did buck the president, the Fed's motivation was clear: to head off a rising inflationary threat. Furthermore, when the Fed stood against the president it never stood alone, but always claimed the support of other political forces—members of Congress and interest groups—that counterbalanced the administration's demands. Indeed, the Fed's consistent value to the president as a scapegoat undoubtedly outweighs the few occasions on which the president has found the Fed intransigent. In interviews, furthermore, the chairmen of the Council of Economic Advisers consistently have argued that a Federal Reserve standing independent of the administration has helped provide stability at times of economic uncertainty. [16]

2. *Sunshine.* Other critics, principally members of Congress and its committee staffs, have urged that public scrutiny of the Fed's debates and decisions should be increased. [17] The Fed's penchant for shielding decisions in secrecy and impenetrable jargon, they charge, make it impossible for Congress to oversee its agency. Reform would mean forcing the chairman to report decisions as the agency reaches them, to target a single type of money

16. See Hargrove and Morley, *The President and the Council of Economic Advisers.*
17. For example, see Henry M. Reuss, "The Once and Future Fed," *Challenge* (March/April 1983): 26–32; and Richard Medley, "Calling the Fed to Account," *Wall Street Journal,* April 25, 1985, 30.

along a more narrow range, and to explain what effects it expects that money supply target to produce in the economy. Opening monetary policy to public debate would, the Fed's critics argue, make oversight more effective.

Throughout the Fed's history, however, most members of Congress have never shown much interest in supervising the Fed. Congressional hearings, furthermore, reveal that most members of Congress understand very little about the details of monetary policy. Fed chairmen during the 1970s therefore found it relatively simple to evade Congress's attempts to force more open discussion of monetary policy. The increased oversight of the 1970s changed the way the Fed recorded its decisions, but Fed officials maintained most of their operating flexibility.

The real impact of increased congressional supervision lay not in shifting the Fed's policy but in improving communication between Congress and the Fed. Members of Congress have indicated to the chairman what they hoped would happen (and, if it did not, what action they threatened). The chairman in turn has laid out the Fed's general strategy and often, as the other side of the bargain, what congressional action would be required to bring interest rates down. The hearings thus have principally provided a forum for sending messages—about congressional expectations for monetary policy and about the Fed's price for easier money.

Despite the urging of some of its members, Congress has never taken a strong hand in directing monetary policy or coordinating it with the budget. Monetary policy issues are interwoven into the fabric of all executive agencies and thus into the domains of many congressional committees. The same institutional problems that prevent Congress from coordinating other functions limit the institution's ability to tackle monetary policy.[18] Congress's messages from the Fed have intermittently been unmistakable, as in the inflation of 1951 and the recession of 1982, but on a more regular basis Congress has been institutionally uninterested in close, regular oversight.

3. *Rules.* One of the best-known suggestions for reforming the Fed, popularized by Milton Friedman but dating from at least the 1930s, is the adoption of a monetary rule. The Fed's penchant for fine-tuning, Friedman and other monetarists contend, produces exaggerated swings in the money supply that worsen inflation and disrupt the economy. These swings could be eliminated, the argument goes, by forcing the Fed to increase the money supply at a steady rate over time. If Congress proves unwilling to pass such a law, Friedman argues, the policy ought to be set by constitutional amendment.[19]

18. See Don K. Price, "Control of the Monetary System," *Harvard Business Review* 40 (July/August 1962): 149–64.
19. Friedman, "The Case for Overhauling the Fed," 7.

As the previous chapter pointed out, however, *any* method of determining monetary policy has political implications. Whether formulated by rule or by discretion, monetary policy produces winners and losers, individuals who find it relatively easier or harder to save or invest, manufacturers who find it relatively cheaper or more expensive to sell their goods, financiers who find their investments relatively more or less profitable. Monetary policy by rule would prevent mistakes resulting from discretion, but it could not make monetary policy less political, and it could not eliminate the pressures from those who perceive themselves as losers to change the policy nor the pressures from the winners to keep it. It could not eliminate the electoral incentives of public officials to try to create a booming economy on which to run for reelection, and it certainly could not insulate the Fed from heavy attacks when high interest rates make monetary policy unpopular.

The Fed's experiment in monetarism from 1979 to 1982, even if not whole-hearted, demonstrated the politically acceptable limits to any attempt to set monetary policy by rule. Members of Congress were intolerant of high interest rates and introduced bills and resolutions to force the Fed to lower them. The message was unmistakable: the Fed would lower interest rates or Congress would reclaim its delegation of monetary authority. It is unquestionably true, as Friedman and his colleagues allege, that discretionary monetary policy has produced mistakes. It is also predictable, however, that members of Congress would never leave monetary policy on automatic pilot. High interest rates, if only for the short term, would surely induce legislators to urge the Fed to back away from monetary targets (as in fact happened in 1982). Furthermore, a monetary policy free from manipulation would put far heavier pressure on fiscal policy. The growth of the Fed's power is inextricably linked with the difficulty elected officials have in making timely changes in fiscal policy, and that makes monetarism even less attractive for elected officials.

4. *Trimming the Turf.* Other critics have argued that the Fed takes on too much in attempting to manage economic growth instead of just maintaining stable prices. A close corollary is that the Fed has built up too large a staff and relies too much on the bank presidents serving on the FOMC. Even in 1962, critics were calling the reserve banks "an expensive anachronism."[20] With the growing role of wire transfers and new forms of electronic payments, banking services are becoming more concentrated and the reserve banks' old functions are diminishing. Some critics contend that the

20. Delbert C. Hastings and Rose M. Robertson, "The Mysterious World of THE FED," *Business Horizons* 5 (Spring 1962): 104.

responsibilities of the reserve banks, especially FOMC votes on monetary policy, ought therefore to be substantially decreased. Monetary policy, critics argue, ought to be made only by politically accountable officials, not by reserve bank presidents answerable to private bank boards. Henry Reuss, former chairman of the House Banking Committee, proposed "adaptive reuse" of the reserve banks: a broader role in regional economic planning, but removal of the reserve bank members from the FOMC.[21]

Closely related are proposals from economists like Herbert Stein that Congress ought to set a new and more narrow mandate for the formulation of monetary policy. First, Congress ought to insist that the Fed renounce fine-tuning by focusing on nominal targets—price level and gross national product (before adjustment for inflation)—instead of "real" targets—like unemployment and output. Second, the Fed should produce its money supply targets on the basis of the targets it sets for nominal gross national product and velocity (the relationship between nominal GNP and the money supply). Such an approach, Stein insists, would have many advantages. It would acknowledge the need, long argued by the Fed, for discretion, but it would also keep the Fed from trying to manage real economic growth, a task which, Stein fears, would have an inflationary bias because of political pressure.[22]

Fed officials would vigorously oppose any such strategy, because they value not only the reserve banks' data but even more their political support. No other governmental agency can boast of a network like the Fed's field offices, powerful and well-positioned supporters, and intelligence networks. Decentralization is the answer on which the Fed's founders settled to broker the dispute between financiers and industrialists, between easterners and westerners. For all of the reasons that decentralization bolsters the American political system, it helps the Fed build political support and deflect attack.

Fed officials, furthermore, oppose these reforms because they recognize they would undermine the core of the chairman's leadership, and hence of the Fed's power. This leadership depends heavily on his ability to broker political support and on his skill in maneuvering the agency through the uncertainties and risks it faces. Fed officials value their discretion above all else, not only because they believe that economic management is best served by the application of wisdom but also because their discretionary power allows them flexibility to build the political support they keenly recognize they need.

21. Reuss, "The Once and Future Fed," 27.
22. Stein, *Presidential Economics,* 336–38.

That still leaves unanswered, however, the basic question: is the Fed—as a powerful, legally independent agency—accountable? Friedman makes a basic point on this issue: the Fed can exercise its "independence" only when there is no fundamental conflict with the rest of the government. "To judge by experience," he concludes, "even those central banks that have been nominally independent" have in fact "been closely linked to the executive authority."[23] Focusing solely on the Fed's legal independence thus risks missing more fundamental and important relationships that bear on its ultimate accountability.

Three issues I have discussed come together at this point. First, the Fed's policymaking is inevitably political, and no institutional (or even constitutional) fix can change that. History demonstrates the folly of thinking that monetary management can be reduced to a process of technical adjustment, for *any* monetary policy has political implications and creates political conflicts. The very attempt to shield such inherently political decisions behind "technical" standards and legal "independence" is itself a political strategy.[24]

The second point is that, in framing monetary policy, the chairman operates as a political leader. He seeks to craft a policy for which he can build political support (and deflect attack). The president is by far the most important of the Fed's constituents, but he is not the only one. Congress has a constitutional, legal, and political interest in overseeing the Fed, and, indeed, there are few interests in the United States that are not affected by the Fed's decisions. The Fed and its chairman make policy by judging both the state of the economy and the balance of political support. Rarely has monetary policy been far out of step with the intricate and complex balance of political forces in the Fed's constituencies.

The final point is that elected officials have shown little taste for taking direct responsibility for monetary policy. The Fed has the discretion it enjoys because Congress chooses to allow (indeed, to encourage) it. The benefits of this discretion to members of Congress have been clearly demonstrated in the Volcker era. They could allow the Fed to take the painful steps that the anti-inflation campaign required, bemoan the awful results of tight money, escape the even more awful political implications of trying to balance the federal budget, and in the end achieve lower inflation and improved economic growth. President Reagan and his staff, meanwhile, could tacitly support the Fed's wrenching policies without having to embrace them publicly.

23. Milton Friedman, "Should There Be an Independent Monetary Authority?" in Leland B. Yeager, ed., *In Search of a Monetary Constitution* (Cambridge: Harvard University Press, 1962), 227.
24. Hargrove makes this point about the TVA in "The Task of Leadership," 89.

The question of the Fed's accountability, therefore, is a complicated one, for two reasons. First, there usually is no clear consensus on what economic policy in general—and monetary policy in particular—should be. Second, elected officials have rarely been willing to take direct responsibility for the content of monetary policy. The tremendous growth of the Fed's power in the 1970s and 1980s had less to do with the agency's megalomania than with the great complexity of economic issues and the political self-interest of elected officials. The Fed's role emerged from the balance of political support its chairmen could build.

Indeed, as the nation entered an era of retrenchment in the 1970s and 1980s, finding a political consensus on economic policy has become ever more difficult. That in turn has produced a political accommodation. Elected officials have relied more on monetary policy because it is a more flexible instrument than the federal budget and because it insulates them from the pain of economic restraint. It might not be too much an exaggeration, in fact, to suggest that elected officials abdicated their authority over extraordinarily difficult economic decisions, and the Fed filled the void. Monetary policy has risen in importance precisely because it fits the needs of elected officials, not because the Fed has built itself into an imperial power.

The shift of economic policymaking toward monetary policy is not without important implications. Maneuvers through monetary policy inevitably mean that sectors of the economy most sensitive to interest rates, especially the construction and automobile industries, tend to be disproportionately hurt when money gets tight. The job of building political support for monetary policy, furthermore, means that the policy often has wider swings than would be the case if the political consensus were more narrow or economic trends more predictable. For elected officials, however, this pain is less than the pain of directly tackling tough economic decisions.

Such a position of predominance is not a stable one for the Fed. The Fed's power continues to rest on its political support, and monetary policy will play the central role in economic management only so long as the Fed maintains public credibility and the backing of elected officials. It will last only so long as the political benefits of the Fed's economic management exceed the liabilities: the pain of high interest rates that tight money sometimes brings and the frustration of elected officials who cannot control the economy directly so long as monetary policy plays the principal role.

As the nation's economic problems became more complex and the political stakes became higher, so too ironically did the Fed's power. The Fed's "independence" has allowed the federal government to take action that the president and Congress could (or would) not. As this book has shown, this does not mean that the Fed has in fact acted independently. Its political interdependence has meant instead that the Fed could never stray far from the political consensus. This style of policymaking, however, does not come without cost. The Fed's legal independence does not so much render it unaccountable as it removes the complex and subtle bargaining over economic policy from public scrutiny. Real accountability for economic policy has become hidden increasingly in a subterranean system in which elected officials can remove their fingerprints from politically dangerous policies they implicitly support.

The generations of complaints about the Fed, its chairmen, and its policies thus reflect more than just a disagreement about the Fed's role and power. They reflect even more the extraordinary difficulty of reaching agreement— among officials and citizens at large—about economic problems when the political stakes are incalculably high.